A Future for Scottish Higher Education

Edited by Ronald Crawford

**Committee of Scottish
Higher Education Principals**

ISBN 0 9521691 5 0

Produced by:
The Committee of Scottish Higher Education Principals

Printed by:
Polton Press, Lasswade

Further copies may be obtained from:
COSHEP
St Andrew House
141 West Nile Street
Glasgow
G1 2RN
Telephone: 0141-353 1880

Copies are priced at:
£10.00 excluding postage and packing – £1.50 for a single copy, £2.50 for multiple copies and £2.50 per copy overseas.

a carefully planned strategy: there are several examples from the past decade of institutions attempting to follow the North American example without properly thinking through whether this was an appropriate model for Britain. The results have largely been unsatisfactory, both for the alumni who may then feel alienated from their *alma mater* and for the institution which may not even have covered its costs. Lessons have been learned, though, and the institutions which have been successful do provide examples for the rest.

Finally, there are "other activities" such as running conferences or summer schools. If your institution has ample high quality residence places, a pleasant location and a supply of staff willing to teach over the summer, summer schools (and/or conferences) can put your residence account into profit (helping to subsidise the price for students) and make a contribution to general income at the same time.

Capital expenditure
Having looked superficially at sources of income which might fund our activities, a little must be said about expenditure, particularly on capital items such as buildings and large items of equipment. Here we find ourselves in real difficulty. The present Government, in its attempts to cut public expenditure, took the advice of the Treasury (they have at least not denied it) that private funds could be utilised in large capital projects such as roads, new hospitals, new schools and so on, thus reducing the need for Government to make capital grants to, *inter alia*, higher education institutions. The Opposition would seem to share this view. Unfortunately, as is often the case in politics, zeal and ideology appear to have replaced common sense. The Private Finance Initiative sometimes seems to have paralysed initiative rather than encouraged it. As is well known, HEIs have a long record of involving private finance in their capital development. Much of the new development of student residences in the past fifteen years has been funded through borrowing. While teaching buildings, research laboratories and libraries might not yet fall into the same category, it is in principle quite possible to set aside a percentage of income (an instantly created "income stream") to service borrowings for such projects. Alas, current constraints on funding are such that finding that percentage of income appears impossible to many heads of institutions. But, as large capital grants from Government would appear to be rapidly becoming the stuff of folk memory, regardless of which political party is in power, the necessary funding will need to be found. My view is that institutions will adapt over time to the need to set aside, say, 10% of annual income to fund capital development in the same way that they adapted

to the introduction of fees for overseas students or the abolition of certain earmarked grants. However, I have serious doubts about the practicability of the PFI approach, given the complexity of the relationships among the so-called partners. Such complexity breeds bureaucracy which costs money: money which HEIs really cannot afford.

Conclusion

Thus, gazing into my crystal ball for advice to pass to Sir Ron Dearing and his colleagues, I try to look ten years ahead, rather than the one or two years of immediate concern. And what do I see?

- a very different and very differentiated tuition fees regime;

- a very uneven landscape of earnings from overseas involvements;

- great differences in the research resources available to different HEIs;

- some (and probably far too few) real earners from entrepreneurial research activities;

- a high level of self-dependence in capital funding.

To many this will be a vision of purgatory; to others a promise of opportunity. Sadly, I believe that it is likely that pending external events will determine the ability of individual institutions to make their own choice of which of these positions they occupy. I am an optimist and an opportunist. I fondly hope that I am joined in my position of promise by as many Scottish HEIs as possible.

References

1   *University of Glasgow: History and Constitution* (Glasgow 1977).

2   George Davie: *The Democratic Intellect* (2nd Edition, Edinburgh 1964).

3   Peter Clarke: *Hope and Glory – Britain 1900 to 1990* (London 1996).

4   Simon Jenkins: *Accountable to None – the Tory Nationalization of Britain* (London 1995).

5   Will Hutton: *The State We're In* (London 1995).

6   Further and Higher Education Act (Scotland) 1992.

7   See the reports in *The Higher,* e.g. 9 August 1996.

8   As is evidenced by the threatened action of New Zealand students against universities which fail to reach standards expected by (part) fee-paying students.

A message from BP

I am pleased that BP is associated with COSHEP in publishing this important book which will undoubtedly make a major contribution to the debate about the future of Scottish higher education.

BP's recent Aiming for a College Education (ACE) initiative had two main aims: to help raise the number of young people staying at school after 16 with a view to entering further and higher education; and to stimulate debate about, and enhance understanding of, issues relating to access and participation in further and higher education.

These aims were tackled in Scotland through action research: seven separate long term projects were funded by BP during 1990-95. These made a real and lasting contribution to raising the educational prospects and potential of young people in Scotland. For example, Student Tutoring, introduced into Scotland by ACE, is now being sustained in higher education institutions across Scotland.

The success of the ACE projects resulted from the strength of the partnerships built up between BP and education providers, including most of the higher education institutions represented by COSHEP.

I am therefore glad that BP's association with COSHEP is continued through the publication of this book by so many distinguished authors. As Scottish higher education looks to the future I am sure this book will help the issues it faces to be better understood.

Kneale Johnson
Programme Director
Aiming for a College Education (ACE)
BP in Scotland

Preface

This book would not have seen the light of day in the absence of the willing support and encouragement of a number of individuals and organisations. First, and most obviously, I have to acknowledge the almost universally enthusiastic responses of my chosen authors, which was more than I dared hope for; their contributions **are** the book and I am the first to appreciate that it was most unfair of me to add to their already impossible burdens in this way.

As anyone who has ever attempted an exercise of this kind will doubtless confirm, it is, however, one thing to conceptualise a book and quite another to bring the idea to fruition. The fact that it has happened is entirely attributable to two generous underwiters – the Carnegie Trust for the Universities of Scotland and *The Times Higher Education Supplement* – and to a magnificent sponsor, BP. To Professor Terry Coppock and Mr Kneale Johnson I owe a special debt of gratitude.

Last but by no means least in my list of acknowledgments, I am delighted to pay tribute in these preliminaries to Bob Fordie, Administrative Assistant in the COSHEP office, whose wizardry on the keyboard resolved the formidable difficulties I would otherwise have faced with the daunting task of preparing the text for printing.

Finally, it is essential for me to emphasise that the views set forth in the chapters that follow are unequivocally and unambiguously those of the individual authors themselves and must not, therefore, be held to represent the position on the issues discussed of either COSHEP or of the institutions in which the authors may hold paid employment, or with which they may be otherwise associated.

Ronald Crawford
Glasgow: February 1997.

Foreword

Professor Sir John C Shaw
Chairman, Scottish Higher Education Funding Council

This collection of essays from key figures in Scottish higher education attests that there is, within an international context, a proud history and distinctive tradition of higher education in Scotland. The wide range of topics covered by the contributors demonstrates the dynamism of a sector which benefits from the diverse nature of its constituent institutions. The present vitality of Scottish universities and colleges proves that they have the capability and desire to meet new challenges and exploit changes in the educational, economic, social and cultural environments.

The overview of the Scottish sector and the analysis of its main features contained in this volume make an important contribution to the debate about the future of higher education at this crucial time, as the sector awaits later this year the conclusions of the National Committee of Inquiry into Higher Education on the shape, structure, size and funding of higher education in the UK over the next 20 years.

A distinctive tradition
Four of Scotland's universities are over four hundred years old, and most of the other higher education institutions trace their roots back to the eighteenth and nineteenth centuries. Teaching and scholarship, as well as research at the highest levels, have existed in Scotland's main population centres for centuries. This contrasts with experience in England, where, until the nineteenth century, universities existed only in Oxford and in Cambridge. The Scottish structure of provision, and a historical commitment to access to higher education as a right for the many rather than a privilege for the few, means that Scotland has long enjoyed high levels of participation in higher education. The Scottish experience of higher education has also always attracted students and scholars from beyond the border.

This engagement in furthering knowledge and pursuing scholarship and research is an important element in providing a cultural context and a historical depth to Scotland's national self-identity. Economically, the higher education system is a vital component in furnishing society with a large proportion of highly skilled, flexible and knowledgeable individuals who will help to secure international competitiveness and thus contribute to improving the quality of life for the population as a whole. And the significant local economic impact of higher education institutions (as employers, as consumers of goods and services, and in attracting students as temporary residents) is reinforced by their valuable overseas earnings for teaching and research.

It is obvious that the ability to play a full part in teaching, learning, scholarship and research in a world-wide context is fundamental to the continuing success of Scottish higher education. Scotland, as a small country geographically on the outer edges of the European Union, has always been international in its outlook and perspectives. The necessity of being able to compete internationally does not need to be argued. Higher education therefore has a major part to play, not just in helping to build a highly educated workforce, but also in contributing to attracting inward investment to Scotland.

Supporting the system

The higher education sector in Scotland currently includes twenty one institutions funded by the Scottish Higher Education Funding Council (SHEFC). SHEFC is the largest single source of funds for these institutions, providing across the sector 45 per cent of their total income. (In 1995-96 over £500 million was distributed for teaching, research, equipment and buildings to the universities and colleges funded by the Council.) The further 10 per cent of the sector's income derived from student fees is directly influenced by the Council's allocation of funded student places.

The Council sees its role as enabling institutions to provide high quality teaching and research; to underpin the competitiveness of the Scottish and UK economies; and to be responsive to the changing needs of society.

Challenges and opportunities

Developments over recent years have required Scottish higher education institutions and the Council to respond to swiftly changing policy objectives. The rapid expansion in student numbers in the late 1980s and early 1990s and the abolition of the 'binary line' have brought many benefits, but have also imposed considerable strains. The end in 1993 of the period of expansion and the introduction of consolidation of student numbers have increased financial pressures on institutions. No longer can reductions in funding per student be accommodated by admitting higher numbers. Universities and colleges are, therefore, required to identify areas of their activities where real gains in efficiency can be made, while ensuring they maintain their academic standards and the quality of their teaching and research. They now have to consider transformational rather than transitional change; to confront the need to consider discontinuing mature activities where they can generate only modest demand, in order to release resources for new, dynamic growth in other directions. And the Council is required to secure continued diversity of role and mission among the institutions it funds.

In his essay on strategic change (Chapter 9), John Sizer, Chief Executive of SHEFC, concludes that continuing pressures on all areas of public expenditure give little prospect of a more favourable position for public funding of higher education in the next few years. Institutions, he argues, must be encouraged to develop and implement innovative strategies for maintaining their responsiveness and vitality while at the same time maintaining their financial viability. The essay describes the framework the Council is using to promote discussion of these issues with higher education institutions.

Further development of the Scottish higher education system will need to take account of and seek to preserve diverse institutional missions. Diversity within the sector is a recurring theme throughout the essays which follow. John Arbuthnott gives a comprehensive overview of Scottish higher education in the opening chapter which is supported by a series of essays covering different aspects of the sector. Richard Shaw (Chapter 4) considers the achievements of and challenges for the 'new' universities – those accorded that status in the period after 1992. Chris Carter examines the key issues in the provision of art & design teaching and research in the Scottish higher education sector (Chapter 14), while Gordon Kirk offers a vision for teacher education (Chapter 13). An outline of the enormous and valuable contribution of the Open University (which is funded, even for its Scottish activities, by the Higher Education Funding Council for England) is given by John Daniel in Chapter 15.

Higher education must also continue to respond to the changing needs of British society and the economy. In his view from industry (Chapter 11), John McClelland argues that investment in higher education must be more sharply focused. His essay argues that, against a background of changing trends in global trade, international competitiveness and the spectacular growth of the Pacific Rim economies, a radical response is required with a redefined UK partnership between higher education and industry. He identifies the need to equip employees with a hierarchy or pyramid of knowledge and capabilities, accompanied by excellent personal communication skills and an internationalist approach to conducting business in world markets.

Scottish higher education makes an important contribution to Britain's competitiveness and quality of life through the research achievements of its institutions. Within its total funding, SHEFC invests £100 million each year in the research capabilities of Scottish universities and colleges. In Chapter 3, Andrew Miller brings a Scottish perspective to an analysis of research activity and funding in the late twentieth century. He argues that, while the contrast between basic and applied research has been blurred and issues of economic growth and quality of life are being addressed through the development of a 'global knowledge network' of research communities, selective support for fundamental excellence remains essential to preserve innovative creativity. The practical application and commercialisation of research is of paramount importance, as is highlighted in William Duncan's essay on the unique contribution which the Royal Society of Edinburgh makes to Scottish higher education (Chapter 17).

During the decade since 1986, the number of students in higher education in Scotland has increased by about 60 per cent. More than 40 per cent of all young Scots now go on to full-time higher education in the UK, compared to 31 per cent for Great Britain as a whole. As well as greater numbers of school leavers now choosing to go to university or college, more than one third of students now enter full-time higher education aged over twenty-one. If Scotland is to remain internationally competitive, educational participation will have to be sustained throughout students' working lives, and the structure of the higher education system will have to encourage and deliver 'lifelong learning'.

Over one third of full-time and more than half of part-time students in Scotland gain their first experience of higher education in further education colleges. Colleges of further education have emerged as competitors of higher education institutions both for resources and for students. The scale of higher education provision in further education is impressive and often understated. In Chapter 8, Tom Kelly explores the important relationships between further education colleges and higher education institutions, and identifies the new 'binary line' between these two sources of higher educational provision.

Students in the geographically more remote parts of the country have also enjoyed improved access in recent years through joint ventures undertaken by existing institutions and through developments such as the University of the Highlands & Islands project (which has secured the Secretary of State's commitment to explore options which build on learning technology and other facilities already established in the region). Describing the University of the Highlands & Islands as Scotland's first regional university – a university of its region and not just in its region – Sir Graham Hills sets out the background and an agenda for the future (Chapter 7).

The expansion within higher education of part-time provision and part-time access programmes has grown steadily through the nineties. In Chapter 16 Maria Slowey paints a 'diverse and vibrant picture' of continuing education activity within higher education. She argues that the characteristics of continuing education today will influence the shape of higher education in the future. Responsiveness and flexibility, equality of opportunity and the dissemination of knowledge and skills to the broader community will be reflected in essential features of higher education provision.

New modes of learning and delivery will help to cater for these emerging patterns of wider participation. Council funding has helped Scottish higher education to develop one of the most sophisticated and comprehensive information technology networks in Europe. Scottish higher education institutions are at the forefront of developments in the technologies of learning. As identified by Alistair MacFarlane in Chapter 5, institutions will need to continue to develop their leadership in this field in order to seize the opportunities presented by the knowledge revolution.

Conclusion

The Scottish Higher Education Funding Council and the Committee of Scottish Higher Education Principals (COSHEP) have common cause in supporting the further development of a world class higher education system for Scotland. Since their respective and recent establishment, the Council has consistently sought a constructive dialogue with COSHEP. Discussions have fostered a level of mutual understanding of issues and a common resolve to achieve solutions. Council members have been made aware of growing concern among institutional leaders for the quality of higher education provision in the present funding environment. SHEFC has sought to explore the potential for establishing jointly with COSHEP a long-term strategic agenda for higher education in Scotland. The Council seeks to understand how it might assist institutions to drive forward the changes needed within this agenda. The relationship between the Council and the institutions it funds is positive and is valued on both sides. Developing this dialogue over the years to come will support the Scottish sector as it confronts the many challenges of securing its quality and distinctiveness.

Such challenges will be highlighted in the forthcoming report of the National Committee of Inquiry into Higher Education. Its recommendations on the future shape, structure, size and funding of higher education in the UK are expected in the latter half of 1997. Its Scottish Committee will advise on those aspects which define Scottish higher education distinctively. At the time of writing it is obviously premature to speculate about the final conclusions, but it is already clear that the recommendations of the National and Scottish Committees will have a considerable influence on how the Scottish higher education institutions operate as well as on how SHEFC defines its future objectives.

The excellent essays in this volume demonstrate the personal commitment of all the contributors to maintaining and enhancing the distinctive tradition of Scottish higher education. All will strive to play their part in ensuring that the Scottish higher education system emerges from this eventful period well equipped to contribute to the future economic, cultural and intellectual life of the nation.

Sir John C Shaw CBE
Chairman, Scottish Higher Education Funding Council

Jack Shaw has been Chairman of SHEFC since its creation in 1992, became Chairman of the Advanced Management Programme in Scotland Ltd., on its formation in 1995, and is a member of the Board of Scottish Enterprise. In 1996 he was appointed to the (new) Scottish Economic Council.

He is a Deputy Governor of Bank of Scotland and Chairman of its subsidiary, NWS BANK PLC.

He held the Johnstone Smith Chair of Accountancy at the University of Glasgow for 6 years until December 1982 and is now a Visiting Professor there. He was President of the Institute of Chartered Accountants of Scotland 1983-84.

Contents

Part II   Sharpening the focus

Part I

Opportunities and threats

INTRODUCTION

Ronald Crawford

Higher Education in Scotland: a "painful transformation"

In its 1991 White Paper *Higher Education – a New Framework* the Government projected a GB Age Participation Index (defined in the White Paper as a percentage of the "averaged 18-19 year old population") of around 33% by the year 2000. In 1994-95 Scotland had achieved an API of 42.7% of young Scots (defined as the number of Scots under 21 as a proportion of 17 year olds) entering full-time higher education. In the same year almost 50,000 Scots of all ages entered full-time HE courses in Scotland and a further 3,000 Scots entered full-time HE courses elsewhere in the UK, with a more than compensating inflow of 8,400 full-time entrants from the rest of the UK into Scottish institutions. In 1994-95 there were 154,500 full-time equivalent students registered on HE courses in Scotland. Altogether 27% of HE students in Scotland were enrolled in FE institutions.

Figure 1 shows – against that background of record numbers – the resources (in terms of state funding) allocated to the Scottish HE sector for **teaching** (ie excluding recurrent funding for research) over the period 1980-81 up to 1996-97 (the latter grant year being an estimated figure). Comparison of the phenomenal increase in the size of the student population from the start of the 1980s with the index of teaching resource over the same period graphically reveals the extent to which the Government has met its overall objective of expanding higher education on a year-in, year-out lower and lower unit of resource. The Government says that it has achieved its aim of value for money – the "even more for even less" mantra – while the institutions of HE claim that it is HE on the cheap and that the policy is in danger of driving some of them to the wall.

All of this might have been foreseen. But it was not. Some argue that Scottish higher education is today paying the price for a lack of clear vision in the 1980s

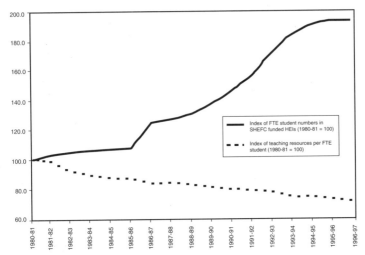

Figure 1: Extrapolation from Annexes B and C of *Expenditure in SHEFC Funded Higher Education Institutions* (SOEID, 1996) – report of Joint SOEID, SHEFC, COSHEP Working Group. It should be noted that student numbers exclude Napier and Glasgow Colleges of Technology up to 1985/86 inclusive. The 1996/97 position is an estimate.

and, it has to be said, of an over-commitment to institutional self-interest at the expense of the overall interests of the Scottish HE sector as a whole. But it is difficult to see how, in the circumstances of the time, it could have been otherwise. In many ways, it was the inevitable outcome of a divided system which, to its credit, the STEAC report of 1985 attempted to correct.

It is certainly not the purpose of this book to draft a blueprint of the future shape and pattern of higher education in Scotland, least of all to second-guess the Dearing inquiry. Rather is it an attempt to present a vision of higher education from the distinctive Scottish angle which the authors see as the way in which our approach to HE is set to develop in the post-Dearing era. HE has made its mistakes in the past. We have to avoid repeating them in the future.

Dearing and Scotland

The idea for this book grew out of an awareness that the inquiry into higher education announced by the Government in Parliament in February 1996 presages what is set to be the most fundamental re-appraisal of HE in Britain since the Robbins Committee report of 1963.

Uniquely for an inquiry of this kind, a Scottish Committee under the convenership of Sir Ron Garrick – there has been a studious avoidance of the term "sub-committee" – has been set up for the purpose of advising the main Committee on distinctive Scottish issues. However, the Scottish Committee is not merely an agent of information; it has its own agenda which enables it to consider, admittedly within the remit of the main Committee, the "potential contribution of, and the requirements for and of, Scottish higher education, in the Scottish, UK and international context" as well as "factors particularly relevant to the future shape, range, organisation and funding of Scottish higher education".

This means that the Garrick Scottish Committee is poised to influence the future direction and pattern of HE in Scotland more fundamentally than any other comparable inquiry since Robbins reported in 1963. It is entirely right that the Government has seen fit to order a review of HE at this time because it is now generally accepted that, regardless of the outcome of Dearing and Garrick, Scottish HE veritably stands at the proverbial crossroads.

A future "less friendly to higher education"?
It is, of course, not only in Britain that higher education is being put under the microscope. In Australia, too, higher education faces tough spending curbs, the much-vaunted Contribution Scheme is, we are told, to be re-constructed and a Dearing-type independent review will take a long-distance look at HE over the next 10 to 20 years.

In the United States most non-private universities are now having to confront the distasteful prospect of waning support for HE. The President of Indiana University, Myles Brand, has eloquently described the problem now facing higher education in the US. His text is worth quoting *in extenso*:

> "The forces of change affecting higher education have been much discussed. . . Since the 1980s, support for higher education has been waning. The evidence, moreover, points to a permanent shift. The federal government is embarked on a program to balance the budget. As a result, student financial aid, research support, and funds for medical education, to name the primary areas, will diminish considerably. Additionally, Indiana, like other states, has assigned a lower priority to higher education than to immediate needs such as the schools, prisons and the criminal justice system, health care . . . There is reluctance to invest in the future. . .

Second, universities, like every institution in America, are facing increased scrutiny and more stringent standards of accountability. . . We may lament this change, but we would be unwise to ignore it.

Third, the world is changing for everyone, not just for us in the university. An ever-increasing range of jobs today requires some kind of higher education and the ability to learn as the job changes or as people change careers. The needs of the society and economy of the future require us to educate a much broader sector of the population in the intellectual skills and habits that will enable our graduates to learn throughout their lives.

Stated directly, the challenge we face is this: How do we respond to a fundamentally changing environment while sustaining our academic excellence and our core values and traditions? The problem underlying this question may be stated yet more urgently: Unless we respond to changes in the environment of higher education, we will not be able to raise the resources we need to sustain our excellence. In resolving this problem, we should not seek to redesign a successful university, but rather to initiate changes that enhance what is good and vital, and create what is necessary to flourish in a future less friendly to higher education." [1]

In Japan, great expectation is being placed on Japanese universities undertaking serious self-reform. The Deputy Director-General of the Higher Education Bureau writes:

"The greatest challenge facing Japanese universities is the enhancement of quality. A number of issues require urgent solution, including a lack of diversity in course curricula, a lax evaluation system and the resulting lack of competition, a closed and rigid system of institutional administration and a weak financial base. . .". [2]

Scottish higher education is facing remarkably similar pressures for change and the diagnosis of the malady is not so very different from that formulated by President Brand. How is it that HE in Scotland should now be entering a critical phase? Why should the outcome of Dearing/Garrick be of enormous potential importance to our universities and colleges? And can we in Scotland similarly conclude that we are facing a future "less friendly to higher education"?

Wandering off course
When Robbins reported in 1963 there were four universities in Scotland and Government commitment to a fifth (from the Royal College of Science and

Technology, Glasgow) had already been confirmed.[3] Over twenty years later, when Scotland had eight universities, the report *Future Strategy for Higher Education in Scotland* was published as a "review of higher education in Scotland" undertaken, at the behest of the Secretary of State for Scotland, by the Scottish Tertiary Education Advisory Council. In the year STEAC reported, 1985, there were 31 HE institutions in Scotland. The membership of the Council was comprehensive and distinguished, including one university Principal and three serving or former college Principals. Rarely has an exercise in well-intended crystal-ball gazing turned out to be so innocently, yet, admittedly with the benefit of hindsight, so disastrously wide of the mark.

STEAC got some things right: notably the desirability of extending formal arrangements for credit transfer and, above all, as already observed, that arrangements for the future funding of HE in Scotland should be devolved to the Secretary of State for Scotland – even though the Council's expressed preference for an "overarching" planning and funding body (SHEPFC), covering the whole of the HE sector, was refused. But STEAC got things seriously wrong on two vital counts: demand for higher education and predicted Government policy on the future of the binary line.

Figure 2: Students in full-time higher education in Scotland (STEAC p. 149)

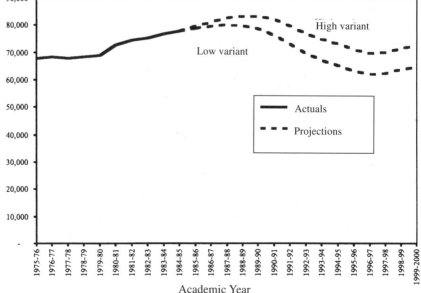

Donald McCallum's STEAC found revised Scottish Education Department projections of demand "broadly reasonable" and concluded that the "number of initial entrants to higher education from traditional sources is likely to decline sharply from the end of the present decade" and, accordingly, suggested that "recruitment should be encouraged from groups which have not previously provided many students for higher education courses." The SED projections which STEAC found "broadly reasonable" were based on the premise that the total number of full-time students (including postgraduates) in HE in Scotland would peak at between c.80,000 and c.83,000 in 1987-88/1988-89 and would then start to fall to between c.62,000 and c.69,600 in 1996-97 – a fall of between 16% and 23% from the peak. Figure 2, abstracted from the STEAC report, graphically illustrates the number projections which informed the Council's recommendations.

As we have seen, however, far from peaking in 1987-1989, numbers of full-time students have climbed inexorably to a staggering 142,700 in 1994-95 – the latest year for which comparable statistics are available from the SOEID. Instead of the 16 to 23% fall predicted by STEAC, the Scottish HE sector has experienced an amazing 58% **increase** over the period from 1989-90 to 1994-95 alone. Put another way, the review that was to influence the future direction of HE in Scotland was wrong in its forecast of demand **by a factor of nearly three**. STEAC set aside much more optimistic forecasts of demand submitted by the Association of University Teachers and by the Standing Committee of the Scottish Universities. STEAC's plea for the stimulation of recruitment from non-traditional sources bore fruit to an extent that even the Council could not have contemplated.

But it was not just the future statistical base of HE in Scotland that STEAC misapprehended. The review's analytical judgement was also flawed. In a chapter entitled "Future roles of higher education sectors" STEAC set out its views on what the sectors within HE should be offering in future and on some of "the underlying principles" which it believed ought to inform Government policies. Here, fatally, the Council failed to grasp the frustrations suffered by the central institutions in their relations with the universities and timidly concluded that they should simply endorse the roles the CIs currently had to the extent that they "should continue on similar lines". The Council concluded that they did not consider "fundamental change" was needed.

To be fair, STEAC was neither the first nor by any means the sole body to underestimate demand for HE in Britain or to fail to anticipate the massive changes that were set to transform higher education in the 1990s. A year earlier, the UGC had responded to Sir Keith Joseph's request that they advise him on the future funding, size and academic organisation of the university system in Britain with the document *A Strategy for Higher Education into the 1990s*. It is of as much practical relevance to the subsequent reality of what actually happened to higher education in the 1990s as a shotgun to an elephant hunter. While admitting that projections of demand were notoriously unreliable and suggesting that they needed regular revisiting – perhaps especially in Scotland – they, with what now appears a breathtaking lack of realism, recommended level funding until at least the end of the decade ("We do not believe that the universities could satisfactorily teach the present number of students with fewer resources than they now have."), a longer planning horizon for recurrent grant and, in words remarkably similar to those of STEAC in contemplating the future of the Scottish central institutions, that the role of the UGC should "remain largely unchanged."

The result of all this was the now almost totally forgotten Green Paper produced by Sir Keith Joseph in May 1985 – *The Development of Higher Education into the 1990s*. Writing in *The Sunday Times*[4] immediately after its publication, Peter Wilby asserted that "anyone who struggles through it . . . will be forced to conclude that Ministers have effectively rigged the figures." He pointed out that the country's future workforce needs were even more difficult to forecast than student demand and that, consequently, contraction policies which involved closing subject departments and even whole universities – which the Green Paper did not dismiss – carried "as many dangers for the nation as for future generations." Who would have then envisaged – a mere seven years later – the passing of legislation the effect of which was to double the number of universities in the country and lead to hitherto unimagined rates of student participation in higher education?

Ball and the "painful transformation"
The tentativeness of STEAC should be contrasted with the vision of Christopher Ball. In his introduction to *Higher Education into the 1990s* (written only four years after STEAC reported, but admittedly in the light of the Government's 1987 White Paper *Higher Education – Meeting the Challenge,* to the formulation of which he made a major contribution), Ball asserts:

"The fundamental challenge facing UK higher education since the middle of the twentieth century has been how to adapt an elite system to provide a popular model; when the history of higher education in the present century comes to be written, I believe that the painful transformation to a popular system will prove to be the key theme." [5]

Painful transformation indeed. In 1991 Ball accepted an invitation to address the Annual Conference of the Scottish Universities at Edzell on the theme *The expansion of higher education: ways and means.* I was then Secretary to the Conference and wrote up the official record of the meeting subsequently circulated to all the delegates. Of Ball's talk I wrote the following account:

"The actual demand for higher education was well above the number of places available. Latent demand was substantial and there was a pool of talent in the country that was well-nigh inexhaustible.

Higher education was undergoing five revolutions at the same time:

- Universities were having to grapple with the notion that serious motivation would itself determine the capacity to benefit – a new interpretation of the Robbins principle that was nothing short of 'amazing'. This was what access was all about.

- There had to be provision for lifelong learning. An initial education no longer sufficed.

- Higher education was facing a new curriculum that was analogous in its far-reaching implications to the New Learning of the 16th century.

- Our processes of learning and the new technologies were a constant challenge.

- **The 'cost-effectiveness' principle (the highest efficiency at the lowest cost) ruled as much in higher education as in everything else."** [6]

My report of Sir Christopher's address ended

"He concluded his remarks by forecasting that before long a new White Paper would re-define higher education on the American model. This would be a logical outcome to the *New Framework* White Paper which simply represented an obvious conclusion of more than twelve years of debate, evolution and development."

In the event, "before long" was little over a year and the "new White Paper" was, in fact, the *Further and Higher Education Acts 1992*. Whether or not UK higher education has had an "American model" imposed on it is, of course, open to conjecture.

The 1992 *Further and Higher Education Acts* ended the binary divide, made the polytechnics universities and devolved the funding of HE in Scotland to a new quango known as the Scottish Higher Education Funding Council. Significantly, however, SHEFC would not be the all-singing, all-dancing **planning** and funding organisation – SHEPFC – which STEAC (and prominent individuals such as Sir Alwyn Williams, himself a member of STEAC, and Sir Graham Hills) had consistently and earnestly desired.

Back on course: a future based on partnerships

In the last analysis, it was the 1992 Acts which made it inevitable that the essentially *ad hoc,* reactive way in which the older universities had previously ordered their collective affairs would have to go. The CVCP could not represent the whole of a sector united under a common funding framework any more than could the Committee of Principals and Directors of the Scottish Central Institutions (COPADOCI) represent the newly created universities who were naturally anxious to join their older brethren in the same representative organisation. Any lingering doubts were quickly dispelled by the Chairman-designate of SHEFC, Professor Jack Shaw, who made it abundantly clear that the Council was prepared to deal with only one organisation which could articulate a common view on behalf of the totality of the sector and could engage in purposeful dialogue with SHEFC. That would be of crucial importance in the particular context of the avalanche of consultative papers which began to flow from the new Council. It was in this way that COSHEP was born.

It is neither naive nor fanciful to predict that higher education in the future will be organised much more positively than at any time in the past on coherent partnerships – not just partnerships between institutions but partnerships that run *across* sectors. For a variety of reasons, such partnerships are, arguably, considerably more credible in Scotland than elsewhere in the British HE system.

If that necessarily speculative scenario turns out to be accurate, the role of the representative bodies – among them, COSHEP, which has the advantage of incorporating all of the HEIs funded by SHEFC but not (or at least, according to some, not **yet**) any of the HE providers within the FE sector – becomes even more crucial. With the benefit of hindsight the lesson of the past is that the Scottish institutions of higher education did not have an impressive record of working in partnership with one another, least of all as a coherent whole. That has changed – dramatically and effectively. When COSHEP sends its annual Public Expenditure Survey submission concurrently to the Scottish Office and to the media, it is commented upon in both *The Herald* and *The Scotsman* leaders. That would have been inconceivable in the 1980s.

Of course, partnerships imply co-ordination, collaboration and, let it be said, rationalisation. They are by no means one and the same thing. It would be silly, for example, to pretend that institutions will be prepared to forego self-interest to the greater advantage of the sector as a whole. Indeed, it now seems more and more likely to many educationists that institutions will be rewarded in future if they succeed in developing missions that are distinctive and, above all, *appropriate* and, even, to be rewarded for having done so.

And so the message of this book of essays is a positive and generally upbeat one. Scottish higher education has a challenging future as never before. Certainly, the road could be rocky in places. But it is a future full of opportunity. Thus far, we cannot conclude that we necessarily face the scenario of President Brand of a future less friendly to higher education. In some ways the future is what the institutions, individually and collectively – admittedly, adequately resourced – make of it. One thing is sure. The **only** way for higher education to survive as a strong and healthy prime national asset is for it – the sector jointly and severally – to maintain its diversity and build on its tradition of high quality. To that end, it is hoped that the contents of this book will prove relevant and useful to the National Inquiry and to the general reader.

Acknowledgement
Thanks are due Dr Gerry Webber of the University of Edinburgh for assistance with the preparation of Figure 1.

References

1   Indiana University, 1996: *The Strategic Directions Charter: becoming America's new public university.*

2   From a letter by Katsuhide Kusahara, Deputy Director-General of the Higher Education Bureau of the Japanese Ministry of Education, Science and Culture in *Nature*, 374, 13 April 1995.

3   It is often, wrongly, assumed that it was the Robbins Report that recommended the elevation of the RCST, Glasgow to a university – the University of Strathclyde. In fact, the decision ante-dated Robbins. See footnote to p 33 of the Report.

4   *The Sunday Times* – 26 May 1985.

5   Ball and Eggins (ed): *Higher Education into the 1990s* – Introduction by Sir Christopher Ball (SRHE and the Open University Press, 1989).

6   Official report of the 1991 Annual Conference of the Universities of Scotland on the theme: "The Expansion of Higher Education: ways and means".

Dr Ronald L Crawford
Secretary to the Committee of Scottish Higher Education Principals (COSHEP)

Ronald Crawford MA, B Litt, Dr *hc* is a graduate of the University of Glasgow where he undertook research in regional Scottish literature. Having spent virtually all of his long career in university administration at the University of Strathclyde, he was appointed foundation Secretary to COSHEP in 1992. He was a member of the Howie Committee which reported on upper secondary education in Scotland in 1992.

1

John Arbuthnott[*]

The distinctiveness of Scottish higher education

At his installation as Chancellor of the new University of Stirling in 1968, Lord Robbins commented:

> "All my life as an academic I have been conscious of a quite special debt to Scottish intellectual influences and a quite special admiration for the Scottish university tradition, both for its achievements and for the educational principles on which it rests . . . and . . . the debt which we owe to those outstanding Scottish thinkers who in the last three quarters of the 18th Century laid the foundations of the systematic study of society, particularly in its economic aspects."[1]

Lord Robbins, a key figure in the development of UK higher education in modern times, recognised the existence of a distinctive and long-standing Scottish university tradition. He chose the occasion of the creation of a new Scottish university to recall that tradition, seeing the establishment of the University of Stirling as a significant point in the evolution of Scottish higher education.

The distinctiveness of Scottish higher education has its roots in its historical origins. In order to identify and understand the Scottish tradition to which Lord Robbins referred, it is necessary to reflect upon the influences that have shaped higher education today. This chapter briefly examines the historical context and highlights some of the most observable differences between Scottish higher education and that in the rest of the UK. It then indicates some of the issues which those in higher education today must consider in order to ensure that Scottish higher education continues to meet the needs of its students and the country in the future.

Historical influence

The history of Scottish higher education goes back to the 15th Century with the foundation of three universities, St Andrews, Glasgow and Aberdeen. The University of Edinburgh was established in the latter half of the 16th Century. From a very early time, therefore, higher education in Scotland was more widespread than that in any other part of these islands.

The Scottish universities were at the heart of intellectual, religious and civic debate throughout their history. However it is arguably the effect of the Scottish Enlightenment and the rapid industrialisation of Scotland's cities that had the most profound effect upon a developing tradition.

In the 18th Century the Scottish universities produced some of the world's leading philosophers and political thinkers, including David Hume and Adam Smith. The activity and vitality of Scottish intellectual life at that time contrasted starkly and favourably with that of Oxford and Cambridge which were then in a period of stagnation.

Robbins also remarked upon this:

> "I think the lamp of learning would have burnt very dim in the English speaking world in those days had it not been for the Scottish universities." [2]

Hand in hand with the advancement of learning, the Scottish universities became closely entwined with the social and commercial world of the cities in which they were located. The universities could not afford the luxury of divorce from the pressing social and economic questions of the time. They were engaged in the life of the city, involved with – and constantly questioned by – their fellow citizens: by clerics and the merchants and tradesmen who made up a growing proportion of the urban population. It was scarcely possible to ignore the commercial and social life of the nation when surrounded by debate upon the nature and purpose of university education. Fellow citizens were not hesitant in their criticism – as a 1761 pamphlet : *The Defects of an University Education and Its unsuitableness to a Commercial people* [3] demonstrates.

The social fabric of universities grew to differ in substantial ways from that prevailing south of the border, creating an additional imperative upon the universities to be involved with the commercial world. By the 1790s *half* of Glasgow University's students came from families engaged in industry and commerce.[4] Such tension was ultimately creative, with *Gown* constantly impelled to engage with *Town* both in discussion and in argument.

The city of Glasgow furnishes many prominent examples of the developing role of higher education. The deep interest and involvement of 18th century Glasgow townspeople in higher education is reflected in the speed and enthusiasm with which they put into action a proposal to establish a *second* university in Glasgow in the 1790s. This university, which was to be dedicated to the principles of 'liberality of sentiment' and 'useful learning', was proposed in the Will of John Anderson, a Glasgow University Professor and a pioneer in widening access to university classes.

For many years John Anderson had opened up a number of his lectures to townspeople. His *anti-toga*[5] classes in Experimental Philosophy, which involved the demonstration by experiment of scientific principles, attracted wide audiences from among the city's artisans and craftsmen.

The establishment of Anderson's Institution in 1796[6] led in time to the development of technical education of all kinds, providing a foundation for the creation, among others, of the Mechanics' Institutes. The development of Adult Education throughout the UK is widely believed to have originated from the example of Anderson's Institution.[7]

It is an interesting point to note that among the progressive educational tenets enshrined in John Anderson's Will were that classes should be open to women. This is possibly the first example of higher education of any kind in the UK being open to women. In the first year of Anderson's Institution in 1796, nearly half of the 972 students were women.[8]

Throughout the history of Scottish higher education the universities and colleges that sprang up were closely allied to community and commercial interests. The role of religion in promoting education, particularly children's education, was fundamental. The Churches directed much of their efforts towards alleviating the misery of the poor in the industrial age and it was widely believed that education was the best means of promoting a Christian civilisation and culture, reducing crime and cultivating a sense of citizenship.

It was in Scotland that one of the world's first teacher training institutions was established – Dundas Vale Normal Seminary, established by David Stow in the

1830s[9]. This was based upon the premise that children needed to be taught by example and the proper training of their instructors was an essential element in this process.

The widespread existence of parish schools provided access to some sort of education for children from virtually every class. While it is true that it took the most determined individual to work their way forward from the lowest classes to finally gain entrance to a university, it was possible, and this was reflected in the wider social 'reach' and composition of the universities.

Over time, many new institutions developed to provide for the demands of a population which saw education as an important path forward in life. Another element of the Scottish experience was the importance of the international dimension; aside from Scotland's links with the European Continent, it should also be noted that throughout the 19th and 20th centuries students came to Scotland from much further afield – such as from India and Japan. The influence of Scots across the world throughout the industrial age is well known.

Scottish higher education today

The historical development of Scottish higher education has led to a sector which is today a central part of Scottish society. Education continues to be seen as essential in the social and economic life of the nation. This ethos permeates the structure and organisation of higher education and influences its relationships with schools, further education, business and government.

Today the Scottish higher education sector is made up of 21 universities and colleges, funded through the Scottish Higher Education Funding Council (SHEFC). There is, in addition, thriving Open University activity and a Scottish Agricultural College. In 1994/95 over 350,000 students[10] studied at higher education institutions. Over 145,000 of these were registered for a first or higher degree, the others – reflecting the wide and vital role of higher education in the community – were studying on a wide range of continuing education and professional development courses.

The composition of the sector ranges from the 13 universities to 8 smaller monotechnic and specialist colleges such as teacher training institutions and Colleges of Art. Between them, the institutions provide education in nearly every discipline.

Administratively, all Scottish education, including higher education, is the responsibility of the Secretary of State for Scotland. The Scottish higher education institutions are funded by the Scottish Office, through SHEFC. Broadly speaking, the responsibilities and the operations of SHEFC are similar to those of the Higher Education Funding Council for England (HEFCE). However, SHEFC is empowered to – and does – respond to specifically Scottish requirements.

Structure and philosophy

The major observable difference in the Scottish higher education system from that prevalent in the rest of the UK is the existence of the three year Ordinary and four year Honours degree, compared to the norm of the three year Honours degree elsewhere. This is not simply an anomaly but part of a coherent structure which complements and builds upon the existing school structures.

The Scottish school structure is based around a broad curriculum with students taking external Standard Grade examinations at the end of the fourth year, and Higher Grade examinations at the end of 5th year. At Standard Grade a pupil is required to study all types of subject, including English, mathematics, a science, a social subject and a modern language. There is an increasing range of other options such as National Certificate modules (awarded through the Scottish Vocational Education Council). However, the overall aim remains that the pupil gains a good grounding in a broad range of subjects.

The majority of students (around 75%) stay on for the fifth year at school, with a proportion going to a Further Education college. In S5 there is a range of National Certificate modules, General Scottish Vocational Qualifications and other options as well as a range of Higher Grade subjects.

It is typically upon Higher Grade results that entrance to university is based, although a number of students choose to stay on at school for a sixth year, taking the Certificate of Sixth Year Studies(CSYS). University entrance is based upon students presenting a broad range of Highers, four or, more usually, five Highers taken in one year of study, showing a breadth of knowledge over different subjects. This is in comparison to the school structure elsewhere in the UK which is aimed at specialisation in 2 or 3 subjects to 'A' Level over a two year period of study. This also means that those students who do not remain at school for Sixth Year Studies but enter university on the basis of Highers are, on average, one year younger than their counterparts in the rest of the UK.

The Scottish university structure builds upon the philosophy of breadth of education, with students studying a wide range of subjects in first and second year, not usually being required to choose subjects for specialisation until the third year. The four year Honours degree is, therefore, based upon the concept of specialisation being most appropriately developed upon the base of a broad general education. Of course, there are exceptions to this rule, particularly when it comes to professional subjects such as medicine. However, it is in the general picture that the differences between the Scottish structure and that in the rest of UK higher education is most apparent.

For a three year Honours degree in other parts of the United Kingdom, students are frequently admitted to a specific course involving only one or two subjects of study, further focusing upon the specialisation already evident at 'A' Level.

There is a particular feature of the Scottish higher education system which must be mentioned, in that it allows for the award after three years of a General or Ordinary degree. This was traditionally part and parcel of a broad based degree system where a General degree was the mark of a person with a good all round education (the *Lad*, and nowadays *Lass, o' Pairts*). The progression of the majority of students to a final Honours year is a fairly recent phenomenon; but the General degree still remains as a respected and valued qualification in its own right. Every year a number of students choose this option rather than continuing to take an additional Honours year. This is in contrast with other parts of the UK, where the award of an Ordinary degree is more usually made when a student is not deemed to have achieved sufficient marks for an Honours degree.

In recent years a national review of the Scottish school system has led to plans to introduce an 'Advanced Higher' to be achieved over two years of study, along with a more open learning structure for the 16-18 age group. This is designed to enable students to follow an approved core curriculum but with a wider range of academic and vocational options and with a number of different 'exit points'. The 'Higher' Grade remains as a core part of the structure. It remains to be seen how this will work in practice, how many students will choose to study Advanced Highers and what the implications may be for the higher education structure.

Sir Ron Dearing's recent review (1996) of the 16-19 curriculum in England and Wales has sought to broaden the range and nature of school qualifications in England, and also seeks to include them within a coherent framework. However, the 'A' Level will remain as the most common school leaving qualification for entrance to a UK university.

Participation rates in Scottish higher education

The participation rates in higher education in Scotland have always been higher than in England and Wales. The current Age Participation Rate (API) in Scotland (that is, the percentage of the population aged under 21 years participating in higher education) is now running at 43%. This is about 10% higher than the average for the UK as a whole. It should be noted that Scotland's Further Education colleges have played a valuable role in encouraging access to higher education, and a substantial proportion of Higher National Certificate and Diploma provision is found in Further Education colleges. Students from these colleges frequently progress to a university, with exemptions from first or sometimes second year of study. This is unlike the situation in England and Wales, where most Higher National provision is located within the higher education sector itself and, therefore, entrance has to be direct to university.

There are many factors which can influence participation: these may include finance and ease of access to higher education, through both a wide base of provision and through initiatives designed to encourage wider access. However, the relative importance attached to higher education by its community is also important through the encouragement of raised aspirations. This can be suggested as an important factor behind Scotland's high participation rate. The historical development of Scottish higher education has led to a sector which is today a central part of Scottish life and one which is recognised as an essential part of its community.

The higher education sector and its economic importance

Higher education in Scotland has been described as the higher education *sector*. The description of Scottish higher education as a sector reflects the extent to which it is regarded as an important part of the economy, and is treated as an industry by economic analysts and commentators. Perhaps, above all, it is the common understanding of the importance of higher education to the economic well-being of Scotland today and in the future that underpins the Sector's strength and standing in the community. The publication in 1995 by the Committee of Scottish Higher Education Principals (COSHEP) of a report[11] studying the business activity of higher education was widely commented on and its findings highlighted and discussed throughout Scotland. The report showed that in 1993/94 the Scottish higher education sector generated an estimated 68,217 full-time equivalent (FTE) jobs in Scotland. This was equal to 4.2% of total Scottish FTE employment in that year. It was welcomed by the Scottish Office as reflecting the success and dynamism of the Scottish higher education Sector.

It is a distinctive feature of Scottish higher education that its role as part of social and economic life in Scotland is so widely recognised. We have an advantage over our counterparts in the rest of the UK in that there is, for example, a greater appreciation of the value of higher education among business and other organisations. The President of Glasgow Chamber of Commerce recently commented that the universities in Glasgow have "created an internationally recognised wealth of academic and intellectual talent capable of keeping the city at the forefront of technological, cultural and commercial developments."[12]

The importance attached to Scottish higher education is also reflected by the attention paid to it by the media. In Scotland, higher education is regarded as *news* – and is reported as such in the main news pages of our daily papers and in the news bulletins of TV and radio. This is in contrast with the rest of the UK where coverage is usually confined to the specialist press and specialist 'education pages'. The fortunes of graduates from higher education are watched with interest and the high rates of graduate employment and positive career progression are not overlooked.[13]

Future consideration

Consideration of the distinctiveness of Scottish higher education is set in the context of an ongoing debate about the future of higher education throughout the UK. A National Committee of Inquiry into Higher Education has been established to take a strategic, long-term and holistic evaluation of the role of higher education in the UK and to make recommendations as to the future of higher education, its purpose and how it is to be funded. The Committee is deliberating upon how best to fulfil the needs of both the country and the individual in its consideration of higher education.

The role of higher education in underpinning the economic and social well-being of the UK is of vital importance. The changing nature of the global economy and what makes a country internationally competitive will have profound implications for higher education. The country producing the people with the highest skills will ultimately fare best in an open, global market. Higher education is a way of meeting the demands of the future.

It can be argued that in many ways Scottish higher education has an advantage over the rest of the UK. The Scottish tradition of breadth and the current flexibility of degree structures can provide a strong foundation for positive developments to meet the future needs of students. The support of the SHEFC has enabled Scottish institutions to take advantage of the UK-wide academic information networks by linking each Scottish institution to each other and to the national academic network. This means that Scotland now possesses a world-leading academic network infrastructure which can form the base for experimentation in the use of new technology in teaching and research.

But we cannot afford to be complacent. The degree structure, its length and flexibility in its teaching will all need to be kept under review. If new funding arrangements require students to share a greater proportion of the costs of their education, they will seek greater flexibility in its delivery. Studying for four consecutive years towards an Honours degree may not meet all students' needs. If Lifelong Learning is to become a reality, institutions will need to find ways to enable students to access higher education throughout their lives and for differing lengths of time. If the existence and standard of the General and Honours degrees are to be maintained, a new approach may be needed which enables students to work towards the achievement of a degree in stages.

The Scottish tradition has been of value and served the people of Scotland well for many years. However the strength of a tradition lies in its ability to evolve over time. It will be how the Scottish higher education sector meets *future* challenges that will define how well it serves its community.

Acknowledgement
I wish to record my grateful thanks to Ursula Kelly of the University of Strathclyde who co-authored the chapter.

References
1   Address delivered upon his installation as Chancellor of the University of Stirling, 1968.

2   Ibid.

3   Reverend William Thom, 1761.

4   Richard B Sher: *Commerce, Religion and the Enlightenment in Eighteenth-Century Glasgow*, from *Glasgow Volume I: Beginnings to 1830,* eds. T. M. Devine and Gordon Jackson, p 315.

5   Derived from *non-togati*, meaning those not wearing the academic gown.

6   Anderson's Institution developed throughout the 19th century to become the Royal Technical College and subsequently the Royal College of Science and Technology. It was recognised as a University College in 1919 and received a Royal Charter as the University of Strathclyde in 1964.

7   For example, George Birkbeck, a Professor in Anderson's Institution, subsequently collaborated in the establishment of the London Mechanics' Institution, now Birkbeck College.

8   Strathclyde University Archives: Anderson's Institution Minute Book, OB1/1.

9   *Training the Teachers: The History of Jordanhill College of Education 1828-1993*, eds. Margaret M. Harrison and Willis B. Marker.

10   Scottish Higher Education Funding Council Statistical Bulletin No.3/96.

11   *The Impact of the Higher Education Sector upon the Economy of Scotland*, Professor I H McNicoll, COSHEP 1995.

12   President, Glasgow Chamber of Commerce, *The Journal,* November 1996.

13   A recent longitudinal study of Scottish graduate destinations *The Class of '92* published by the Scottish Graduate Careers Partnership (1996) has shown that four years after graduation, unemployment among the 1992 cohort was only 2% (some of which was clearly frictional rather than structural) with 'an upward movement in salary bands in all the subject groups'.

Professor John P Arbuthnott
Principal and Vice-Chancellor, University of Strathclyde

Professor Arbuthnott became Principal and Vice-Chancellor of the University of Strathclyde in 1991. Formerly Convener (1994-1996) of the Committee of Scottish Higher Education Principals, he is currently a member of the Dearing National Committee of Inquiry into Higher Education.

2

Stewart Sutherland

Quality and standards

In the spring term of 1996, in the University of Edinburgh, there was not a single week in which we did not have the company of one Teaching Quality Assessment team or another. At the same time staff across the institution were preparing submissions for the Research Assessment Exercise and two departments had either just had, or were preparing for, the visit of Professional Accreditation bodies. Coincidentally we did manage to do some teaching and find some time to attend to our multi-million pound turnover research base. Happily that term we were spared the additional attentions of the Quality Audit Unit.

However, in terms of opportunity costs alone, I am forced to ask whether we have got the balance right between doing (teaching and research) and checking up (Quality Audit, Teaching Quality Assessment, Research Assessment Exercise, and Professional Accreditation).

There was clearly a belief that we had not, for through the relevant Secretaries of State, the Government set up a group under the chairmanship of Sir William Kerr Fraser to consider whether the varying pressures of Quality Audit, Teaching Quality Assessment and Professional Accreditation could be brought into more rational and efficient relation. The Research Assessment Exercise belongs to another set of interest groups and was excluded from that review.

Sir William was given an unenviable task which could have had great and positive outcome. However, the working group was, in the jargon, representative of the 'stakeholders' i.e. interested parties. The result is a report which represents at best a balance of the interests represented round the table, and more probably an aggregation of those interests. It is clear that the discussions of the group were characterised by lower-case and possibly lower-grade 'politics' and when the report was presented to the Committee of Vice-Chancellors and Principals we were told in no uncertain terms that the Report had been compressed into a single entity with the help of 'blood, sweat and tears'. It remains to be seen whether blood, sweat and tears have adhesive powers, or are merely the stains of war. As it currently stands, the Report holds out little hope of alleviating the distracting, and, I believe, unfruitful pressures of our current obsession with 'Quality Assurance' which I exemplified at the beginning of this paper.

By implication I have indicated that what is currently bedevilling the debate is that it is caught in a power struggle between interested parties. In fact this has an element of truth in it for the quality assurance industry is now quite large, and significant budgets are at stake However, this is too simple as an analysis, for the cross currents are very complex – and even worse, we are trying to navigate through them on the basis of imprecise terminology and confused thinking. I want to devote the rest of this paper to a clarification and discussion of some of the basic ideas at play and to point to some of the implications of that for the process of ensuring quality and protecting standards within universities.

Accountability and assurance
The first sign of confusion is that those currently responsible for designing the system do not indicate clearly whether the various processes to which we are subjected are designed to meet questions of accountability or questions of assurance. The notion of accountability is really quite straightforward and has been well-defined within the public sector with regard to financial accountability. In the latter context universities meet significant responsibilities *via* a not over-elaborate but effective system of Accounting and Designated Officers. However, it is also perfectly reasonable to ask whether in terms of the quality of academic activities the public purse is receiving value for money. Equally, and this lies at the core of the relevance of all this to academic autonomy, it is further reasonable to ask whether the responsibility for setting and maintaining academic standards entrusted to universities through relevant Charters and Acts of Parliament is a task of stewardship for which adequate forms of accountability exist.

One very good test of any specific proposals which arise from the implementation of the Report of Kerr Fraser's group will be to ask which of these strands of accountability that particular proposal helps us discharge.

My fear is that unless the group responsible for implementation is unusually punctilious in carrying out its remit (i.e. is uncharacteristically free of the successful pressures of interest groups) then the accretion of additional burdens imposed on universities will dwarf and compromise attempts to answer the legitimate questions of accountability.

The reasons which will be given for this, should anyone be bold enough to ask, will involve much use of the term 'assurance'. Associated with this will be much fudge which despite being intellectually inedible will be digested with relish in some quarters. The difficulty with the term 'assurance' is that it requires syntactic completion. The verb 'to assure' from which it is derived is transitive: we do not assure, in the abstract, we assure someone about something. More importantly, to set out to provide assurance in general is not just to misunderstand the rules governing the use of the word, it is to set off on a short walk to neurosis. Let me illustrate.

If one asks of Quality Audit and Teaching Quality Assessment, 'Do they provide assurance?', of course it is impossible to answer sensibly. The point is that in order to avoid that sort of nonsensical question we must first ask, 'Whom are we trying to assure about what?' This is a question which many in the quality assurance industry conspicuously fail to ask themselves clearly and as a consequence they find themselves without a real measure of their performance. Thus instead of first clarifying what it is that, for example, the Secretary of State or the Funding Council wish to be assured about and designing processes to meet that, the tendency is to provide catch-all forms of 'assurance'. The task then becomes something like assuring Orwell's Big Brother that of course one is a loyal, hard-working, relevance-seeking, teaching-devoted, credit-accumulating, semesterized university. The trouble is that it is not Big Brother (? Sister) that we speak to, only his officials, agents and computer terminals. We are never quite sure that this is what **he** wants or what **he** regards as a test of loyalty/assurance. (This contrasts quite markedly with the tests of accountability which, for example, apply to our financial responsibilities.) Very cleverly, Big Brother informs us through his officials, 'You can have your academic autonomy, I would not dream of interfering. Just one thing, however: **Do not forget to assure me.** Now go ahead and design your own assurance mechanisms, and before you ask, no, I will not tell you precisely what I want to be assured about. However, if you do not measure up, there may be penalties.'

Quality Assurance, if it remains in this current ill-defined form is not good news, and indeed should carry an intellectual health warning. If we do not know the question which we are answering we are unlikely to be able to define a process to give an adequate answer.

There are some of Big Brother's officials or self appointed interpreters who do have a solution to this problem. **They** are much clearer in what they want. What they desire is an end to this pretence of academic autonomy. What they want is the power of **Inspection**. This has the considerable advantage, from their point of view, that one need not specify what it is that one wants to be assured about, nor even whom it is that ought to be assured; rather one can send an inspection team to have a look in the hope that something will turn up! More of that anon.

Quality and standards

Accepting as we surely should that universities should properly be accountable, not simply for the financial propriety of their operations, but also for the value for money shown in the academic processes and ends towards which very substantial sums of public resource are devoted, we must now draw a clear distinction between the uses to which the terms 'quality' and 'standards' are put in this debate.

The systems currently in place in higher education, under the titles 'Quality Audit', and 'Teaching Quality Assessment' deal with quality understood as process. That is to say, the questions which are asked have to do with the provision made for teaching, whether directly in the classroom and laboratory, or indirectly in the library and through information technology and other support systems. The quite separate clutch of questions which address the standards set as output measures of academic success are not covered by current systems. Quite bluntly, it has not been deemed either prudent or possible sensitively to ask about the standards set by Institution X or Department Y in measuring what counts as satisfactory completion of a course, or appropriate standard for the award of a First Class Honours degree.

There are swings and roundabouts to be encountered in this area. On the one hand, if one is to talk in any meaningful sense of academic autonomy, one must be talking of the responsibility of universities to set academic standards. On the other hand, it is surprising that it is at a time of the huge expansion of higher education, that the proportion of students being awarded First and Upper Second Class Honours degrees is also rising. *Prima facie*, that seems implausible. My interim position is that there are real questions here, but that there is also a slippery slope which is beckoning.

A gradient was given to this slope during a meeting between John Patten, the then Secretary of State for Education, and his counterpart the Minister for Education in Malaysia in the latter's office in Kuala Lumpur in April 1994. The occasion was the visit of a United Kingdom Higher Education delegation led by the Secretary of State to discuss areas of mutual interest and to promote British Higher Education in Malaysia and Singapore.

The focus of interest of much of the discussion was upon the quality and standards of British Higher Education in the post-expansion era. In the process of outlining to the Minister the various forms of quality control in British Universities, it became apparent that the key question which he was asking was not about quality of process, but about comparability of standards of degrees between the significantly increased number of institutions with the title 'university'.

The next step on the slippery slope was that in his address the following week to the conference of Universities and Colleges in England run by the Higher Education Funding Council for England, the Secretary of State passed this concern to the Institutions and asked what evidence could be given of 'broad comparability' of standards of degrees in British Universities, in a new expanded and diverse higher education system. This was in the circumstances a very reasonable question. There was not, however, an equally reasonable and convincing answer.

Further slippage occurred as the Higher Education Quality Council – to whom this issue was referred – realised that there was no easy and widely acceptable answer, and for various reasons did not choose to pursue the option of trying to identify minimum threshold standards to which all university degrees subscribed. Instead, the slope became steeper as the attempt was made to market and define a more general concept of 'Graduateness' which, it was hoped, would be the benchmark according to which the standard of a British Degree could be recognised. Interesting work has followed this initiative, but there is no likelihood that it will provide a satisfactory answer to the questions raised by John Patten, and his colleague Tim Boswell, then carrying the ministerial portfolio for higher education, let alone even approaching the concerns voiced by the Minister of Education in Malaysia and all those for whom he, perhaps unwittingly, spoke.

What had been revealed, not surprisingly, was that Ministers in this country wished in fact to be reassured that the Government's policy to expand higher education had not resulted in a loss of standards understood as academic output measures. (The concern with quality understood as process did not loom large in the ministerial mind – something which CVCP has not realised as it attempts to argue against cuts on the basis of loss of quality understood in this way i.e. as quality of student life). In a system which had properly premised expansion on diversity there was no adequate, or for that matter widely acceptable answer to the question of 'broad comparability' of standards. However, it was very difficult to say so in so many words and therefore the slope became steeper.

Traditionally it had been argued that the external examiner system had provided the necessary quality control to underwrite claims to 'broad comparability', and on the whole it had – provided that the word 'broad' was given sufficient prominence. There is not, however, the same confidence that that system as it currently stands can bear the weight. Scenarios are therefore now being painted in which the way to deal with this problem is to develop a national register of trained external examiners. Apart from the practical problems of doing this, which are considerable, the element of downward gradient in this lies in the path which leads from a national external examiner system to a system of national exams and thence to a National Higher Education Curriculum. So much for academic autonomy at institutional level. On top of that issue of principle, there is no possibility that a national curriculum in molecular and cell biology could simultaneously meet the needs of students in those subjects in, respectively, the University of Edinburgh and the University of Auchterturra, and *mutatis mutandis* for a national curriculum in mathematics to serve simultaneously and equally effectively Imperial College London, and the University of Poppleton.

There are two problems with this slippery slope, apart from the fact that we do not know where it will end up. The first is that the proposals which this line of discussion generates are out of touch with reality. The second is that to ask the question of 'broad comparability' of degree standards of what is properly an increasingly diverse system is to ask the wrong question.

Summary and conclusions

I have argued that the first condition of measurable success in this area is clarity of language which as ever presupposes clarity of thought. In search of this a fundamental distinction was drawn between quality measures which are concerned with process and provision, and standards which are measures of output. The work of the Funding Councils through their respective Quality Divisions, and of the sector through Academic Audit, followed by Quality Audit organised by the Higher Education Quality Council, has focused upon quality and process rather than standards.

A second key distinction was drawn between 'accountability' which has a degree of clarity about it and 'assurance' which as used I regard as a fog hiding a precipitous slope. The example which I gave of an attempt to dispel the fog i.e. one of the few occasions on which those who must be assured did actually make clear what they had in mind, allowed us to see that Ministers probably accurately mirroring wider concerns, were most interested in standards and how they compared between institutions. Unfortunately, the elaborate and expensive systems which we have in place do not answer that question. This poses a series of further questions, the most important of which is currently, 'In that case, whose questions are we answering, and what precisely are those questions?' The prominence given to and the unclarity implicit in the use of the term 'assurance' was the basis of my argument that a great deal of the difficulty in which the system finds itself lies in our unwillingness to press these questions home.

In the meantime, the system has found itself confronted with a question which has not been answered: Is there still in an expanded higher education sector broad comparability of standards for the award and classification of degrees?

In fact the answer to this question is, 'No', but there are good reasons for this which I shall rehearse in due course. In passing, however, we ought to note that the route of attempting to define minimum or threshold standards which are implicit in the award of any degree e.g. literacy, numeracy, and level of knowledge and understanding of a subject or group of cognate subjects appropriate to higher education, has not been followed. Nonetheless, given the will, some important work is possible which would help clarify a benchmark for a minimum standard could be applied to the award of university degrees in the United Kingdom.

To return to the main strand of argument, there are at least four good, and if properly understood, valid reasons for the conclusion that there is not broad comparability of standards across university degrees in the United Kingdom. They are all consequences of the expansion of the higher education sector. That comment requires two points of elaboration to ensure that I am not misunderstood. The first is that this is not an essay primed by the nostalgia of the more-means-worse brigade. The second however, is that more-means-change in both perception and aspiration in a way which has not yet adequately insinuated itself into the agenda of what is publicly discussable.

Thus, I have no doubt that the expansion of opportunity in post-school education was both inevitable and desirable. The growth has been dramatic. In 1945 the percentage of the age cohort entering Higher Education was just over 2%: the recent figure issued by the Scottish Office Education and Industry Department is just over 42%. That this has been accomplished so efficiently is a great tribute to all concerned – not least the Universities. The downside, however, is that we have not properly taken on board all of the implications.

One evident sign of that is that even after the most recent expansion involving the creation of approximately fifty new universities, the Ministers responsible still believed it appropriate to ask the question of 'broad comparability' The answer to that question, should be a very quiet 'No', and a very loud, 'Because that is the wrong question'.

The first and main reason for such a double-headed answer is bound up in the principle 'more-means-change'. Not only was it inevitable that the expansion of the system did bring change, it was right that it should do so, and wrong that in some contexts we should be encouraged to think otherwise. The three additional reasons for this answer are each an elaboration of the implications of diversity.

It is the case, and inevitably so, that the level of entry qualifications of a much larger and more diverse cohort of students entering university would change and that therefore the starting point and level for some degree programmes and some universities would be lower. Granted the diversity of age and background of students entering the system, and also the diversity of school provision which this represents, this is just as it should be, as opportunities are widened. It is obtuse, however, to suggest that this will have no impact on the levels which some will achieve in three or four years of university study (accepting also that there will be notable exceptions to this rule of thumb).

Further, and this is surely built into the development of a mass higher education system, the abilities which this much larger cohort bring collectively to university study will be more variable. The evidence of the most successful mass higher education system in the world – the USA – bears this out. More means change in this sense also, and it would be quite wrong to assume that the degree major programme in mathematics appropriate in the Massachusetts Institute of Technology could be transferred without change to the new branch campus of the University of Paduka.

The additional obvious reason for that and the final of my four points, is that the needs of diverse student bodies – as diverse as they are likely to be as they stretch from MIT to Paduka branch campus – are almost bound to be different. Thus the university education offered to each will be and ought to be different. In the light of what we see across the Atlantic to be both the meaning and benefits of a mass higher education system, to ask whether there is broad comparability of standards across a United Kingdom mass higher education sector is to ask the wrong question.

The design of Quality Audit and Teaching Quality Assessment systems shaped to measure process rather than output (standards) is an implicit recognition of this. As we are on the threshold of designing a new national system, it is opportune as well as essential for the higher education sector to be 'outed' on this one.

The future
My proposal is that any future system should be focused largely on the acceptance by the sector of appropriate forms of accountability. This, I believe, is compatible with all the stress which I have given to the notion of diversity.

Universities are accountable for their use of significant public funds in pursuit of their proper academic objectives. They are accountable, that is to say, for showing appropriate value for money, and this includes providing effective and appropriate patterns of teaching, and having rigorous means of discharging their responsibilities for setting standards.

All of the above is, of course, to be seen in the context of what the jargon calls 'mission'. There is an important and overlooked point here. In the end, accountability of the sort which I have just summarised is through the respective Funding Council to Ministers who stand representative of the public purse (i.e. the taxpayer). The view which I am proposing would require the Funding Councils to make an explicit judgement, not simply about effective use of public funds, but also about the acceptability of the mission of the institution and its ability to carry that out.

There is a separate form of 'assurance' of which much is made and that is to students and potential students and whoever may be sponsoring them. I have two comments on this – other, that is, than to underline its importance. The first is that although this is used as a justification of current cumbersome systems, I would feel less sceptical about that if there were some clear, well-researched data which showed that there was a significant demand for, or at least good evidence of significant consultation by students and their advisers of Teaching Quality

Assessments and Audit Reports – and that they had some impact on student choice.

The second point is that what we should have in place is what was certainly part of the initial remit of Audit, namely, a version of the WYSIWYG principle. The version applicable here is something like WTPIWYG – what-they-promise-is-what-you-get. Partly here of course the protection is legal and relates to the Trade Descriptions Act, but essentially it is a matter to which any worthwhile profession should pay careful attention. We should not advertise what we cannot/do not deliver.

There are of course those who make much of the need to 'assure' employers and businesses of one form or another. I think that there is an important issue here, but occasionally generalised statements are made about the needs of employers which ignore the huge differences between companies and their very varied needs. Sometimes it is argued, for example, that the needs of employers do not include detailed understanding and grasp of subject matter and related skills, and for some this may well be true. Experience elsewhere, for example amongst some of the large pharmaceutical companies, suggests quite the reverse.

More important, however, is the fact that employers do have clear ways of showing satisfaction or the reverse. The market operates and operates very strongly. One positive step would be for employers and universities to make clear statements about special relationships and link programmes which they have. Perhaps, however, the most important step is to ensure that employers' representatives on university governing bodies and departmental and faculty advisory groups explicitly recognise and discuss these issues. This would be much more specific in its impact and certainly much more cost effective.

The stage which national discussions have reached following the Report of Sir William Kerr Fraser's group suggests that we must now lay down some guidelines and criteria for developing next steps. My proposals are as follows:

1   The focus of future developments should be upon satisfying the legitimate demands for accountability, rather than the vaguer insistence that we must 'assure'.

2   We are properly accountable to the Funding Councils and through them to Parliament to show Value For Money in the processes which we employ and managing and delivering teaching and research.

3   In comparable fashion the Funding Councils have a duty to assure themselves that the respective Missions of the diversity of Universities

    are in each case an appropriate basis for the allocation of resources under the relevant Acts of Parliament governing the operation of Funding Councils.

4   We are also properly accountable for showing that we have mechanisms in place to set and monitor standards for the award of degrees appropriate to those Missions.

5   There should be a means of ensuring what I have called the WTPIWYG principle, i.e. that universities clearly demonstrate to students what the benefits of matriculation are, and deliver accordingly.

6   In some ways the most important accountability role is to the general public through the various professional associations and institutes that, for example, the education provided to future doctors, vets, nurses, lawyers, engineers, architects, and so on is at least adequate and in most cases better than that.

7   Finally, an institutional plea. Helpful in various ways, as aspects of current provision are, what they conspicuously fail to address is the need of good management and good governance for an evaluation of a department as an entity. What we have at the moment is one group evaluating a department from the point of view of its research performance, another group quite separately reviewing its teaching performance, and, if appropriate, yet another group accrediting it as a provider of professional education. All academe is being halved up, as the Romans used to say of Gaul, into three quarters, and yet, what we most need is a coherent single picture of the integration of these elements within departments and faculties.

Professor Sir Stewart Sutherland FBA
Principal and Vice-Chancellor, University of Edinburgh

Stewart Sutherland taught philosophy in the Universities of Wales and Stirling. In 1977 he was appointed to the Chair of Philosophy of Religion at King's College, London, thereafter becoming Principal (1985). In 1990 he moved to the post of Vice-Chancellor, University of London (1990-94), concurrently (1992-94) also Her Majesty's Chief Inspector of Schools. Since 1994 he has been Principal and Vice-Chancellor of the University of Edinburgh. He also serves on the Council for Science and Technology, the Hong-Kong University Grants Committee, the Higher Education Funding Council for England, and is Chairman of the Council of the Royal Institute of Philosophy.

3

Andrew Miller

Research – a Scottish perspective

Research is the highest form of intellectual activity. It has profoundly affected our lives, yet we do not know how it works. The search for new knowledge is deeply self fulfilling; even the anticipation of the discovery of new knowledge can drive individuals to extremes. Researchers tend to form academic tribes[1] with a greater loyalty to their research discipline than to their university. What is this thing called Research, who does it, who pays and what effect does it have? Is all as it should be with research in Scotland and its universities? This is a brief up-date.

What is research?
Research aims at the discovery of new knowledge. The Robbins Report[2] defined research as "intellectual activities that serve to increase man's (sic) power to understand, evaluate and modify his world and his experience." In the last few hundred years research has vastly increased the sum of human knowledge and we are now said to be living in a knowledge-based economy. However, there is no recipe for research. The biologist J.B.S. Haldane warned that the universe was probably not only "queerer than we think but queerer than we can think".

Working scientists usually hold the common sense realist view that they are striving towards a better and better understanding of how the material world functions. Social scientists emphasise the determining effect of social context on research and that ideas or mental models intended to explain the material world are corrigible. Progress is an illusion they say, and in science, 'anything goes'[3]. Drawing attention to the advances of modern technology elicits the response that many theories which 'worked' have later been revised. As an (ex-) working scientist, I will not review the reams written around this topic,[4,5,6,7,8,9] particularly 'Sokal's Hoax'[10] but opt for a critical realist view.

Academic science is traditionally described as communal, universal, disinterested, original and sceptical (spells CUDOS!)[11] with value assessment by peer review based on contribution to advancing the discipline. In the last few years, however, a new research culture has evolved emphasising the context of application, managed research teams, social accountability and reflexivity with quality assessed by reference to the market, value for money, competitiveness and social acceptability[12].

Knowledge is information held by humans. We broadly recognise two types – factual and tacit. Factual knowledge can be digitised and codified. Examples are the accepted facts of history, the regularities in the natural world as expressed in scientific laws, mathematical and logical theorems, dictionaries and so on. Factual knowledge can be stored independently of humans and transmitted; its significance has been increased by susceptibility to IT. All factual knowledge is corrigible though some is known with a high degree of certainty and precision. Factual knowledge can be further divided into two types – empirical regularities noted by observation and theories or models devised to explain the regularities. Tacit knowledge is a skill incarnated in a person taught by training[13]. Examples are riding a bicycle or tuning an x-ray monochromator.

I will be discussing mainly factual knowledge in the natural sciences, human sciences and humanities though, given Chapter 12 (Laver), mostly the former.

A second important distinction is between pure and applied research. The so-called Frascati definition[14] recognises basic research, applied research and experimental development. A UK Government report in 1991 noted that the Frascati definitions described the **nature** of the research activities and suggested instead, a classification that emphasised the **primary purpose** of the activity. Basic or curiosity-driven research is carried out with no thought as to its application. Applied research is goal directed. Either of these can be strategic – that is, targeted.

There are two distinct components in research. The first is highly creative. It is to spot a regularity in the data or to have a new idea, theory or mental model to explain it; the second is to test these. Research can be confused with mere testing. Many people can be trained to test ideas, few come up with new ideas and very few indeed come up with new ideas which survive testing. Most scientific advances seem to be made by only 5% of scientists; they are the real creators whom we must protect[12].

The first step is creative, novel, original, innovative and shares many of the features of artistic creation. Anything goes, and the social context is highly influential. Albert Szent-Gyorgyi said that scientific creativity was "seeing what others see and thinking what no-one else thinks".

The second step needs restrained and disciplined checking with statistical analyses of the extent of fits between observed and predicted data. Anything does not go. Fecundity is relevant – the way in which the idea opens up new avenues of exploration and understanding and explains wider ranges of data. Verification and even falsification are too absolute terms, but the outcome is objective in the sense of being open to inter-subjective scrutiny.

Experimental scientists worry about the precision of their results and whether or not they have taken account of all the correction factors for which they should make allowance in their measurements. The driving force behind the demand for increased precision[15,16] has often been social and political – centralising states with bureaucracies managing trade, taxation and the military, or large-scale commercial enterprises with their need for standardisation and mass production. Basic scientists require precision for deciding between competing theories used for prediction or extrapolation.

Theoreticians worry about the uniqueness of their theory. Could an alternative theory – worse, somebody else's theory – explain the data just as well, or better. There are recipes for testing but not for ideas – *pace* de Bono et al. Research, because it is going into the unknown, is not predictable. High temperature superconductors, discovered in 1986, were not foreseen by a high-level UK physics committee in 1985.

Research and Teaching

The Economist[17] has commented that universities can claim to be the main source of new knowledge. Research Council and Government Department Laboratories and those of major charities concentrate on research while schools and colleges teach. Is a high research profile necessary for a university?

Jowett, the 19th century Master of Balliol, held that research could be an excuse for indolence. Even in 1914 the Professor of Physics at Oxford said that ". . . the wish to do research showed a certain restlessness of mind."[18] Research grew in importance in universities after Humboldt, who, in founding the University of Berlin in 1809, asserted the affinity of teaching and research. A lively PhD programme grew up serving the needs of the growing German chemical industry. When the UK became aware around the first world war of its need for research to underpin industry, the DSIR was founded in 1915.

When the number of universities in the UK was almost doubled in 1992 by the abolition of the binary line and the award of the title University to the Central Institutions in Scotland and certain Polytechnics in England and Wales, the criterion of research was not taken as essential for promotion to a university. Some ask 'Why don't universities concentrate on superb teaching as in the Harvard Business School or the Liberal Arts Colleges in the USA?'. It would, however, be quite wrong to think that the teachers in the Harvard Business School do little research; many are world leaders in their field. And the LAC staff are often on nine month teaching contracts to which many of them add funded research (or summer teaching) programmes.

The Teaching Assessment exercises have given students a much better deal from Teaching than a generation ago as Neil Keeble pointed out[19]. Money speaks, and if teaching quality were more strongly linked to funding, the benefit to students would be even greater. (It might also divert unrealistic research ambitions). Research and teaching are mutually enhancing and there is a good correlation between Departments which teach well and those doing good research. There is no doubt that we have still a lot to learn about the psychology and sociology of learning and hence optimal strategies for teaching[20], particularly with IT. However, students whose course gives them something of the research ethos will benefit educationally. This is nothing to do with training students to become researchers. A research approach is an excellent training for any future career. This ethos comes best from active researchers.

How to fund the best researchers
It goes without saying that industry, charities and Research Councils have their own agendas in funding research. But can they or universities find the real creators?

In the UK universities, the **dual support** system for research means that

- The Funding Council is responsible for (the research part of) academic salaries, 'well found' laboratories , libraries and IT infrastructure.

- The Research Councils fund specific research projects competitively in a bidding process.

Funding Council support for research in each university department is calculated by multiplying the Unit of Research Resource for the subject by the number of academic staff who are research active in the department and again by a factor which is proportional to the research Grade (1-5) awarded to the department in the Research Assessment Exercise. In Scotland the proportionality between the different Grades is, sensibly, exponential with a constant ratio between Grades. The RAE is on a UK-wide basis – and long may it continue so.

This system is quite selective and brings complaints from institutions who do little research. However, it is important to fund top-class research adequately. This retains diversity of mission in the higher education system as was clearly intended in 1992 when institutions with little research were admitted to the system. It does not mean funding only a group of (say) ten top research universities in the UK (so in Scotland, only Edinburgh and St Andrews[21], thus omitting the best biochemistry and aquaculture departments in the UK!). Research funding should go to University **Departments** or centres of excellence wherever they may be, including, particularly for goal-directed research, in the newest universities. When resources are short, selectivity is essential to preserve the top quality researchers and their teams. Mediocrity is dispensable.

The research assessment process was criticised as encouraging short-termism and mission drift and as too cumbersome to be cost effective. The last RAE cost Universities an estimated £12M and the Funding Councils £1M – about 0.6% of the research funds distributed over 4 years[22].

Since curiosity-driven research is, by its nature, unpredictable, the question of how the research funds are most effectively distributed is an interesting one – how do we find those who make the advances? Some quite radical proposals have been made.

Should all research funds be transferred from the Funding Councils to the Research Councils?[23] Not as long as the Funding Councils allow academics the freedom of curiosity-driven research and can resist nudges towards stalinisation. It was claimed that the dual support system gave vice-chancellors too much freedom for which they were insufficiently accountable, so in 1992, the direct costs and some indirect costs associated with Research Council projects, previously the responsibility of the Funding Councils, were transferred to the Research Councils. The effect of this transfer was reviewed[24] and it seems likely that the way of calculating the indirect cost will be changed.

Should the Medical Research Council grant system be abandoned allowing some £50,000 per year to be distributed to each of 5000 medical academics?[25].

Should the resource-intensive selection amongst alpha-rated projects be jettisoned in favour of a random choice of alphas?

Should the limitations of peer review be better recognised and should anonymity of reviewers be abandoned?

Research Councils spoke of 'timeliness and promise' and peer review based on scientific merit. However, decreasing funds has meant that policy increasingly determines choice of research problem.

In 1971 Lord Rothschild recommended a 'customer-contractor' principle for research. Academics were anguished and I remember a notice pinned to Miriam Rothschild's office door in the Zoology Department in Oxford reading 'I am not my brother's keeper'. In 1994, the UK Government, through the Office of Science and Technology (OST), initiated the Forward Look and Foresight Exercises designed to analyse the primary purposes of research and to seek consciously to identify research areas which, with foresight, one might see as having the potential to impact on society in 20 years time.

Foresight does not just apply to the sciences; there are many examples of work in the humanities which could transform society – for example, the effects of research in linguistics and phonetics on speech technology and communication, the philosophy underpinning bioethics to guide the application of biotechnology, logic in computer technology and robotics, and in the social sciences to understand the assimilation of technology by societies. Research is done *by* humans and ultimately is *about* humans in their physical and biological world[26]. SHEFC is discussing how it might encourage foresight by modified funding formulae.

Martin et al[27] describe the new culture as a social contract in research in which there are more expectations that basic research should generate economic and social benefits in return for the substantial public funds it receives. Ziman[11] and Oxburgh[28] worry that this new research culture in academia may erode objectivity and stifle creativity if it is over-managed, particularly in the interests of government policy, political fashion or commerce. These new pressures may also increase scientific fraud and competitiveness can lead to secrecy. New Research Culture, New Danger!

I suggest distributing most research funds by open peer review, in keeping with the mission of the funder, to those with a good track record, retaining some funds for speculation on unknown applicants and staying alert to once-productive researchers running out of steam.

How much should be spent on research? Save British Science say there is not enough. Of competing economies, the UK spends the lowest fraction of GDP on academic research except Italy and Japan. The 1996 Forward Look paper reported a fall in government support for R and D over the last ten years, though this was in the dominant military and government departments. There was a slight increase in support for university and research council research. An important recent survey of research in the UK, the NAPAG report,[29] concluded that the level of support for research in the UK was so low that the national economy was being put at risk in spite of the fact that research has fared rather better than teaching in the last few years. NAPAG despairs of the adequacy of the dual support system and suggests that a proper level of competence in scholarship be preserved by ensuring that university departments not active enough to attract research funding from the Funding Councils be given research money to keep staff up with their subjects. Of course all HE teaching must be scholarly, but surely this is a charge on the Teaching budget in HE to support what differentiates HE from FE. The research budget is already under enough strain.

This strain is also apparent in a survey of research equipment in universities[30]. It found that one fifth of equipment was of poor quality (even endangering health and safety), that four fifths of laboratories see lack of equipment as holding up research and it points out that the UK is in danger of losing multinational companies since they prefer to relate to state-of- the-art laboratories.

So, the evidence is clear: that the UK public spend on research is too low.

Who should pay for research – public or private?
Who benefits from research? Pavitt[31] maintains that the benefits of research are a **public good** in the sense that they are readily transmissible without further cost and infinitely reusable, but they are not a **free good** in that it does take an investment on the part of the beneficiary to reap the benefit. Once the results of research are in the public domain they are formally open to all. However, they can only be interpreted and applied by trained minds. Research know-how is held by global networks of experts. Acceptance into these networks is informal,

based on peer esteem. A country with no members in the network cannot access the world knowledge base. Also, the law of intellectual property[32] has developed.

Economists argue about the 'decline' of the UK[33,34] and about the relation between science and technology and economic growth[35,36].

Kay and Llewellyn-Smith[36] hold that the benefits of research are real though often general rather than specific. Electricity was discovered by Faraday and others in curiosity-driven research projects. The transistor, and hence the ubiquitous computer, would have been impossible without investment in the rather esoteric subject of quantum mechanics. Scientific research has brought immeasurable benefits to mankind so it should be supported by public money. More recently, Pavitt has shown that the applications of research in the physical sciences are more general and those from the biological sciences are more specific[31].

Industrialists generally want graduates to contribute to the profitability of the company as quickly as possible. Some large companies do their own in-house curiosity-driven research. This is less because they think that researchers might produce money spinning ideas than because good researchers are usually sharp minds which can be consulted on any topic (keep scientists on tap not on top) and also because tame boffins, who are members of the unofficial networks mentioned above, maintain accessibility to the global networks.

Mary Warnock in her 1994 Norbrook Lecture[37] examined the research spending by UK companies in 1992. 336 UK companies were surveyed. Only 11 compared with the 200 top spenders on research and development in the world. The top spender in the UK was ICI which was 47th in the world. UK firms spend an average of 1.6% of their income on R and D compared with 4.6% by the world top 200. Hence industry is not likely to be a major supporter of R and D in Scotland. Even when companies do support research they reasonably retain the power to delay publication of the research results. Industrial support for research can threaten academic autonomy. Who pays the piper calls the tune. Warnock believes that excellent research is most likely from curiosity-driven work so public funding with accountability is essential. I would add that there are many projects of great social importance that industry would be unlikely to support and SMEs, which employ 80% of the Scottish workforce, do not have the resources anyway.

Several eminent scientists were unaware of the potential use of basic research, notably Rutherford on nuclear physics and Kelvin on x-rays. Most researchers, including the greatest, are flattered to be told that their work could be useful. Galileo's first telescopes were used by merchants to observe the approach of ships bearing fresh cargo and to sell off the old stock cheaply before their rivals; Kelvin laid the Atlantic cable; Newton was involved in the competition to devise a means of measuring longitude and so on[38].

There are many examples of our knowledge advancing through technology rather than through basic research. The so-called linear model of progress from basic research to technology and thence to economic progress has correctly been criticised. Terence Kealey[39] makes this point strongly but also argues that public funding of research is not advisable since – as measured by original publications – private funds purchase more research than public funds. He believes -by extrapolating some observations about the past – that if public funding of research was withdrawn, it would be replaced by more efficient private funding.

I disagree with Kealey. Research is a social activity, not totally determined by inexorable laws. Kealey amasses many examples to 'prove' his point but counter-examples can be adduced where basic research *was* the origin of technological development. X-Ray crystallography is the basis of materials science, chemistry and structural molecular biology. The rapid development of crystallography after 1912 was possible because three-dimensional symmetry space-groups had been worked out by mathematicians in the 19th century. Many varied methods lead to progress and one successful approach does not exclude others.

A report prepared for the UK Treasury[27 and see 40] concludes, after a detailed survey of the last two decades, that public funding of basic research does lead to economic advantage which present calculations probably underestimate. "The main finding to emerge . . . is the central importance to industry of the new knowledge emanating from basic research carried out in academic and government laboratories"[27].

Private funding can lead to efficiencies because of the closer attention of the funder. But this has to be set against the limited interest of the funder. Companies have to justify their spend to shareholders and charities to their subscribers. Pharmaceutical companies will support basic research in molecular biology because they can reasonably expect a spin off. But will they support work on artificial life, the environment, preventative medicine, safety standards, consumer and employee protection or social inequality?

Kealey takes little cognisance of the dramatic changes in modern society[41] which make the past a poor guide to the future. 'Even the future is not what it used to be'[42]. Pavitt[43] gives examples where the 'linear model' does work, quotes Mulvey's finding that when the G7 countries increased their support for research, industry did so too and refers to 'western' countries where the universities get around 80% of their research support from government. Support from industry is marginal. Public support is therefore crucial and to put it at risk would be courageous only in the 'Yes Minister' sense.

Research in Scotland

Scotland has 12% of UK full-time academics, 11% post-graduate (research) workers and had 12% of the UK Departments rated 4 or 5 in the 1992 RAE. It is third in the world for research publications *per capita*.[44] It receives 12% total UK Funding Council resources for Teaching, 13% for Research, 11% from Research Councils, 14% from Government Research Departments and 14% from the European Union[45]. These figures, for 1994-5, suggest that Scotland, which has 10% of the UK population, more than holds its own in research in the UK.

The small size of Scotland as a country is being exploited by the universities in a series of research initiatives. SHEFC has encouraged universities to collaborate (not just in research) by offering top-sliced funds to competitive bids. There are many motives for collaboration – complementarity of expertise, sharing expensive facilities among them. Researchers in mainly teaching institutions can collaborate with those in research led institutions. SHEFC have particularly stimulated the search for economies of scale and the protection of small subjects to ensure a healthy and efficient portfolio of expertise at higher education level in Scotland. Scottish universities also collaborate globally.

SHEFC have also funded the Scottish Universities Research Policy Consortium. This involves the 13 universities and its objective is to develop a generic framework for the institutional management of research, identifying policy options and providing background documentation[46]. There is cross-membership between this group and the Research Advisory Group of COSHEP. SURPC is due to report in December 1996.

There is also cross-membership between SURPC and another SHEFC initiative on Contract Research Staff. This studies the implications of the CVCP/COSHEP

-Royal Society Concordat on Contract Research Workers and is due to report in mid-1997. It will rightly stress the need to appreciate and protect the careers of this highly productive group. The financial consequences will, I hope, be accepted by all funding bodies.

A further development in Scotland has been the emphasis on the commercialisation of the science base supported by Scottish Enterprise and the Royal Society of Edinburgh[44]. The aim here is narrower and more immediate than that of the Foresight Exercise. It is to ensure that the healthy academic science base in Scotland is scrutinised thoroughly for possible commercialisation of the research results. Industrialists are keen to become party to the knowledge networks to which I referred above, to give a competitive edge to their business. Academics, despite a contrary reputation, are actually rather pleased if their work can be commercialised. UK bureaucrats notoriously turned down requests by researchers to commercialise penicillin and monoclonal antibodies leading to annual losses to the UK approximately equal to the MRC budget. I am sure that if courses in commercialisation – accountancy and finance, business, management techniques, intellectual property rights and patents, sources of start-up money – were made available in universities to new science graduates and post-doctoral scientists, this would boost the commercialisation of science. Full commercialisation of science is no doubt better done by the financial professionals. However, it is imperative that some profits from commercialisation are fed back to the science base, if only to preserve the geese that lay the golden eggs. Brilliant, though rare, examples are the Wellcome Trust which annually puts £250 million into research, and Ken Murray of Edinburgh whose hepatitis vaccine has contributed £20 million to his university.

Conclusions
Curiosity is as much a legacy of our evolutionary history as hunger, sex or fear[47,48]. It has got us where we are and is imperative to ensure a future in a world with global warming, HIV and BSE. Curiosity-driven research, mainly carried out in universities, feeds and is fed by goal-directed research. It strengthens the national economy. The basic/applied contrast has blurred. The new research culture uses the global knowledge-network to address economic growth, long-term survival and the quality of life. However, it also remains an intellectual and technological adventure, integral to human culture and self-fulfillment. It is increasingly concerned with ethics – "Science without conscience is but the ruin of the soul"[49] – and, it might be added, the ruin of the planet.

Public funding and the university dual support system maximise the likelihood of innovation – both have been curtailed recently – but charities and industry are also key funders. Selectivity must preserve the creators. Over-bureaucratic management is counterproductive. Scottish research is highly active with much to contribute to our future – if it is allowed. We do not yet have a biology of PPE but forty-five years ago we did not have the double helix.

References

1   Becher, T., *Academic Tribes*. Open University Press. 1989.

2   The Robbins Report, para 553, London HM Stationery Office, 1963.

3   Feyerabend, P., *Against Method*. London: New Left Books. 1975.

4   Newton-Smith, W., *The Rationality of Science*. Routledge and Kegan Paul, 1981.

5   Kuhn, T., *The Structure of Scientific Revolutions*, Chicago, 1963.

6   Popper, K., *Conjectures and Refutations*. Routledge and Kegan Paul. 1962.

7   Loese, M. A., *Historical Introduction to the Philosophy of Science*. Oxford. 3rd. Edition 1993.

8   O'Hear, A., *An Introduction to the Philosophy of Science*. Oxford. 1989.

9   Papineau, D. (Ed). *The Philosophy of Science*. Oxford University Press, 1996.

10   See the correspondence in the *New York Review of Books*, 8 Aug and 3 Oct 1996 on Sokal's spoof article accepted by the magazine Social Text.

11   Ziman, J., *Is science losing its objectivity?* Nature, **382,** 751-75.

12   Gibbons, M. et al. *The new production of knowledge,* Sage publications, 1994.

13   M Polanyi, *Personal Knowledge*, Routledge, 1958.

14   OECD Frascati, 1963.

15   Norton Wise, M., *The Value of Precision*, Princeton University Press, 1995.

16   Mayo, D.G., *Error and the Growth of Experimental Knowledge,* Chicago University Press, 1996.

17   'Teaching spires', *The Economist,* 24 August 1996, p 14.

18   Phillips, D. C. in *Universities in the Twentieth Century* Paul Hamlyn Foundation, 1994, p 40.

19   Keeble, N., *The Times,* 12 July 1996.

20   Hughes, C. and Tight, M., *Linking University Teaching and Research*, Higher Education Review, Vol 28, No 1, 1995.

21   *The Times* League Tables 1996-97.

22   A Report for the Universities Funding Council on the conduct of the 1992 Research Assessment Exercise.

23   Richmond, M., *Science and Public Affairs*, Autumn, p. 2, 1996.

24   Review of the Dual Support Transfer. Coopers & Lybrand Report for the Office of Science and Technology, 1995.

25   Horrobin, D., *The Lancet* (in press).

26   I am indebted to Prof John Laver for discussions on this topic.

27   Martin et al. *The Relationship between Publicly Funded Basic Research and Economic Performance* (p. 37), A SPRU Review, 1996.

28   Oxburgh, R., Presidential Address to British Association, 1996.

29   *Research Capability of the University System.* NAPAG Report, 1996.

30   Survey of Research Equipment in UK Universities, PREST Report, 1996.

31   Pavitt, K., Academic Research, Technical Change and Government Policy, Steep Discussoin Paper No 24, Science Policy Research Unit, October 1995.

32   Farrington, D. J., *The Law of Higher Education.* Chapter 8, Butterworth, 1994.

33   Wiener, M. J., *English Culture and the Decline of the Industrial Spirit 1850-1980.* Cambridge University Press, 1981.

34   Alford, B. W. E., *Britain in the World Economy since 1980.* Longman, 1996.

35   Edgerton, D., *Science, Technology, and the British Industrial 'Decline' 1870-1970.* Cambridge University Press, 1996.

36   Kay, J., and C., Llewellyn-Smith *Fiscal Studies* **6**, No 3, 14-23, 1985.

37   Warnock, M., *The Veterinary Record*, 22 Oct 1994, p 396-399.

38   Sobel, D. *Longitude.* Fourth Estate. 1996.

39   Kealey, M., *The Economic Laws of Scientific Research,* Macmillan Press, 1996.

40   Klug, A., *New Scientist,* No 2042, p 47, 1996.

41   Sykes, R. *Daily Telegraph*, 26 June 1996.

42   Attributed to Hermann Kahn.

43   Pavitt, K., *New Scientist*, No 2041, p 32-35, 1996.

44   Commercialisation of the Science Base paper, August 1996.

45   I am grateful to Sue Dyer for help with these statistics.

46   Laver, J. *The Scottish Universities Research Policy Consortium, The Times Higher Education Supplement*, Sept.6, 1996, page 12.

47   Hull, D. L., *Science as Process*. Chicago University Press, 1988.

48   Plotkin, H., *Darwin Machines and the Nature of Knowledge*. Penguin Press, 1994.

49   Francois Rabelais.

Professor Andrew Miller
Principal and Vice-Chancellor, University of Stirling

Professor Miller is a biophysicist interested in biological fibres – muscle and collagen, X-ray diffraction and synchrotron radiation.

Prior to taking up his appointment at Stirling, he was, succesively, Vice-Principal (Research) and Professor of Biochemistry at Edinburgh University, Director of Research at the European Synchrotron Radiation Facility, France, Lecturer in Molecular Biophysics, Oxford University and Staff Scientist, MRC Laboratory of Molecular Biology, Cambridge.

He is an Honorary Fellow of Wolfson College, Oxford, a Fellow of the Royal Society of Edinburgh and Convener of the COSHEP Research Advisory Group.

4

Richard W Shaw

Catch 22: The newest universities

Common heritage

The five post-1992 Universities in Scotland share much of the same heritage. Prior to the abolition of the binary line they were all long established degree and postgraduate level institutions with these awards being made under the Charter of the Council for National Academic Awards (CNAA); they all, at least latterly, were funded directly through the Scottish Office Education Department; they all were committed to vocationally oriented programmes of study; they all had a commitment to widening access to higher education; they all drew strongly on their local and regional area for students and encouraged a variety of links with their communities and local businesses. While they were all committed to and engaged in research and scholarship broadly defined by CNAA – as indeed they had to in order to satisfy degree and professional accreditation – the Scottish Office Education Department tended to discourage academic research, unless it could be shown to be relevant to teaching programmes.[1] Of course, each institution had its own personality, its particular academic course profile and distinctive history; nevertheless the common heritage is both clear and, at least in the mid 1990s, more striking than the differences among these five universities compared with the pre-1992 universities.

A record of achievement

Three of the new universities, Abertay Dundee, Paisley and The Robert Gordon University share histories stretching back into the nineteenth century. Abertay Dundee was founded in 1888 as Dundee Technical Institute "to consolidate much of the then existing vocational education provision in Dundee"[2]. Paisley, which is celebrating its hundredth anniversary in 1997, was similarly founded to provide 'an institution of art, science and, so far as possible, technical instruction adequate to the wants of the community'[3].

Robert Gordon's College was established in 1881 and combined with Aberdeen's Mechanics Institute in 1884 to form a larger technical institution.[4] Dundee Technical Institution and School of Art (from 1901) and Robert Gordon's College (from 1903) were among the first Central Institutions (CIs) with funding from the Scottish Education Department. Their achievement of this status was virtually contemporaneous with that of Heriot-Watt College and the Glasgow and West of Scotland Technical College later to become Heriot-Watt and Strathclyde Universities respectively. Paisley had to wait until 1950 before becoming a CI and benefiting from the consequent increased financial security.

The two other new universities in Scotland, Glasgow Caledonian University and Napier University Edinburgh have a somewhat different history. The former was created in 1971 as Glasgow College of Technology by the then Glasgow Corporation by transferring advanced provision from existing further education colleges. While newly created as an independent institution its roots, of course, extend much further back. Napier College of Science and Technology was also established as a local authority college in 1964 and subsequently merged with Edinburgh College of Commerce in 1974. Glasgow College of Technology and Napier College of Commerce and Technology were transferred from their respective local authorities to Scottish Office responsibility as Central Institutions in 1985. The two institutions subsequently adopted the polytechnic title unlike the three older Scottish institutions that were to become post-1992 universities. Glasgow Polytechnic merged in April 1993 with The Queen's College Glasgow (whose origins can be traced back to 1875) – another SOED funded institution – to become Glasgow Caledonian University.

All five of the post-1992 universities can proudly point to their roles in widening educational opportunity and in serving their communities in responsive and innovative ways. In part, this reflected their own, and indeed Scottish Office and local authority, commitment to locally based vocational education and, in part, from the mid 1960s, to the developing ethos of the Council for National Academic Awards under which and in partnership with the institutions an expanding range of first degree and postgraduate programmes evolved. Prior to the creation of CNAA the three older institutions offered a range of sub-degree, professional and London University degree programmes and qualifications. The advent of CNAA provided a new opportunity and, in common with the emerging polytechnics south of the border, the late 1960s and early 1970s saw the development of new degree programmes. Overwhelmingly these were concentrated in engineering, science, social science and business related subjects.

The concentration on these subject areas reflected Scottish Office policy which restrained any ambition to diversify into arts and humanities as happened in some of the English polytechnics. The Scottish institutions built on their existing foundations and the commitment to applied and practical aspects was reinforced in many cases by the inclusion of compulsory work based experience in the curriculum in the form of sandwich degrees. Indeed at Dundee Institute of Art and Technology in the early 1970s 'all of the college's degree courses except the BSc in Science were of the sandwich type, reflecting the college's close links with industry and its aim of producing graduates able to begin their employment with a minimum of further training'.[5]

The development of these new degrees was associated with rapid expansion of full time and sandwich student numbers and a switch of emphasis away from day release and evening students. Happily there are signs that the wheel is turning full circle with a major expansion in part-time student numbers, in many cases based on evening and weekend provision and distance learning. This is a welcome manifestation of the development of lifelong learning.

Although it may seem that a decline in day release students would reduce the link between the institutions and employers this turned out not to be the case. As early as 1963, Dundee, Paisley and Robert Gordon's established formal industrial liaison services. At Paisley this was subsequently developed into the Technology and Business Centre with a remit of facilitating short professional development courses, consultancy and applied research services to industry, commerce and the public services. Univation Ltd at Robert Gordon's provides the corresponding service. As well as these more general centres the post-1992 universities have developed specialist units reflecting their own particular niches. Perhaps the best known is Robert Gordon's Offshore Survival Centre created in 1972 which now operates as RGIT Limited having also diversified into medical and occupational health services. At Abertay Dundee the units include the Scottish Institute for Wood Technology and the Waste Water Technology Centre. At Glasgow Caledonian and Napier they include the Centre for Industrial Bulk Solids Handling and the Scottish Electronics Manufacturing Centre respectively. At Paisley corresponding units include centres specialising in Environmental and Waste Management and Electromagnetic Compatibility.

While the many linkages with industry, commerce and public services represent a continuing tradition they also reflect the universities' adaptability to changing needs. This is also shown in their willingness to provide work based learning on site either in the form of programmes of study or in the accreditation of work based learning. Examples include Glasgow Caledonian and Paisley's work-based and on-site programmes at British Aerospace and at IBM.

A major innovation spearheaded by the post-1992 universities is the development of credit accumulation and transfer schemes within the SCOTCAT framework. Glasgow Caledonian and Paisley Universities initiated their schemes as soon as CNAA regulations for Scotland were available and Napier has subsequently followed suit. Robert Gordon's chose to embed their CATS developments within their new academic structure. Using the framework and starting from a zero base at the beginning of the 1990s Paisley expanded its CATS enrolments to approximately 2500 by 1995/96 with nearly 2000 of these studying part-time mainly in the evenings. The SCOTCAT framework has also assisted the development of seamless transfer of HNC and HND students from further education colleges to the post-1992 universities. In the cases of Glasgow Caledonian and Paisley the relationships have been taken further, through the former's Affiliated College scheme and the latter's Associate College scheme. Although the closeness of the relationships between further (and higher) education colleges and the post-1992 universities varies, it is clear that for many students following the further education route into tertiary education there is a clearly available and managed pathway to degree levels of study in the post-1992 universities.

The history outlined so far is one of continuous development with a consistent theme of commitment to increasing educational opportunity and working in a flexible and innovative way with business and local communities. While these remain as core commitments the picture is incomplete without reference to long standing and recent burgeoning international initiatives. These include the recruitment of overseas students; the development and operation of distance learning programmes; partnerships with universities, colleges and other institutions involving franchising, student and staff exchanges; staff development programmes; research collaboration and consultancies. Among the initiatives are Paisley and Robert Gordon's distance learning programmes where the combined enrolments now exceed 1600 students. All the post-1992 universities have activities overseas with Glasgow Caledonian reporting that its "diverse range of partnerships and initiatives" include "over 80 countries around the world".[6]

While a review of some of the important activities of the post-1992 universities reveals much of their character growth has also been a key feature with student numbers more than doubling since the early 1980s. The post-1992 universities have certainly played a very full part in the development of a mass higher education system.

The recent history of the post-1992 universities in Scotland, beginning with the achievement of 'accredited' status with the CNAA at the end of the 1980s, includes some radical changes. Accreditation meant that the five institutions for the first time became formally responsible for the approval, monitoring and quality assurance of their academic programmes, albeit under the umbrella of the CNAA Charter. This was followed by the 1991 White Paper and the Further and Higher Education (Scotland) Act 1992 leading to full degree awarding powers and university title. For Glasgow and Napier Polytechnics both degree awarding powers and university title were 'automatic', in line with the White Paper's proposals that all polytechnics be granted these powers and title. For the other three institutions it was necessary for them to make their cases to Government. As a result, Dundee Institute of Technology, Paisley College of Technology and the Robert Gordon Institute of Technology were all granted full degree awarding powers, and Paisley and Robert Gordon gained university title alongside the polytechnics in 1993. Dundee Institute of Technology had to wait until 1994 before it, too, achieved university status.

In the case of Glasgow Caledonian it combined the transition to a university with the merger with The Queens College, Glasgow. Not only did this create a 'new' and much larger institution, it also reinforced the vocational mission of the former polytechnic and considerably strengthened the combined insitution's health sciences activities. Paisley's vocational mission was similarly strengthened by its merger with Craigie College of Education in Ayr. In September 1996 four of the post-1992 universities, Glasgow Caledonian, Napier, Paisley and Robert Gordon's were awarded contracts for nurse and midwifery education, once again extending their activities, reinforcing their vocational mission and giving another substantial impetus to their growth.

The record of achievement of the post-1992 universities has a strong theme of continuity allied to a history of growth, adaptability and innovation.

The future
The CATCH 22 in the chapter title refers to the choices in the direction of development for the new universities. Should they continue to focus on vocationally related education; on widening access and promoting lifelong

learning; on teaching and learning as their primary role; on applied and related strategic research; on consultancy and continuing professional development for local and regional industry and their communities? All five of the post-1992 universities are proud of their contributions in all these areas so why not stick to these areas of acknowledged success – or in management speak – why not stick to the knitting?

The dilemma arises largely because of the relative perceived status in Scotland and Britain more generally accorded academic versus vocational study; exclusiveness versus openness; basic versus applied research; research versus teaching and learning; international and national versus local activities.

The higher status traditionally has been given – with the notable exceptions of medical and legal education – to the more academic subjects or specialisms within subjects relative to the more vocational and technical subjects. The universities that by and large take the most academically qualified students have higher status than those whose mission is to widen access and expand educational opportunity. Similarly, the traditional pecking order of universities is largely determined by their reputation and record as research rather than as teaching institutions. Within many, if not most pre-1992 universities this is reinforced by promotion practices which have highlighted research above other contributions. International links often enjoy more prestige than similar local links. Being ancient helps too!

Given the traditional values which are deeply embedded in society and academia itself it is hardly surprising if some new universities and staff within them aspire to becoming more academic; to raising the traditional academic entry qualifications for students; to emphasising research; and to developing international linkages. Such aspirations are strengthened by the publication of league tables which largely accept the traditional values. Further reinforcement comes from the prospects for institutions and departments of increasing much needed income from research and international activities. Indeed, some would argue that the financial motivation to develop these activities is the primary one. For some individual staff the desire to engage in research and perhaps international activities is reinforced by the recognition that their own marketability and promotion prospects are frequently enhanced by success in these areas. Indeed, it can be argued that the pressures are such that convergence with most universities adopting similar strategies is a likely outcome unless there are significant changes in funding or other policies at a national level.

Despite the pressures towards convergence, and they are undoubtedly real, there are other factors which suggest that the post-1992 universities will seek and achieve only a limited convergence. This comment is, of course, made before the outcomes of the Dearing Committee's investigations are known.

The first factor is the commitment of many staff to vocational education, wider access, teaching before research, and to serving local and regional industry and communities. It should be noted that the commitment referred to may be to one or some of the aspects listed and not necessarily to all of them. For example, some of those most strongly committed to vocational education and the preparation of undergraduates for their chosen careers in areas such as engineering may be sceptical of policies that widen access in case this lowers standards.

Despite the 'inherited' commitments referred to it is possible that these will become progressively weaker as existing staff retire so that status, additional funding and the personal career interests of staff will indeed lead to convergence between the missions of the pre- and post-1992 universities. A key factor in determining the outcome of this widely perceived tension is whether there is in reality a conflict between the 'inherited' values of the post-1992 universities and 'new' values adopted from the pre-1992 universities.

It is therefore worth exploring whether self interest can be a second factor limiting the pressure towards convergence between the old and the new. Before proceeding further it is necessary to consider what 'convergence' may mean. At its most simple it involves the post-1992 universities in seeking "to emulate some of the older universities in their desired student profile"[7] and in developing major areas of research excellence. As a generalisation it means that the post-1992 universities would seek to follow the path taken by the 1960s Robbins universities and perhaps create more of the same. In practice the levels of success of the universities created in the 1960s and indeed of some of their longer established sisters is by no means uniform. For instance, despite departmental centres of excellence across the sector, overall research income is very unevenly spread in both Scotland and the UK generally among the pre-1992 universities. Similarly, on another 'traditional' indicator the pre-1992 universities, subject by subject, have varying academic entry qualifications. It is in this context and in a very different environment to that experienced by the 1960s universities and their older sisters that self interest for the post-1992 universities has to be assessed.

In a report to the CVCP, Connor, Pearson, Court and Jagger[8] use a typology that identifies four "clear groups of qualitatively different kinds of university": the traditional elite; the quasi-old; the quasi-new; and the real-new. The 'traditional elite' are characterised as a "small number of universities, currently the more prestigious ones, which have hardly changed at all in the last five years". They continue to recruit students mainly straight from school with 'good' 'A' levels' or Higher grades usually from a wide catchment area. Typically they have little vocational orientation outside the professional areas of medicine, law etc. They place a strong emphasis on research and growth is likely to be concentrated at the postgraduate level.

The 'quasi-old' are characterised as "a much larger number of universities which have traditionally recruited school leavers". According to the report they are "struggling to compete with" the traditional elite and to widen their appeal are developing more vocationalism and increasing flexibility in the curriculum and delivery of learning "but are facing internal tensions between traditional cultures and values and newer development."

The 'quasi-new' are former polytechnics and colleges that are "trying to emulate some of the older universities in their desired student profile, in particular their entry standards" while also developing "new kinds of provision to continue to attract non-conventional students".

Finally, according to this typology there are the 'real-new' which are broadening their profile, "strengthening local identities and links, moving further towards vocationalism, developing more access arrangements and a flexible range of delivery mechanisms".

While the typology cannot do justice to the rich variety of individual university profiles it is instructive. According to the authors the problematic groups are the 'quasi-old' and the 'quasi-new' both apparently sitting uncomfortably with potentially confused missions. For the post-1992 universities, of course, their choice, at least in this restricted typology, is between 'quasi-new' and 'real-new'. However, there may be a lesson from the alleged predicament of the quasi-old. If the authors are correct, even for pre-1992 universities which have had the benefit of many years to establish their place in the traditional hierarchy, and historically with a substantial element of research funding guaranteed without any questions, the new mass higher education system with attendant cost pressures and competitive research selectivity poses significant difficulties. How much harder must it be for the 'quasi-new' universities without these advantages to succeed with the more traditional part of their mixed strategy.

On this interpretation it would seem that perhaps the most sensible strategy for the post-1992 universities is to adopt the 'real-new' approach. The point here is that this conclusion derives not so much from carrying forward a commitment to wider access, vocationalism and flexibility, although that may be important in the strategy's success, but rather from an identification of self interest. Essentially the authors are suggesting that the probability of prospering for post-1992 universities is increased by wholeheartedly embracing the 'real new' approach. If this is the case then perhaps convergence is less likely – some or all the post-1992 universities will indeed seek to be different!

Much of this analysis is persuasive as far as it concerns the identification of target student groups. There is a strong case for focusing on particular segments of the student market. For the post-1992 universities these may include students seeking clearly vocationally orientated courses; students who have successfully completed advanced certificate and diploma programmes in further education colleges; continuing professional development students seeking flexible and relevant programmes tailored to their needs; company partnerships to deliver agreed programmes of study for employees. At least to date in Scotland this 'real-new' strategy is being adopted. Where convergence is perhaps more tempting is in the areas of research and internationalisation. In both cases the pull of esteem and financial interest may coincide.

All the post-1992 universities have developed international activities and it seems likely they will continue to do so. In educational terms there is a benefit to all students from widening perspectives and foreign students certainly contribute to a stimulating academic environment. Staff similarly benefit from contact with colleagues from different educational environments whether it be in research, or teaching and learning collaborations. There may also be financial benefits from the recruitment of overseas students whether to study in Scotland, or as part of partnership programmes in host countries, or on distance learning programmes. Although the extent and nature of international activities may vary both among the post-1992 universities and between that group and pre-1992 universities the potential educational and finance benefits will ensure that there is an international dimension to most if not all universities' strategies – educational benefit, high esteem and financial self interest coincide.

As far as research is concerned, the twin problems for post-1992 universities are the apparent biases in research selectivity exercises towards basic and more theoretical research as opposed to the more applied end of the spectrum and the high degree of selectivity practised by SHEFC. From a relatively low starting base the post-1992 universities face considerable difficulty in a financially strained environment in being able to make the necessary investment to achieve success. However, by a selective internal approach the investment problem may perhaps be overcome. If this is the perception then the pull of esteem and financial interest may coincide. This view is reinforced by some of the outcomes in Teaching Quality Assessment, which suggest that a vibrant research and scholarship environment is supportive of a stimulating teaching and learning environment. Insofar as this is correct, the post-1992 universities, with their strong commitment to their teaching and learning mission, must seek to enhance their research activities. The questions become not 'whether' but 'how far' and of 'what kind.' It may not be realistic to seek to become strong research universities but it may be sensible to build selective research strengths in some disciplines, specialisms within disciplines, or in interdisciplinary areas. The Government's Technology Foresight initiative and the widespread desire to bring the academic science and technology base closer to industry may indicate some worthwhile and important criteria in developing such strategies. It is arguable that suppport and encouragement for such an approach may offer good value for money to the public purse in developing potential centres of excellence, in supporting the mission to work closely with local industry, and at the same time in enhancing the teaching and learning role of the institutions.

The perspective adopted in this chapter has been an institutional one. As autonomous institutions the post-1992 universities are responsible for determining their own character and direction. However, it would be inappropriate and incomplete if the wider institutional framework and external stakeholders' needs were not explicitly considered . Indeed any analysis of self interest requires such consideration.

External stakeholders include students and potential students; employers in industry, commerce, public and private sector services; local and regional communities; the Government; Parliament, and a Scottish Parliament if the latter is created; SHEFC; quality assurance agencies and professional bodies.

While universities determine their own strategies they do so within the framework established by Government and under the funding regime determined by SHEFC. Both the Government and SHEFC indicate priorities which may include incentives to expand in some subject areas, such as science and engineering, and to increase numbers of part-time students. Similarly, the Government and SHEFC may encourage growth in full time student numbers as they did in the early 1990s or put a cap on numbers as they have in the mid and later 1990s. At another level Government and SHEFC by their policies can push institutions into strongly competitive behaviour as happened in the early to mid 1990s or tilt the balance towards more co-operative behaviour as is happening under SHEFC's Metropolitan Area Networks and Regional and Strategic Change initiatives. This may extend further to include policies encouraging or discouraging mergers or other formal relationships. Indeed policy concerning relationships between universities and further and higher education colleges is a major issue for the Government and the Dearing Committee in the new mass higher education system.

While the framework set by Government and SHEFC is a crucial determinant of strategy, the subject profiles also depend on the changing patterns of student and employer demand. The recent rapid growth of business and computing and information science departments and faculties reflects student demand. Whatever strategic choices are made they must adapt to, and hopefully anticipate, the changing demand patterns.

There are choices, and they are not always easy!

References

1	In contrast to the situation in England for comparable institutions the Scottish Office did not specifically fund research

2	Dundee Institute of Technology, *The First Hundred Years 1888-1988*, 1989.

3	University of Paisley, *The First Hundred Years:* Evelyn Hood (forthcoming, 1997).

4	*Scientia et Opera,* R B Strathdee, Robert Gordon: Technical College and Institute of Technology, 1971.

5	Dundee Institute of Technology, *The First Hundred Years 1888-1988*, 1989.

6	Glasgow Caledonian University, *Annual Report 1995.*

7	H Connor, R Pearson, G Court, N Jagger, *University Challenge: Student choices in the 21st Century.* A Report to the CVCP, The Institute for Employment Studies, Report 306, 1996 pages 49-52.

8	H Connor, A Pearson, G Court, N Jagger, op. cit.

Professor Richard W Shaw
Principal and Vice-Chancellor, University Of Paisley

Prior to moving to Paisley as head of department of Economics and Management in 1984 Principal Shaw lectured in economics at the University of Leeds (1964-69) and the University of Stirling (1969-84). He was appointed Vice-Principal at Paisley in 1986, Principal in 1987, and Principal and Vice-Chancellor of the University of Paisley in 1992. He was elected Convener of COSHEP in August 1996.

5

Alistair MacFarlane

The knowledge revolution

Learning, teaching and technology

Learning is an interactive and dynamic process, in which imagination drives action in exploring and interacting with an environment. It requires a dialogue between imagination and experience. Teaching provides the relevant experience and mediates the ensuing dialogue. Our limited raw information-processing capability requires us to interact with only a severely restricted part of our environment at any specific time. Thus when we learn we can only learn about, and acquire a facility in dealing with, a highly limited version of part of the world. Knowledge thus comes in chunks. The severely limited, circumscribed and simplified situations which we can attend to, or learn about, at any specific time we will call a *microworld*. This idea is central to the discussion of the ways in which technology could be used to support learning which is given here. As we learn by interacting with our various environments, day after day, year after year, we weave from our experiences an intricate web of beliefs, concepts, descriptions, prescriptions, rules and procedures, facts and dodges. We weave microworlds into our macroworld, constantly modifying, stitching, repairing and creating our abilities to understand, to explain and to cope. This process is active, constant and never-ending[1]. The primary role of technology in teaching, and in the support of the learning process, is to create appropriate microworlds, and to facilitate and mediate a learner's interaction with them. The wider role of technology is to create networks of interconnections – between groups of learners and teachers, and between learners and a variety of shared environments. The primary role of teachers is to manage and facilitate the learning processes of their students. The wider role of teachers is to create and develop effective and efficient environments for the support of learning.

As we move into the next century, technology thus provides us with both a challenge and an opportunity. The challenge is to find out how to construct and deploy highly supportive environments which could be used to provide self-paced tutor-supported learning deliverable in a highly flexible way to individuals, or to collaborating groups, and in a variety of locations and over a distance as required. The opportunity is to radically change the ways in which we aid the learning process in order to give students a much higher degree of individual support, and a much more flexible approach to the management of their learning experiences. Only by seizing this opportunity will we be able to expand participation in higher education while maintaining quality, and only by an imaginative use of technology will we be able to make the ideal of life-long learning for large numbers of people a reality. The ideas for the machine-aided support of learning which are developed here, and the ways in which they are described, are biased heavily towards scientific and technical subjects. It is believed, however, that the principles which underlie them are general, and so could be adapted for use in a variety of fields of learning.

Information and knowledge
Although there is no room here (or need) for a technical discussion, it will be useful to spell out the sense in which the terms *information* and *knowledge* are to be understood. Information is a quantitative measure of shape, pattern or order. It is a property of a material object (or of energy, as in a modulated radio wave) and so is objective. It can be moved around in space, and stored in a physical substrate. In interacting with the world we encounter and use information in two ways[2]. One way characterises *the world as sensed* – it provides, for example, the information needed for identifying and characterising objects, and for building models of them. The other way characterises *the world as acted upon* – it provides the information needed for an action to have a desired effect. Thus information can be both *descriptive* and *prescriptive* – one use of information is associated with specifying *perception*, the other use with specifying *action*. Prescriptive information specifies a *process* which runs on an *information processor.*

Knowledge integrates abstractions from experience into a capacity for effective action. Any practically useful characterisation of knowledge must be integrated with an appropriate characterisation of the learning process. Knowledge we take to be the capacity for action, and intelligence the degree to which this capacity is used effectively. Thus knowledge is associated with an agent, is a process, and is information used to achieve action. Because knowledge is information of a special kind, it can be physically instantiated (in books, media, computers) where it can be interactively accessed by an agent, so supporting the agent's learning.

Learning and its phases

The development of thorough conceptual understanding involves a series of learning *phases* – preparing to tackle the relevant material, acquiring the necessary information, relating it to previous knowledge, transforming it through establishing organisational frameworks within which to interpret it, and so developing personal understanding[3]. If this process is to work effectively, teaching – however it is delivered – must be *designed* to support these phases of learning. The required support can be described in terms of necessary *teaching functions* which to some extent parallel, but also overlap, the phases of learning. These functions include:

- orientating – setting the scene and explaining what is required
- motivating – pointing up relevance, evoking and sustaining interest
- presenting – introducing new knowledge within a clear, supportive structure
- clarifying – explaining with examples and providing remedial support
- elaborating – introducing additional material to develop more detailed knowledge
- consolidating – providing opportunities to develop and test personal understanding
- confirming – ensuring the adequacy of the knowledge and understanding reached.

After the initial phases of preparing for learning, the conventional process of acquiring new knowledge begins with a teacher *presenting* appropriate course material. The new knowledge has to be carefully selected to ensure relevance and potential interest, and then presented in a way which helps the student both to relate it to prior knowledge and to see a clear logical structure within it, as a first step towards establishing a personal organising framework. Then the process of *clarifying* begins. Through explanations and examples, students are encouraged to begin developing their own personal understanding of the topic. If the prior knowledge is inadequate, remedial support will be required at this stage, to allow a firm base on which to build explanations and further clarification. Once the initial grasp of the material is sufficiently firm, opportunities have to be provided for *elaborating* the knowledge by examining nuances of meaning, and by incorporating more detail and additional examples or evidence. Thereafter, the knowledge requires *consolidating,* by encouraging application to new contexts and periodic review of what has already been presented. Ultimately, there needs to be a final consolidation which allows the students to integrate the course as a whole and that is often linked, through assessment procedures, to the final teaching function – *confirming* that knowledge and understanding have reached an appropriate level. Such confirmation is involved in certifying standards to the outside world, but is also part of quality control to ensure that teaching has been effective.

Within conventional teaching methodology, the initial stages of orientating, motivating, presenting, and explaining or clarifying, are carried out through lectures. Further clarification and remedial support is obtained from textbooks or through tutorials, which also involve elaborating and consolidating. Laboratory classes and field work introduce additional knowledge and skills, together with opportunities for consolidation and elaboration in relation to the lecture course. The additional reading suggested by lecturers and tutors continues the process of elaboration, while much of the consolidation comes from worked examples in the sciences and coursework essays in many courses. In all areas of study, assessment requirements are used to encourage consolidation through the periodic review of lecture notes and the more thorough revision process which precedes examinations. Student progress needs confirming through comments on coursework and the results of periodic tests, while degree examinations are used formally to confirm the levels of skill and understanding reached by students. Finally, course evaluations are required to confirm the quality of the teaching. The provision of teaching and the support of learning should be seen in terms of a complex, interacting *system*. Assessment is only one of the factors influencing learning. The outcomes of learning depend on the combined effects of the *whole learning environment* provided by an institution and its courses (teaching, discussion classes, resource materials, and assessment procedures). The provision of an effective and economical system requires a careful analysis of requirements and functions both at institutional and course levels.

While the conventional teaching methods continue to fulfil these functions, it is now imperative to consider whether there should be widespread adoption of more efficient and cost-effective ways of encouraging and supporting student learning. There needs to be a re-examination of both the purposes and the techniques involved in conventional teaching methods, and a widespread adoption of new methods which support the additional transferable skills now being required. In particular, it is necessary to consider carefully how, and to what extent, we can make use of technology in improving the provision of teaching and the support of learning.

Learning support

Effective action is achieved via *schemata* – the rules and procedures which are assembled to guide action. Learning results from the progressive development and refinement of concepts and schemata, and leads to the acquisition of coherent frameworks of reasonable beliefs together with the necessary skills to put them to effective use. Descriptions and prescriptions are the warp and woof of our web of understanding. In interacting with a microworld we need to both comprehend it and to be able to act effectively upon it. To comprehend it we need a necessary set of concepts, and to act upon it we need a necessary set of schemata. Understanding of a microworld is manifested by an ability to:

● use the concepts assimilated and the schemata created in the learning process to successfully interpret data, explain sets of related events, and solve problems posed in terms of the microworld

● cope with new situations described in the microworld

● explain new situations arising in the microworld

● act in these new situations with satisfactory consequences.

To deal with a specific microworld, one can conceive of creating an *intensely supportive environment for learning* using computer-based systems which support and aid the human reasoning process, and communication systems which augment this by providing flexible access to tutors and to fellow learners. Such an environment allows one to interact with structured objective knowledge in such a way as to absorb concepts and develop schemas, derive an understanding of their use, and to test that understanding by appropriate investigations and exercises. It could support learning *on both an individual and on a group basis*, allowing the users great flexibility in finding their way through the structured objective knowledge which is made available to them, yet also allowing an instructor to monitor and, if necessary, direct the progress of each individual student.

Given such a system to use, the teacher's principal roles are:

● structuring knowledge in such a way as to make it interactively accessible

● facilitating the learning process

● managing the learner's interaction with structured and interactively-accessible knowledge.

The teacher no longer acts primarily as a transmitter of information, allowing some learning support functions to be supplied by a machine. An important implication of this form of learning support system structure is that *remote* tutoring can be provided.

The *functional* structure of a learning support system must provide, among other things:

● development of an understanding of the *concept set* for the microworld

● development of an ability to use the *schemata set* for the microworld

● a *flexible narrative* to lead, guide and support the learner

● a *reference system* to provide – on request – definitions, explanations, guidance and to help to place concepts and schemata in an appropriate *context*.

It must be emphasised that machine-based learning-support environments of this sort are seen as *supplementing*, and not as displacing, the essential role of the human teacher. Their use will free vital human skills for face to face and small-group tuition, of which so little is now available at so many levels of education. The use of technology for learning support could evolve in such a way that the *group* becomes the natural learning unit, where pupils and students reinforce increasingly each other's learning experiences, guided by both their peers and by their teachers.

There are wider implications to what is being proposed. Three of these are:

● tutorial support delivered over a communications link into such supportive environments, based on portable computers in the home or workplace, could be the prime delivery mechanism for advanced professional training

● the provision of powerful knowledgeable machines (which is one way of looking at a learning support system), with which one could interact easily, could go a long way towards overcoming the increasing fragmentation of knowledge into highly specialised domains

● powerful learning support environments coupled with remote tutoring could provide small and medium sized enterprises with affordable training schemes.

Knowledge economies

The above discussion envisages the emergence, for educational purposes, of a system which includes a mixture of human and machine agents subject to a variety of goals and descriptions. In discussing such a system, it is useful to use the word *economy* in its old-fashioned sense of an organised system of agents which displays explicable regularities (not always predictable in their details!). We can then say that the future of higher education can be considered in terms of *building knowledge economies*. These will involve computers, networks, communications and multi-media software, and will interconnect schools, higher education institutions, and the workplaces of industry. Any effective use of such networks must take appropriate account of the ways in which human agents interact, of different human communication modalities, and of the crucial distinction between tacit and explicit knowledge.

Following the sketch of the processes of learning support which has been given above, a possible scenario for developments in teaching, learning and training is now described as they might develop over the next two decades. In doing this, the following technical assumptions have been made:

- the technology of learning support environments will have been developed and will have become widely deployed in the forms both of computer-based systems providing interactively developed knowledge of a wide range of microworlds, and in the form of networking giving easy and flexible access to tutors and fellow learners.

- Widespread networking will exist, with multimedia capability. All higher educational institutions will be connected to a powerful academic network, and all individuals participating in higher education or continuing professional training will have access to such networks over commercial service networks from their workplace or from home.

- All higher educational institutions will have powerful local distributed computing systems connected to a national academic network. All teaching staff will have access to workstations and personal computers with multimedia capability. The local academic networks will have powerful knowledge servers providing a wide range of teaching and learning support material.

- Powerful multimedia authoring systems will be widely available, which will have a high degree of standardisation or reciprocal compatibility and transference, and these will be in widespread, routine use.

- All participants in higher education – staff, students, and those pursuing off-campus continuing professional training – will routinely use desktop and portable computers with multi-media and networking capability.

When a knowledge economy of this form has been developed, we would expect to see individual higher educational institutions importing from and exporting to each other a wide range of educational material, and also delivering into schools and the workplace. A possible set of teaching areas in such a teaching economy could be:

- specialist
- core, and
- foundational,

where **specialist** could involve subjects like astronomy imported into physics departments from specialised astronomy centres, Japanese for scientists and engineers imported from Japanese departments, and so on. **Foundational** material of very high quality, such as mathematics for engineers and scientists, could be supplied in high volume into a large number of institutions. **Core** would denote those areas of work where the individual institution saw itself as supplying its own added value, tailored to its own students' individual needs.

Generic changes in terms of shifts along a teaching/learning spectrum

The benefits which will have arisen from the use of innovative methods, and from the use of technology in a learning-support process, can be considered in terms of a number of types of *generic change* which we will call *shifts*. The term shift is used to emphasise that each form of change can be thought of as associated with a progression along a spectrum of teaching/learning support, which ranges from simply imparting information at one end of the spectrum of possibilities to comprehensively managing the complete learning-support process at the other end.

These forms of generic change, their role in developing teaching methods, and the associated benefits which will have been obtained, are as follows:

(i)   **a shift from synchronous single-location learning support to asynchronous networked learning support:** The severe space and time constraints of traditional presentation methods using lectures and laboratories will have been replaced by a shift to self-paced supported learning using a variety of possible support and delivery mechanisms.

(ii)   **a shift from passive learning to active learning:** Learning will be seen as an active process in which concepts are acquired, incorporated into appropriate schemas, and tested in action.

(iii)   **a shift from static presentation to dynamic presentation:** Cheap methods of producing, transmitting and storing acceptable quality video and animation will have greatly improved the presentation of a wide range of material.

(iv)   **a shift from the use of real objects to the use of virtual objects:** The use of virtual objects – that is, objects whose behaviour is simulated by computer, and which are interactively accessible – offers huge scope for linking theory and experiment in teaching science and technology.

(v)   **a shift from impassive delivery to supportive delivery:** Well-designed computer-based learning-support systems will have been made highly supportive in dealing with a learner's difficulties. This will provide great scope for remedial teaching.

(vi)   **a shift to multi-media:** The imaginative and skilful use of a wide range of media will provide huge scope for imaginative teaching. Video, animation and audio will be of great value in improving presentation quality and learning effectiveness in every subject area, but will have particular value in science and technology where the spatial visualisation of complex phenomena plays a key role in learning.

(vii)   **a shift from unidirectional presentation to interactive presentation:** Interactivity offers great scope for benefits in clarification, elaboration and consolidation, and is the key to the production of highly supportive learning environments. Great benefits in quality and effectiveness will be obtained, provided by well-designed support systems.

(viii)   **a shift from broadcast delivery to personal delivery:** The possibility, given skilful design, of developing learning-support systems which tailor their response to an individual's needs and performance will have been shown to be of great value in combining volume benefits with quality benefits.

Changes at institutional level

As they respond to the pressures on them to increase their output while maintaining quality, and as they draw on an ever-widening spread of abilities and backgrounds in their intake, institutions will generate a much greater degree of flexibility in their teaching arrangements.

A fully developed learning-support methodology which will allow a very high degree of self-paced, exploratory learning will be created and studied in order to identify those features of the environment which best support learning. In institutional terms, material will be highly modularised, and new mechanisms devised for supervision and assessment. A whole spectrum of working methods will be investigated and appraised – from individual working with a remote supervisor or tutor, through small group working, to the use of asynchronously accessed lecture material in video form. Management systems will be devised and tested to track an individual student's progress and to provide straightforward yet intensively-supported access to remedial teaching.

In organisational terms the technical complexity of the support systems will have changed the roles of computing services and other support systems at institutional level. At regional and national level, organisational arrangements will have been created to ensure that standards are generated and adhered to which will permit and facilitate an effective and efficient sharing of scarce resources both in manpower and materials.

Changes at teacher level
Teachers will be involved increasingly in the support, development and management of learning environments. The organisational implications of this shift will be very great. Much training will be required and teachers will have to adapt to greatly changed working styles. Teachers will be involved in communities spanning many institutions and operating on a national basis.

Changes at student level
The changes at the individual student level will be profound. Students will be taught how to manage their own learning processes to an unprecedented degree. They will learn how to swim in a sea of information, to use the rich resources of a supportive learning environment, to self-pace and self-structure their own programmes of learning. They will be able to choose from a spectrum of learning styles ranging from self-instruction with tutor support to group working of various types. The effectiveness of each individual student's learning process will be efficiently monitored, and appropriate arrangements provided for each individual student to interact effectively with supervisors and tutors.

Although lectures and laboratory classes will continue to play a role in the teaching process, it will become clear how all those activities which are currently carried out in groups could be more effectively and appropriately carried out in a supportive learning environment. The role of the lecture will be radically re-assessed, and re-presented for many purposes in an appropriate free-access format enriched – as relevant – with film and simulation material. The use of flexible interactive simulators will replace much of the traditional laboratory material. There will be seen to be great advantages in devising ways of supporting small groups working closely together; such methods of working will usefully develop and enhance the social and communication skills which will be demanded increasingly by employers.

Conclusions

Large-scale changes to anything as complicated and as important as the country's educational and training systems will be complicated, prolonged and disruptive. It will have to be carried through in the face of the ever-present realities imposed by costs, space, time, organisational and institutional constraints, and by individual attitudes. Nationally co-ordinated changes to our teaching systems on the scale which will be necessary to maintain or increase quality, while further increasing volume, will require an unlikely degree of collective political will. A more probable outcome will be a set of piecemeal, disjointed, *ad hoc* responses to increasing economic and political pressures, as institutions fight to compete effectively in a developing educational market, while generating their own internal arrangements for innovative teaching, and negotiating a series of collaborations with like-minded partners. Whatever actually happens over the next two decades, some things seem reasonably certain – technology will have a key role to play in the effective provision of high quality learning environments, finding out how to do this in an effective way which commands general support will be a complex and painful process, and the relatively small scale and coherence of the Scottish system should provide us with an opportunity to give a lead in these exciting developments.

References

1   Quine, W.V. and Ullian, J.S. (1978) *The Web of Belief* New York: Random House.

2   Simon, H.A. (1982) *The Sciences of the Artificial* Cambridge MA: MIT Press.

3   CSUP REPORT (1992) *Teaching and Learning in an Expanding Higher Education System* Committee of Scottish University Principals Working Party.

Professor Alistair MacFarlane CBE
Formerly Principal and Vice-Chancellor, Heriot-Watt University

Professor MacFarlane is an Honorary Fellow of Selwyn College, Cambridge, a Fellow of the IEEE, of the Institute of Measurement and Control, and of the IEE; and Consultant Editor of the International Journal of Control. He was elected to the Royal Academy of Engineering in 1981, made FRS in 1984, FRSE in 1990, and awarded a CBE in 1987. The Institution of Electrical Engineers awarded him its Achievement Medal in 1992 for work in automatic control, and the Faraday Medal in 1993 for outstanding contributions to electrical science. He has been Chairman of the Scottish Council for Research in Education since 1992, and Chairman of the Scottish Library and Information Council since 1994.

6

Graeme Davies

Funding: the Tablets of Moses?

If one of my august predecessors as Principal of the University of Glasgow had been given the gift of foresight, he would surely have been puzzled by the phenomenon of his successors in Glasgow and the other Scottish higher education institutions (HEIs) being publicly so grateful for an announcement of Government funding for higher education (in 1997/98) where the annual allocation would actually take account of inflation: no real increase but at least not a cut. Surprised perhaps that the country has come to such a pass, he would no doubt be astonished at the column inches in newspapers and *The Times Higher Education Supplement,* the hours of debate in Senates and Courts and the accusations and counter-accusations of politicians which are all devoted to one topic: the funding of higher education.

A brief foray into the history of the University of Glasgow shows that funding difficulties are indeed nothing new. The University was bailed out by the City Magistrates in the 1570s. Its staunchly presbyterian character then served it ill after the Restoration of 1660. It was, ". . . short of income and sunk in debt"[1], until good fortune returned after the 1689 Revolution. Even in the 19th Century, there was evidence of state "interference" in the affairs of the universities. The munificence of the Crown in endowing professorships in the four universities throughout the 18th and early 19th centuries had ceased and there was no prospect of Government support, other than at what proved to be a high price. Present-day observers of the relationship between the Scottish Higher Education Funding Council (SHEFC) and the Committee of Scottish Higher Education Principals (COSHEP) and of the Scottish Office may read George Davie's comment on the 1850s[2] that, "Both Government and Opposition were agreed, as a matter of public policy, on the inadvisability of (the Government) subsidising the Scottish education system so long as it remained virtually independent and attached to un-British standards", and consider that things are perhaps not as bad as they might seem. We have the Committee of Enquiry into Higher Education (the Dearing Committee): our predecessors ended up with a Royal Commission which may eventually have paved the way for Government support but at the cost of "anglicising" higher education in Scotland.

The Funding question

My brief, though, in writing about the funding of higher education, is not to dwell on the past but to look at the present and speculate a little on the future. Funding higher education is not a difficult issue *per se* but, in a pluralistic society like Britain, is as much a political issue as it is an economic one. The accession of Mrs Thatcher in 1979 has led to the modern political orthodoxy that low personal (and corporate) taxation is "a good thing". Taxes are, of course, used to fund government spending. Put crudely, in an ideal fiscal world, tax revenues should at the very least match outgoings. Given the cyclical nature of the economy ("boom and bust" – neatly summarised recently by Peter Clarke[3]), that ideal has rarely been achieved with the net result that excess of expenditure over revenue is funded through the Public Sector Borrowing Requirement (PSBR). So, in order to reduce levels of taxation but faced with uncertain revenues and with no more nationalised industries to be sold, the simple method is to reduce public spending. Thus, the funding of higher education becomes the subject of political whim. Set against the context of overall resources which are shrinking and in the absence of any real long-term Government policy, HE has to take its chance with schools, health, social security, defence, local government and so on in the lottery that is the annual Public Expenditure Survey (PES) round.

Previously shielded from the exigencies of the real world, "Universities were to be no different from any other part of the public sector"[4], Simon Jenkins's general thesis – that Thatcherism, instead of freeing institutions (such as universities) from state controls and constraints, has in fact led to greater state control ("accountability") – is hard to deny, although his view – which, in a Scottish context, we might ascribe to "Disgruntled, Auchtermuchty" – that UGC/ SED = good, UFC/SOEID = the slippery slope and SHEFC/SOEID = the end of the civilised world as we know it, does not really stand up to close scrutiny. Indeed, the throw-away and rather glib comments of supposedly serious and "heavyweight" commentators that, "Universities and the old polytechnics, now all 'Universities', have been turned into factories for the production of degree-holders"[5] are, frankly, nonsense. There is a good deal less interference in 1997 in relation to the academic programmes of HEIs than there was in 1987 or 1977.

There is little doubt that in latter years the UGC exercised forms of benevolent despotism. While the "consolidation" of undergraduate funded numbers may mean that the funding of new course development may need to be at the expense of other activities, HEIs formerly funded by SOEID at least no longer have to seek Government approval for new courses. Nonetheless, and I say this with some trepidation as the ex-Chief Executive of two funding councils, ever tighter purse-strings and the overwhelming reliance of all HEIs on Exchequer funding, do seem to mean that the perception (perhaps to a degree misguided) in HEIs of being powerless in the face of Government is greater in 1997 than in 1987 (1977 now seems like prehistoric times). The question is, though: can HEIs break free from the iron grip of the Exchequer?

The American experience

One way to lessen dependence on public funds is to become wholly privately funded, along the lines of American institutions like Harvard, Dartmouth or Vassar. There, £12,000 plus per undergraduate in tuition fees for liberal arts subjects makes the Funding Council's gross units of resource seem somewhat niggardly. That, of course, is not the whole story as up to 60% of undergraduate students in a private college such as Vassar will either have their fees reduced or have a bursary provided to help pay those fees. Nevertheless, the British Government might try tax concessions (tuition fees as a tax allowance for personal income tax purposes), which would not necessarily cost the Government much in relation to lost revenue. Institutions might also gain additional tax breaks, as might potential donors or benefactors.

But history and culture in Britain are rather different than in the USA. There, the relative youth of the federal structure and the country's republican form of government mean that there is no long tradition of a monarchy and a state government and bureaucracy to support it. The creation of a national (and central government-driven) system of state benefits, including almost free higher education, in return for higher levels of taxation than had previously been the case, would have been almost inconceivable in the USA, given the relationship between State and Federal Government. As a result, there is no generally held view in the USA that it is a fundamental responsibility of the state to provide for all, rather than for provision to be made by private individuals or commerce and industry as is the case in America.

Giving (and paying) is part of the American way of life in a way which does not exist in Britain (or, indeed, in many other North European countries).

Endowments, either individual or corporate but linked to tax concessions, continue to bolster the finances of American institutions (along with the realistic but high tuition fees) in a way which has been since the end of World War Two largely culturally alien to individuals and industry in this country. Although there have been generous exceptions (the Nuffield Foundation; donations which have allowed the foundation of new Oxford colleges and so on), the fact remains that such donations are exceptions and, if you are a less than charismatic Midland university, about as likely as winning the jackpot in the National Lottery.

Funding "from other sources"

I would stress that I am not for a moment suggesting that British higher education should move to the American model of reliance on large-scale corporate sponsorship as such sponsorship may well bring its own difficulties in relation to academic freedom, interference from paymasters and accountability (well satirised in Jane Smiley's fictional Mid-Western campus which forms the setting of her novel, "Moo"). But, if funding from the state continues on its downward path, we cannot escape the obligation to look at increasing funding from all other sources, if we are to continue to offer high quality teaching and research. The 1992 Further and Higher Education Acts were a clear signal from Government of its views in this regard in that the Acts contained an instruction to the respective funding councils, ". . . (to) have regard to the desirability of not discouraging any institution . . . from maintaining or developing its funding from other sources"[6]. Such "other sources" are expressed in my own (and other) University's income and expenditure account under four main headings, viz:

> Academic fees and support grants
>
> Research grants and contracts
>
> Other services rendered
>
> Endowment funds and donations

Academic fees and support grants – overseas fees

In this context, academic fees can be taken largely to mean tuition fees. If fees payable on behalf of British and EU students are discounted, the largest category of students are those from overseas. Given the current competition to recruit such students, it seems strange to think that this source of income has only been in existence in this form since 1981 when the then-Government created the distinction between home and overseas students in relation to the payment of tuition fees. Overseas fees rapidly moved to a level which was asserted to be "full-cost" by the Department of Education and Science, which was responsible at that time for "recommending" fees to institutions.

Overseas fee income has become a significant element in the balance sheets of many (most?) HEIs , with increasing efforts being made to recruit what everyone hopes is an infinitely expandable number of students but which many people privately fear will prove to be a bubble which will eventually burst. Scottish HEIs have at least come together under the aegis of the recently formed Scottish Education and Training Export Group, which exists to promote the high quality and standard of a Scottish education to potential students abroad.

But where are the students? Some markets have withered away while others have grown: fashions for courses have also changed with Business Studies, for instance, replacing Engineering, at least in terms of a growth market. If I take one example, and if that example is South-East and East Asia, that is because large efforts are expended in this area where sustained economic growth has meant that there is a seemingly insatiable demand for graduates. Local institutions have been unable to cope with the demand which has meant that many students have gone abroad in order to obtain a degree. However, there have been signs in parts of the market that either demand for particular subjects is waning or that students are turning elsewhere. There is increasingly fierce competition from competitors such as Australia. There is also the situation that, "where everyone is a graduate now", some of those graduates will seek to obtain competitive advantage over their fellows by enhancing their qualifications with a further degree, particularly an MBA. British universities have been quick to capitalise on such opportunities, firstly through hyping the value of an MBA as a generic qualification and then through offering such degrees on a part-time, mixed-mode, distance-learning, franchised and so on basis. A quick scan through *The Straits Times* (Singapore's daily newspaper) reveals both the breadth of what is being offered and the range of competition.

Singapore is a good example because, as an essentially English-speaking country with its roots both in Chinese culture and the British educational system and with a booming economy, it has been a fruitful market in the past but is likely to prove less so in the future. While the demand for graduates in Singapore is likely to continue, the Singaporean Government may well choose to increase the number of local universities from the present two institutions, which, it has to be said, have resources and facilities of a standard which British vice-chancellors and principals can only imagine in their dreams. While that Government is also likely to continue to provide overseas scholarships to the elite of local school-leavers, there are signs that such students increasingly prefer the well-equipped laboratories of CalTech, the computing facilities of Stanford and the libraries of Yale to the comparatively investment-starved campuses of Britain.

The two Singaporean universities may also find themselves under increasing pressure to widen their income basis by recruiting overseas students. Well-equipped, well-resourced in terms of residences, entirely English-speaking, and academically of a high standard, they may well begin to compete in Hong Kong, Malaysia, Korea, Indonesia, Thailand, Vietnam and so on alongside universities from the UK, the US and Australasia.

While the competitive advantage of a British higher education based on tradition, quality and high standards continues to be eroded, there is also increasing pressure on UK HEIs to compete on the basis of price. Fee discounting is already a widespread practice, at least unofficially, and has recently been put forward by the British Council as a policy to be scrutinised in its efforts to promote UK higher education abroad. Faced with cuts in UK Government funding, it can hardly be surprising that increasingly desperate measures like deep discounting and reducing the length of periods of study are being adopted. But at what long-term price?

Some institutions have taken the bold (or is it iron?) step of establishing overseas operations, either in partnership with local institutions or businesses or independently. While such enterprise is to be applauded, at least in theory, recent experience[7] suggests that hasty decisions may have been made without there having been proper appraisal of the long-term returns likely to be realised on the initial investment. Unless you are an institution with a genuinely world-wide reputation (Oxford; Cambridge; LSE; Harvard; Yale), it is really quite difficult to imagine a local operation in, say, Malaysia or Abu Dhabi based on the "reputation" of a university from two globally obscure towns somewhere in the English Midlands being a long-term moneyspinner. Potential students in such countries are rather more aware of academic reputations (for excellence in teaching and research) – for which read labels – than many of their British counterparts. In this intensely brand-conscious age (a global phenomenon among the young), it is Emporio Armani (say the LSE) – of which everyone has heard, which not everyone can afford but to which everyone may aspire – which sells as an object of desire and not, alas, Poppleton (our obscure Midland university).

As a source of funding, therefore, overseas students or overseas activities look suspiciously prone to the law of diminishing returns where increasingly frenzied activity on the part of HEIs (and, nowadays, increasing numbers of FE Colleges) seems unlikely to counter long-term decline.

The other great "moneyspinner" which has led to a rush of activity is of course the full-fee postgraduate course, which can be conveniently packaged in bite-sized chunks, each commanding a healthy fee. MBAs on a part-time basis and MBAs by distance learning have mushroomed in quantity at such a speed that increasing doubts are being expressed about quality. Not surprisingly, the MBA "Old Guard" views this proliferation of its "product" with some alarm, given that an MBA, once sought after by big companies, has now become commonplace. Once again, the London Business Schools, Cranfields and INSEADs, which have the name and reputation, may prosper but are many of the rest liable to do much other than struggle in the longer term?

"Top-up" fees

There is undoubtedly a market for other high-quality postgraduate courses which can be broken down into parts which may then be marketed separately on the basis of continuing professional development. Such courses, however, demand investment (of staff time – academic and support materials etc) because high prices should mean high quality. A reputation for high price and low quality will soon spread. Nevertheless, some glimmer of hope would seem to exist in this area. But I would suggest that any Principal or Vice-Chancellor who aspires to success first studies the course catalogues of the real professionals in this area: for example the Industrial Society, the Office for Public Management or the Civil Service College. Only the best will do.

There is then left the vexed question of "top-up" fees which have been mooted both by new universities in England which have suffered badly in relation to core HEFCE funding and which are, simply, short of money and also by some large research-based universities which recognise that the resources needed to keep them ahead of the game in teaching and research are increasingly hard to find.

The dangers are well known: if not everyone introduces such fees, will that drive students to institutions which do not charge the fee? Unless you are Oxford or Cambridge, the answer to that question is probably "yes". Would the introduction of a top-up fee then let the forces of darkness, also known as the Treasury, reduce funding to higher education accordingly? Not necessarily, but the way in which lottery funds are being increasingly used to substitute for what was Government public expenditure on areas like sport and the arts should give pause for thought. Further, it is important not to forget the inclination to this made public by the current Government in various Ministerial pronouncements. What would students (or, more likely, parents) be getting for their money? There is no doubt that a requirement to hand over hard cash concentrates the mind wonderfully in relation to simple issues like value for money. Anything less than "excellent" in teaching might well come to represent a second rate "product" scorned, even in the January sales[8]. Will the ability to pay become more important than academic ability? Theoretically, the answer to that question should be "of course not" but it is hard to dispel doubts about taking the money and running, based on simple human nature. Will such fees simply deter the mature or non-standard entrants for whom many institutions, particularly those in Scotland, have done so much in the last fifteen years? I fear that the answer to that question will probably be "yes".

No single institution has committed itself so far to such fees. Members of the so-called "Russell Group" have recently been engaged in a delicate quadrille of the, "will you? won't you? if you're not, I'm not", type, which probably means that nothing will happen this year, or next year, or possibly the year after. In the USA, there is a widespread belief, based on hard economic reality, that material success (based on some form of career) is significantly enhanced through being a college graduate. In simple terms, a degree "adds value". Large debts incurred to fund first degrees and then graduate programmes are a fact and a way of life. Graduates recognise that a proportion of their income for the next ten or fifteen years will need to be devoted to paying back loans. But higher salaries provide the means to do so. "Working one's way through college" is accepted as perfectly normal and, while it may be anathema to educationalists and pedagogues for distracting students from their studies, many of their jobs depend on students earning money to help pay their way. The less intensive and modular nature of American first degrees is, of course, rather more conducive to allowing this to happen than an intense three or four year Honours course. As I said earlier, there is a significant cultural difference between the USA and the UK in relation to the question of "who pays?" Moves in the American direction involve more than higher education although it brings the issue into sharp focus and will undoubtedly do so when the Dearing Committee starts to consider the whole issue of funding. To those of us in the business there is a growing awareness that financial pressures are driving many of our students down the road of paying their way.

Research grants and contracts and other services rendered

Although the sums involved in research income and expenditure may be substantial, I feel fairly confident in making the assertion that no institution makes significant surpluses from its research activity. There is a distinction to be drawn between research *per se* (defined in the 1996 Research Assessment Exercise as "original investigation undertaken in order to gain knowledge and understanding. It includes work of direct relevance to the needs of commerce and industry, as well as to the public and voluntary sectors; scholarship; the invention and generation of ideas, images, performances and artefacts including design, where these lead to new or substantially improved insights; and the use of existing knowledge in experimental development to produce new or substantially improved materials, devices, products and processes, including design and construction") and what might be thought of as "problem-solving". Some institutions are adept at the latter with the surpluses generated being used to add to general income as well as to provide resources for investment in new activities. "Problem-solving" often appears as income from consultancies or from "other services rendered". Properly costed and realistically priced, it represents a commercial side to the activities of HEIs of which they are sometimes accused of being incapable. But this is an accusation which cannot be sustained in many cases. For example, my university, which has consistently been in the top five in the UK for its income from industry, currently holds 340 contracts with industry and commerce worth more than £20 million. Together with Strathclyde University it is responsible for more than 5% of the collaborative research between universities and industry in the UK, placing Glasgow in third position in the league table of university cities. This and other universities also play an important role in technology transfer although the rewards are not spectacular – our current annual income is only around £400k from 20 licensing agreements and 105 patents. Unfortunately, the problem is one of scale in that the surpluses needed to make up for shortfalls in Government funding would require a level of activity for which most institutions are not resourced, either in relation to staff or space/facilities/equipment.

Commercialisation

Hence the interest in the further "commercialisation" of mainstream research activity where the intention is that greater focus be given at all levels to examining the commercial potential of research activity. In itself, this must be a laudable aim although I need hardly state the obvious point that you have to have something to "commercialise" in the first place. As is often the case with initiatives being promoted by Government Departments, there is some danger of emperor's new clothes syndrome where people get so caught up in the idea of "commercialisation" as an end in itself that the need to invest in the research itself in order to sustain the approach is sometimes forgotten. Of course, the provision of 'R' funding by the funding councils should allow some selective investment to be made. Funding council money, although calculated on the basis of selective RAE performance, is not so constrained that the "growing" of young researchers or new research cannot be funded as well as the 'R' which formed the basis of various RAE submissions.

Dual-funding

The dual-funding principle is of vital importance to all HEIs in this regard in that its disappearance to be replaced by all Government funding for research being channelled through, say, the Research Councils (the "simple funding principle") would undoubtedly lead to further concentration of research funds in the Oxford – Cambridge – London "golden triangle". The current system will at least guarantee that all institutions in Scotland should continue to receive some funding from the Funding Council, however small, to support research.

But all institutions must also surely recognise by now that supplementing their income through gains in SHEFC 'R' funding is only likely to result in relatively small increases. While the overall volume/quality of research may have increased by, say, 15% between 1992 and 1996, the funding available to SHEFC has not increased commensurately. While the single-mindedness of individual institutions is perfectly understandable – one institution's gains are, after all, another institution's losses – what we should be collectively concerned about is increasing the resource which is available to all, not crowing over doing better than the university down the road. Thus, the solution to the funding problem does not lie simply in increasing the volume and quality of research, although both of these aims are well worthwhile in their own right. And there is no doubt that spin-offs may well one day result in the royalty from a best-seller and providing a significant real addition to income which is not offset in any way against entailed expenditure.

Endowment funds and donations

For some institutions, income from endowments represents a significant element of their annual budget. However, much of this income is entailed in that it may only be spent on specific items such as student bursaries or named lectureships. Nonetheless, HEIs do receive donations and bequests and there is no doubt that alumni do represent a possible source of funding. Such fund-raising does require

Professor Sir Graeme Davies
Principal and Vice-Chancellor, University of Glasgow

Sir Graeme was until September 1995 Chief Executive of the Higher Education Funding Council for England (and previously, the Universities Funding Council and the Polytechnics and Colleges Funding Council). He moved to the Funding Councils from being Vice-Chancellor of the University of Liverpool, a post he held from April 1986 to June 1991. Previously he was Professor of Metallurgy in the University of Sheffield having taken up that post in 1978 after 16 years in the Department of Metallurgy and Materials Science in the University of Cambridge where he was also a Fellow of St. Catherine's College. He was educated in the School of Engineering of the University of Auckland, New Zealand.

Currently he is Chairman of the Scottish Office's Scottish Education and Training Export Group and of the Universities Superannuation Scheme Ltd. He sits on the Science and Engineering committee and the Committee for International Co-operation in Higher Education of the British Council, the Scottish Enterprise Technology Ventures Group and the Council of the Committee of Vice-Chancellor and Principals.

7

Graham Hills

The University of the Highlands and Islands: Scotland's first regional university

Regional universities

A regional university might be glibly defined as being *of* its region and not just *in* its region. It is there to serve its region and its peoples as a centre or centres of the higher education appropriate to that place and time. Inasmuch as all regions seek to have high quality schooling, high quality libraries and other such facilities, so they can now expect to be linked to the global knowledge networks of the global village. Its peoples should not have to travel long distances to access the best of the knowledge base. They can confidently expect it to come to them. The matter of how that is best done is the substance of this paper.

The concept of the regional university is recent but not new. The rapid growth everywhere of higher and further education has prompted many towns and cities, hitherto regarded as outside the university framework, to consider coming inside and aboard. The minimal catchment population considered to justify such a development in the 1990s is thought to be between 300,000 and 400,000. Across Scandinavia, northern North America, the Australian outback and other sparsely populated regions there is an active movement to promote the foundation of new colleges and universities. In Britain well over a dozen regions, from Cornwall to Suffolk and from Swindon to the Shetland Isles, are all vying for a place in the intellectual sunshine. Notwithstanding stout opposition from the existing universities, many of them late arrivals themselves, these regional initiatives are unlikely to be denied.

This is so because the nature of industry, of work and of leisure has changed greatly and will continue to do so. The transportation revolution and, even more so, the information revolution have combined to reduce the obstacles of distance and time. The economic and other benefits of the new technologies, high and low, will not be confined to the big cities and their conurbations. As Japan's export industries have demonstrated, distance is easily overcome. The Internet and its derivatives are, of course, available everywhere. Inasmuch as lifestyles can also be created deliberately, so arcadian settings and even remoteness can acquire charms denied to them before.

This is not the place to list the economies and diseconomies of scale factors in education but the use of auditorium lecture theatres for teaching purposes has to be an act of desperation. At best it can only be a poor way of conveying knowledge. It cannot be a place for active learning and self-development. There is certainly room for smaller colleges devoted to small-group teaching and learning, and to the development of personal skills and personality. The continued success of the small liberal arts colleges in the United States is evidence of this. But here the case for a small, new university of the Highlands and Islands rested upon its economic impact. As an industry in its own right, higher education is always good business. As an economic multiplier, its effect is all the greater.

The Highlands and Islands of Scotland
The Highlands and Islands have a special and honourable part to play in this most recent explosion of higher education. Their regard for education and especially higher education is well known and is of long standing. For centuries there has been a steady migration of gifted students from the Highlands and Islands to the lowland universities and beyond. In the early 1980s, when the APR (Age Participation Rate) in England stood at a miserable 14%, it was already 21% in Scotland as a whole and 32% in the Highlands and Islands. These figures have grown sharply in the last decade but the differential remains.

This regard for scholarly attainment is cultural and causally related to the quality of primary and secondary schooling. It is also the result of the egalitarian attitudes underlying Scottish politics. The social pyramid in Scotland is low and would be lower still but for English infusions. The marked absence of an 11+ examination hurdle and the persistence of a broad subject base up to the age of school leaving and university entrance have conspired to sustain a steady flow of suitable candidates into higher education, much to Scotland's benefit. But Scotland's gain was the Highlands' loss for, by and large, these successful students never returned to live in the glens and the islands where they were born and bred.

The emigration of these graduates into the professions, into government, into the services and not least into education, has been remarkable. For the places they leave it might be regarded as a wasting ailment but it is even more remarkable that from those places still the students flow. This reverence for education may, of course, be an act of resignation. It could be a response to earlier repression. Whatever the reason, the Highlands and Islands remain a potent source of human talent and of young people eager to be educated to the highest level of their considerable ability.

It is easily argued that this was best done and could still be best done by educating these young aspirants at the existing universities of, say, Aberdeen, Glasgow or Edinburgh. There is no doubt that these universities have inspired and educated many generations of young men and women from the Highlands and Islands. Perhaps they should long ago have established in Inverness a university college or colleges but that was not the thinking of the time. It certainly remained an option for the present proponents of a new university in the Highlands and Islands to invite an existing university to nucleate a satellite campus in Inverness or elsewhere but, by that time, other options had appeared.

One of these was to allow for the expression of the Highlands and Islands culture itself. The arguments in favour of this option were several. In many peoples' minds there was a presumption that whatever the older universities were prepared to do, it would be for their benefit rather than for that of the Highlands. Indeed, it seemed that it was only when an independent university had been mooted was there a serious response from the others. There is another, complementary view, supported by the Second Law of Thermodynamics, that satellites never prosper. They are invariably a means of draining talent from the newer partner to the major partner and seldom the other way round.

To those charged with delineating the new university there were less prejudiced reasons for preferring a new body. The period 1985-1995 saw enormous changes in educational technology. Their effective exploitation will require equally large changes in educational attitudes, structures, courses and degrees but there was no sign that the older universities were in the mood to implement these changes. As in all times of rapid development, there is merit in coming late and avoiding most of the baggage of the past. Given the potential of information technology and computer assisted learning, it seemed wise to 'go for' these enabling technologies and more easily so without the luggage of older attitudes.

Going it alone
The prospect of founding a new, independent university in the Highlands and Islands was first mooted long ago. The declaration of Sir Thomas Urquhart

(figure 1) is but one of many serious intents preceding the Scottish Enlightenment. However, it was during and after the First World War, when many if not most young men of the Highlands and Islands were conscripted into the armed services, that the gap in prosperity and sophistication opening up between the Highlands and Islands and the rest of Scotland became sufficiently evident for serious consideration to be given to the formation of a new university. Although Inverness is the natural focus of such a university, it was not always favoured by the neighbouring communities on the Atlantic rim. There was also at this time a growing anxiety for the future of Gaeldom, for the culture and language of Scotland's earliest surviving community of pre-Roman peoples. The idea of a small university college devoted to the language, and offering a wide range of vocational and other courses taught in the language, began to germinate and by the 1980s was flourishing. It took root at Sleat in Skye where Sabhal Mor Ostaig College is already a success. It sees plenty of scope for growth and is not short of customers. It already aspires to postgraduate studies in its specialist field and some of the most imaginative concepts for a University of the Highlands and Islands stemmed from Farquhar Macintosh and his colleagues on Skye.

Higher Education in Cromarty
Sir Thomas Urquhart's plan for a University, 1653

I would have encouraged likewise men of literature, and exquisite spirits for invention, to converse with us for the better civilizing of the country, and accommodating it with a variety of goods, whether honest, pleasant or profitable; by virtue whereof, the professors of all sciences, liberal disciplines, arts active and factive, mechanic trades, and whatever concerns either virtue or learning, practical or theoretic had been cherished for fishing their abode in (Cromarty.)

I had also procured the residence of men of prime faculties for bodily exercises such as riding, fencing, dancing, military feats of mustering, imbattleing, handling the pike and musket, the art of gunnery, fortification, or any other thing that in the wars belongeth either to defence or assault, vaulting, swimming, running, leaping, throwing the bar, playing at tennis, singing and fingering of all manner of musical instruments, hawking, hunting, fowling, angling, shooting, and what else might any way conduce to the accomplishment of either body or mind, enriching men in their fortunes, or promoving them to deserved honours.

Logopandectesion, Book 6, section 20.

Figure 1

Perhaps these separate and sometimes conflicting aspirations were a factor in the failure of Inverness to be invited to host a fully-fledged Robbins university when in 1964 several towns were examined as sites for Scotland's eighth university. In the contest between Inverness, Stirling, Dumfries, Falkirk and others, Stirling was the winner, to many people's dismay as yet another university in the Lowland Belt.

The arguments in favour of the new university at Inverness were cogent. Some of its proponents also foresaw the possibility of a distributed university with a virtual centre nearer the west. Many of those involved in the early planning exercises were still alive and kicking in 1990 when it was decided to strive once more. Funding to explore the matter was found by the newly established Highlands and Islands Enterprise (HIE) and it commissioned a report. The report recommended a new kind of university, a collegiate federation of some 10 campuses, linked by the most powerful information highway, much of which was already in place. Its theme was to be less one of distance learning, as with the Open University and the outreach programme of Aberdeen University, and more one of learning locally at distant centres, nevertheless collectively operating as a single university.

The basis for the new university was to be the existing further education (FE) colleges in the region, together with a number of research centres. These are already to be found at Lerwick in Shetland, Kirkwall and Stromness in Orkney, Stornoway in Lewis, Thurso in Caithness, Dunstaffnage in Argyll, Moray in Elgin, Inverness itself and also Perth, the "Gateway to the Highlands". The colleges and research institutes were already thriving and looking for opportunities to offer courses in higher education (HE).

The concept of a comprehensive university in addition to these colleges seemed absurd. On the other hand, the possibility of the colleges collaborating to create first a considerable FE presence and then an integrated HE presence seemed attractive and entirely feasible. The prospect of a seamless robe joining HE to FE would be a bonus and a welcome way of avoiding the irritating dividing line that persists elsewhere. Furthermore, the process of growing HE onto the existing colleges was financially possible in a way that no new foundation, even a satellite, could be.

Given, then, the political advantages and the financial reality of growing a university organically, it was decided to press on with the design and creation of a new university.

The new agenda for universities in general

For the reasons set out above, it was not feasible and not desirable to attempt to clone an existing university. Scotland certainly did not need another traditional university and, in any case, such a university would not serve the economic and cultural needs of the Highlands and Islands on an appropriate time scale. It was therefore decided by an 'Action Group' representing Highlands and Islands Enterprise and the regional councils to go for a new kind of university which would make the most of the new educational ideas and technologies.

What were these new ideas and technologies? They included, among others, open learning, computer aided learning, the advantages of a more general first degree (Learning for Life), the flexibilities of modular, unit-based courses and qualifications, a better balance between knowledge and skills and, in the Mode 1/Mode 2 debate[1], a shift towards Mode 2. An eye was to be kept on the need to offer students global experience and on the importance of values.

If IT was to be the driver, then it would be essential to have a clear view of the new mechanics of learning. A consultant, Richard Hooper, was commissioned to make an audit of the pros and cons of heavy investment in IT. Among the many aspects he identified was the virtuous cycle of learning (figure 2) and a matrix of learning procedures and their effectiveness (figure 3).

The crucial outcome of this analysis was the always suspected conclusion that the live teacher in the classroom or lecture theatre is the *least* effective way of imparting information and knowledge as information. That this was still the main method of teaching at all levels, even after the 500 years that has elapsed since the invention of the printing press, is still a painful reminder of the innate conservatism of the university community. This is not to deny the prowess of the inspirational lecturer but only to assert that he or she is rarer than we care to admit and even then the purpose of the inspirational lecturer is more to motivate than to inform.

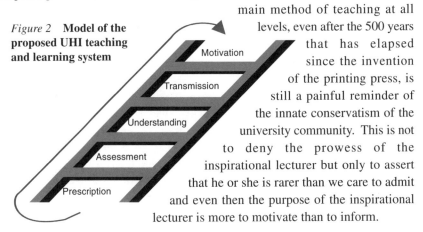

Figure 2   **Model of the proposed UHI teaching and learning system**

Motivation

Transmission

Understanding

Assessment

Prescription

Figure 3   **Technologies matched to functions within teaching & learning**

	Live Teacher	Laboratory Exercises	Student/Peer Group	Print	Audio	Video	Computer Off-line	Conferencing Audio Computer Electronic Whiteboard
Motivation	✔	✗	✔	✔	✔	✔	✔	✗
Transmission	✗	✔	✔	✔	✔	✔	✔	✗
Understanding	✔	✔	✔	✗	✗	✗	✔	✔
Assessment	✔	✔	✔	✔	✗	✗	✔	✗
Prescription	✔	✗	✔	✗	✗	✗	✗	✔

The agenda for UHI

Quite quickly, therefore, it was decided to soft-pedal the lecture, to seek to avoid large-class teaching altogether and to use wherever possible computer aided learning for the transmission of information and knowledge. Indeed, it was seen as a Scottish target for the new university to abandon, as its mainstream activity, the acquisition of large volumes of knowledge and, rather, to encourage the development of skills, especially intellectual skills, to encourage small-group teaching, learning by example, case studies, analysis, exposition and research exercises, all to involve sympathetic tutors rather than didactic teachers. This was to be a tall order but a worthy objective.

The central plank of the pedagogic basis of the new university was therefore seen as a first degree of a broad-based nature, owing more to the liberal studies, intellect-based programme of the USA than to the highly specialised, knowledge-based programmes of the UK (especially England). The old Scottish MA is not quite dead. Its intended revival by Glasgow University is good news indeed.

A general first degree has been advocated before. It was to be the main theme of the new Keele University, the cold-shouldering of which eventually led to its reversion to a traditional university. A broad-based first degree does not preclude specialist study at undergraduate level but even then it is still only a major among minor subjects. The place for thorough specialism and proficient professionalism is at postgraduate level. It is no surprise to anyone with experience of North America that it is the graduate schools which are the power houses of American science, technology and the arts. They – and not the undergraduate programmes – are the seedbeds of Nobel Prizes and they are the source of America's intellectual vigour.

The new University of the Highlands and Islands is therefore envisaged, in computer-speak, as a platform of locally important knowledge-based and skills-based activities. The themes will be local but the context global. The target student community will be largely the aspiring young but the university will also offer open entry to adults, returners or browsers. It will also offer to incomers the opportunity of learning in the Highlands about the Highlands, its way of life and specialist subjects relevant to it. For those subject specialisms of all kinds, particularly those of interest to residents, use will be made of the subject specialists in other, probably neighbouring, universities. But wherever possible, the subject specialisms will be built on a sound general basis. This sequential progression from the general to the special seems so self-evidently sensible as not to require further justification. Already, much of the world – and not least the universities of the Old Commonwealth – are turning in this direction. The Honours Degree is a British anachronism and always has been. It is too big a step for most students not intending to specialise in a single subject and too small a step for those who are. Rather arrogantly, therefore, the University of the Highlands and Islands is seen as a stepping stone to sanity and reform.

Postscript: the new university as a paradigm for others
Part of the argument in favour of a new kind of university rests on the belief that diversity is a virtue and the only sensible basis for evolutionary change. Voting with the feet is a certain and largely trouble-free method of instituting change, especially rapid change. No persuasion was required to effect the change from black-and-white television to colour TV, or to prefer the compact disc as the best vehicle (so far) for recorded music. The customers came, they saw and they bought, an entirely bottom-up response to opportunity. On the other hand, Lee Kwan Yew's exhortation to Singaporean graduates that they should marry other Singaporean graduates fell on deaf ears.

But no matter how desirable a broader spectrum of higher education in Britain might be, reform of the British model is near impossible because too many careers, fortunes and past glories are locked up in the *status quo*. Our monolithic organisation of well over one hundred old and new universities is a recipe for conformity and, therefore, of stagnation. According to chaos theory, which is concerned with the eventual effects of prolonged positive feed-back, it is also a recipe for disaster. The alternative, of easy choice among a wide range of options, is the surest and safest way to effect painless evolution and thereby to bring systems up to scratch. The University of the Highlands and Islands is therefore to be seen as a small but deliberate step in this direction.

The projected University of the Highlands and Islands is, of course, not alone in questioning the *status quo*. The academic ethos which permeates all of British higher education has recently been brought into question from another viewpoint. A recent book *The New Production of Knowledge* by Michael Gibbons *et al*[1] draws attention to an alternative basis of undergraduate education. Termed Mode 2, it is in sharp contrast to what is currently the norm and referred to by the authors as Mode 1.

In the simplest terms, Mode 1 is the subject-based and internally referenced *raison d'être* of universities as we know them. It is long on objectivity and short on values. It is knowledge-based rather than skills-based. Moreover, its knowledge base is constantly fragmenting into newer, smaller, homogeneous elements, eventually walled in by language, concepts and habit. The A-level courses and their examinations are pure Mode 1. They rest largely on an academic view of life, they require a good memory and they are entirely predicated on university entrance.

Mode 2 is quite different. It values team work, transdisciplinary studies and is skills-based rather than knowledge-based. Its strengths lie in its heterogeneous knowledge base, in its divergence and in its recognition of subjective elements. Its research will be mission oriented rather than blue-skies. It will have no truck with peer review (You scratch my back and I'll scratch yours) but rather with measurable success, value for money as well as for ecology, ethics and other societal systems.

John Ziman, ever a discerning observer of the academic scene, is a staunch defender of Mode 1 in the face of Mode 2. However, his concern, "Prometheus Bound"[2], that the post-academic science of Mode 2 might drive out the best of Mode 1 is, we must hope, unfounded. Undoubtedly Mode 2 describes the world outside the university, the world that all our graduates will need to inhabit and in which most will expect to find jobs. For their sake, as well as for the world's sake, it is important that they be aware of its values, its skills and its requirements. That the universities have studiously ignored it is at least one of t he reasons for the difficulties experienced by graduates as they enter the work place and for the disappointment felt by employers who grumble that graduate entrants need to be retrained (and often re-educated).

The fact is that we all need the basics for life-long learning offered by exposure to a Mode 2 curriculum. Some of us, a significant but not large minority, will need more, much more, if we are to become competent, professional doctors, lawyers, scientists or historians. That additional education and training is the proper business of the graduate school.

Again, therefore, one arrives at the conclusion that the sequential experience of a general education and then a specialist education is the most sensible basis of higher eduction. This is not to deny that the virtues and values of Mode 1 are real and not just those of special subject interests. In their championing of the search for truth, of objectivity, free discourse and orderly controversy, they should permeate all that we do. But in the early years, young undergraduates deserve a bigger picture, a context in which to build their understanding and, above all else, the intellectual tools of life-long learning and job worthiness.

It is therefore to be hoped that the University of the Highlands and Islands will be the first avowedly Mode 2 university in Britain. Mode 2 is enjoyable and easier in ways that Mode 1 is not. It is as much a learning mode as Mode 1 is a teaching mode. And we are told we must become a learning society.

To end this postscript it is necessary to declare that this article and the view it propounds are only those of the new university's academic adviser who also wrote the first report. They may well be changed by experience and themselves overtaken. This learn-as-we-go method of planning is now dignified by the title soft-systems methodology[3]. So we are in good company.

Addendum

Since this article was written, the proposals for the new university have taken a giant step forward, following the announcement, on September 30 1996, that the Millennium Commission had awarded the project £33.35 million for buildings, IT equipment and other services. Together with the matching funding required by the Commission and other such monies, this will provide some £100 million wherewith to launch the new university.

It is worth re-emphasising that it will be avowedly different from its traditional counterparts in aims, procedures and style – a harbinger of things to come.

References

1   *The New Production of Knowledge,* Michael Gibbons et al (Sage 1995).

2   *Prometheus Bound – Science in a Dynamic Steady State,* John Ziman (Cambridge University Press, 1995).

3   *Rational Analysis for a Problematic World,* Edited by Jonathan Rosenheard (John Wiley 1989).

Professor Sir Graham Hills
Academic Adviser to the University of the Highlands and Islands

Sir Graham was educated at London University, largely at Birkbeck College, where he took his first degree in Chemistry, his research degree in physical chemistry and his higher doctorate in electrochemistry. He began his academic career at Imperial College and from there was appointed in 1962 Professor of Physical Chemistry at Southampton University, where he was successively Dean and Deputy Vice-Chancellor. In between times he was a Visiting Professor in Canada, the United States and Argentina before in 1980 becoming Principal and Vice-Chancellor of Strathclyde University in Glasgow. He was Secretary of the Faraday Society and President of the International Society of Electrochemistry and of the Society of Chemical Industry. He was a member of the Prime Minister's Advisory Council on Science and Technology, Scottish Governor of the BBC and a Board Member of Scottish Enterprise. He is at present Chairman of Quarrier's Homes and of the Glasgow Regeneration Fund.

8

Tom Kelly

Further or Higher?
Links between FE colleges and HE institutions

This chapter is a personal perspective on the developing relationships between Further Education colleges[1] and degree awarding institutions in Scotland. The focus is on Higher Education (HE) provided by the colleges rather than access courses or other provision for first admission to HE, important though these are. Another necessary omission is reference to the Open University which is, of course, a major provider of HE programmes and also validates awards for courses provided by others in Scotland.

The scale and nature of colleges' HE provision has changed markedly in the 1990s as a consequence of Government policies and of strong student demand. This has led to new patterns of both competition and collaboration between colleges and higher education institutions. Major changes in Government policy are in prospect as a consequence of the Dearing and Garrick Committees of Inquiry into Higher Education. Meantime, even within the constraints of the current policy of consolidation/capping of student numbers in HE, important new possibilities are being opened up including the UHI Project.

HE in colleges
The main provision of HE courses in colleges is for SCOTVEC HNC and HND qualifications as shown below:

Student enrolments on HE Courses in Scottish FE Colleges 1994-95[2]

Qualification Aim	Full-time	Part-time
HNC or HND	23, 145	17, 577
First Degree	369	1, 195
Others (including professional, SVQ4/5 or postgraduate qualifications)	631	11, 692

Higher National Certificate (HNC) and Diploma (HND) provision is both FE (because it is vocational) and HE (because of the standard of courses). (A "programme of learning" falls within the 1992 Act[3] definition of FE if it- "prepares a person for access to Higher Education" or "offers vocational education". In the same Act "Higher Education" is defined as "courses at a higher level in preparation for a Higher Diploma or Certificate" of a standard higher than courses in preparation for examinations for SCOTVEC National Certificate.) The numbers of full-time and part-time students on degree courses in colleges remain a very small proportion of the totals.

There has been no SOEID master plan for HE provision in colleges. Until 1995-96 colleges were free to determine the balance between HE and the other vocational FE provision they offered. The most obvious change before and since incorporation of colleges has been the rapid growth in numbers of full-time students. The total of full-time students in FE colleges doubled between 1992 and 1995 while numbers of part-time students remained roughly the same for 3 years and increased, by 12.5%, only in the last year.

Students in HE in Scottish FE Colleges[4]

Year	Full-time	Part-time
1991-92	12, 374	25, 044
1992-93	15, 192	27, 688
1993-94	20, 342	26, 914
1994-95	24, 460	30, 746

This dramatic growth was the result of a combination of policy triggers (introduction of student support for full-time study at HNC, expansion of all HE encouraged by high levels of mandatory tuition fee, and removal of Scottish Office controls on HNC and HND courses), SCOTVEC's reforms (unitisation and greater local responsiveness) of HNC and HND programmes, and unexpectedly strong student demand for full-time study at all levels of HE.

SOEID's recurrent funding formula for colleges emphasises efficiency and promotes overall growth in activity. It is intended to allocate the available funds rather than "model" requirements for HE or vocational FE. In 1994-95 growth measured by SUMs (the Student Unit of Measurement representing the learning activity for 40 hours of study by one student) was 18.1% for HE and only 1.4% for vocational FE. Overall growth in colleges' publicly-funded activity was 6% with efficiency gains of over 4%[5].

From 1995-96 onwards the sector as a whole cannot increase the volume of HE activity. HE is now capped by a condition of recurrent grant requiring colleges not to exceed the number of entrants to HE courses in 1994-95 and by more stringent conditions to be met before SOEID will approve the introduction of any new degree courses. These restrictions bear most heavily on colleges which have developed a high proportion of HE provision. Within the SOEID grant funding formula, there is a calibration unfavourable to HE (a full-year programme of HE is counted as 15 SUMs whereas a full year programme of vocational FE counts as 21 SUMs). SOEID continues to urge increases in part-time provision though this had borne little fruit by 1994-95 (the last year for which there are detailed figures as yet).

Configuration of colleges

It is perhaps surprising that so major a change in delivery of HE was accomplished without major changes in the configuration of colleges. The colleges across Scotland are highly varied in size, balance of provision and catchment as a consequence of previous local authority, mainly regional council, decisions or strategies. For example, Aberdeen and Dundee have a single large college, Edinburgh has 3 multi-purpose colleges in its area and Glasgow has both 5 specialised colleges in the city centre and 5 "community" colleges in the suburbs. 25 of the colleges are in towns which have no university campus. Orkney and Shetlands Islands Councils retain their colleges offering FE as local authority provision. Colleges no longer have fixed boundaries or "catchments" and some of the new education authorities have no FE college or campus in their areas. This is being addressed – in two cases – by plans for new campuses of existing colleges.

Despite the major change of ownership, following incorporation of colleges in April 1993, Further Education in Scotland is still a national service locally provided. The Further and *Higher Education (Scotland) Act 1992* transferred to the Secretary of State for Scotland the duty to "secure adequate and efficient provision" of FE in Scotland. Nonetheless, in practice there is a great deal of scope for colleges to be flexible and highly responsive to student needs and employer requirements within the framework of SCOTVEC qualifications, and the policy and funding controls of the Secretary of State.

The new divide

The 1992 legislation redefined the boundary between colleges and higher education institutions. The divide – some call it the "new binary line" – between colleges and institutions is more marked in Scotland than elsewhere in the UK. Universities and other higher education institutions have or can acquire degree-awarding powers (5 "new" universities and 2 institutions have acquired such powers since 1992), grant funding is provided by the Scottish Higher Education Funding Council (SHEFC) for teaching and research, and oversight of quality and standards is a combination of internal "peer" review and assessment by SHEFC and audit by the Higher Education Quality Council. The 43 colleges incorporated in 1992 operate mainly within the framework of SCOTVEC qualifications and awards (though other awarding bodies are used too), receive recurrent funding from SOEID, and are subject to quality control requirements of SOEID including periodic inspection by HM Inspectors of schools. In the 1992 Act, provision was made for HE in colleges to be funded by SHEFC though this has not been pursued. The main divide between colleges and institutions remains the source of grant funding.

Market share

Inevitably the colleges are competitors with higher education institutions for resources and for students in HE. The extent of the market – and respective shares of it – can be measured in different ways. For example, the latest figures – for 1994-95[6] – show that FE colleges have about 17% of full-time and 52% of part-time students in HE in Scotland. However, colleges' share of entrants to full-time HE in Scotland at undergraduate level was 33.6% (and its share of these entrants who are Scots domiciled was over 40%). In short, over one third of full-time and more than half of part-time students in Scotland now gain their first experience of HE in colleges.

In terms of Government policy, this has had two significant effects. Firstly, the Secretary of State's initial guidance of July 1992 encouraged SHEFC to promote shorter or diploma courses in the institutions. This need has now been amply filled by college provision. Secondly, the greater participation possible because college courses are shorter has enabled the Government to attain its target for the Age Participation Index (API) of over 40% nearly 5 years early[7].

In the immediate future, and even before the Dearing and Garrick Committees report, there will need to be some adjustments to reflect changes in student demand for HE. For participation, there is a sharp upturn in the numbers of 17 and 18 year olds in Scotland (an increase of 12% in 1998 compared with 1995).

Nor is there any sign that aspirations of adult students to enter HE and go on to degrees has diminished – despite some employer signals of graduate over-supply.

The arithmetic of funding more HE is stark. For the grant and student award cost of 120 extra full-time places, colleges can offer an annual intake and potential output of 60 HND students (and more for HNC alone) as against 30 Honours degree students. Of course, the situation is not quite so clear cut. An increasing proportion – over half in 1994-95 – of colleges' students completing HNCs or HNDs ("diplomates") go on to further full-time study[8]. Many go on to degree courses at degree-awarding institutions and may be allowed to enter the second or third year of degree programmes. The need for provision in colleges and institutions to be more closely co-ordinated seems more likely to increase while consolidation/capping continues and ever more students aspire to attain degrees.

Course links
Recent surveys of formal links between colleges and degree-awarding institutions emphasise that in Scotland the majority of such links take the form of "articulation agreements"[9]. A typical articulation agreement makes use of the SCOTCAT framework and the potential for progression through HNC/HND/ Degree/and Honours Degree. Different entry points and possibilities for progression may be offered according to the content and fit of the programmes students have followed in the college. These agreements make it easier for HE students to find gates and pathways to degree courses which might otherwise be closed. "Exclusive" agreements (less favoured in Scotland so far) may provide stronger guarantees of places for students who progress to degrees, and make easier joint planning of teaching and shared use of specialist facilities such as libraries, workshops or laboratories.

Increasing numbers of colleges have articulation agreements with a number of degree-awarding institutions. The number of such agreements – and of students who take advantage of them – is not easily accessible. Inspection reports on colleges mention agreements only in passing in the commentary on colleges' programmes and do not list or evaluate these overall. More is emerging from a current research project at Glasgow Caledonian University[10] and from reports of HEQC on the external collaborative provision of degree-awarding institutions.

Colleges have an incentive to seek such links in order to overcome the clamp SOEID has imposed on new degree course provision in colleges[11], and to satisfy the aspirations of full-time students to progress onward from HNC/HND to degrees. Moreover, colleges and institutions can expect continuing exhortation to increase part-time HE provision. This has been sought for some years but is proving difficult to achieve in the current regime of student awards and absence of capital grants for IT needs of students who might take up distance-learning or study at home.

Academic links

So far, course links have developed as private agreements between colleges and institutions. A clearer picture of these, and the implications for students, is starting emerge from studies in Scotland[12]. Local agreements with colleges will always be needed so long as degree-awarding institutions design, deliver and validate their own courses and awards. Colleges need to negotiate passage, and terms of transfer, between the national SCOTVEC framework and colleges' HNC/HND courses, and the institutionally controlled courses and awards for degrees. SCOTCATS has provided a currency, or means of calibration, to make that task less cumbersome or one-sided. The starting point of the relationship is one of college as seeker and institution as giver. Partnerships should become more active and effective but can do so only if the college is treated as a more equal partner.

Is there any prospect of a genuinely comprehensive and national framework of HE courses and awards in Scotland? At the sector level, HEQC and COSHEP have led the way in promoting the SCOTCAT framework for credit accumulation and recognition. Only one institution in Scotland is not a party to the existing framework.

Plans are now afoot to enlarge the framework to include qualifications below HE. Credibility and recognition in the rest of the UK, and further afield, will be vital for both vocational and academic qualifications. Inevitably, however, the adjustment needed would be greater for the universities and other degree-awarding institutions. They hold the keys to degrees and "degree equivalence" and may resist opening more gateways (for example, to higher level Scottish Vocational Qualifications which have been little used so far but may become more important).

The focus should be on what is best for students but this is not straightforward. Should the emphasis be on student "choice"? This would favour a range of non-exclusive opportunities in several institutions. Or should it emphasise continuity of programme of study and guarantee of places? In which case the preference could be for a firmer, bilateral arrangement with a single institution.

At first, after incorporation, it seemed likely that there would be at least one major re-alignment or merger across the new "binary divide". Colleges could see new academic horizons and opportunities in starting as "affiliate colleges" and then becoming more closely integrated with one university. Progress in this direction seems to have faltered. The sharp separation of lines of funding and policy constraint of capping and consolidation may be the main reason. Another reason is the tighter control SOEID can exert on the strategies and plans of individual colleges than can SHEFC on the institutions it funds. Colleges' Boards of Management may not "effect any material change in the character of their college" without prior approval of the Secretary of State (Section 12(7) in the 1992 Act[13]).

Recent work by IES for CVCP[14] points to the advantages degree-awarding institutions can secure from associations or "preferred partnerships" with colleges. These include improved recruitment of students particularly in hard to recruit but priority subjects such as science and engineering, a wider "community" role, and opportunities for concentrating more teaching effort at the more advanced and "honours" levels of degree courses. There may also be gains – though these are more speculative – for staff of institutions in becoming more familiar with the national vocational programmes and qualifications of FE, and the employer needs colleges seek to serve.

It suits all concerned to discuss the issues in terms of collaboration or strategic change initiated by the partners rather than mergers, (or, worse, takeovers) initiated by others at the centre. But the challenge to reduce unit costs of teaching and to get better utilisation and returns on expensive premises and equipment is getting more intense. Higher than ever efficiency gains and the need to call on private sources of finance for investment should make shared cost solutions much more attractive.

So far, it is easier to see prospects of advance in limited areas, such as IT (for example linking up colleges to the SHEFC-funded Metropolitan Area Networks for SuperJANET). Incentives as well as opportunity may be needed if sharing of teaching between colleges and institutions is to develop. There are differences of style, tradition and oversight by other bodies which will need major investment of time and effort to overcome.

Some local solutions may emerge. So far, there have been small prods and financial rewards from SHEFC to institutions, and even smaller prods and no real financial encouragement from SOEID to colleges. Enthusiasm for "initiative" funding is bound to be diminished by fears that new schemes will just be top-sliced from ever more reduced baselines of the main grants for teaching.

The University of the Highlands and Islands (UHI) project

The University of the Highlands and Islands Project is the one departure from the cap on expansion of HE in colleges. The Project is discussed more fully elsewhere by Sir Graham Hills *(see chapter 7)*. The issue here is how the intended transition to a university from a network of colleges fits into the wider pattern of HE provision in Scotland's colleges.

At this stage the scheme has two elements – a major infrastructure project in which the prime movers are Highlands and Islands Enterprise and local authorities, and a collaborative educational project of the 7 FE colleges and 4 other partners. Most of what has been announced so far – and nearly all the capital promised – contributes to the infrastructure element. HIE is not empowered to provide education and confirms that it sees the Project as "contributing to all of (its) Network's key economic and community objectives"[15].

By the year 2000 a great deal of new social and IT infrastructure will be in place, assuming – as seems reasonable – that the other funding will be found to accomplish the projects for which the Millennium Commission has promised £33 million. Management of the project is being taken over by a new body, the UHI Foundation (intended to be the eventual university Court) with UHI Ltd "the company set up to make the university happen" as its executive board.

It is less clear what will have been accomplished for the educational element of the Project by 2000. By then only the first cohort of students embarking on the new collaborative degree programmes at colleges in 1996 will be receiving their awards from validating universities.

Some steps are being taken to accelerate academic integration. An academic has been appointed as Chief Executive. Instead of the previous Academic Council, a new "partnership agreement" is envisaged to set the terms of collaboration between the colleges and research establishments for the next phase "and to pave the way towards an eventual federal constitution"[16]. The decisive issue is likely to be how soon the track record of the colleges in providing degree programmes will justify degree-awarding status for a dispersed, federal institution of the kind proposed.

By the year 2000 it seems certain only that the FE colleges in the network will have the opportunity to introduce new degree programmes, and to develop and use a new kind of IT infrastructure for teaching within – but not necessarily beyond – the Highlands and Islands. Whatever else, the colleges' contribution to HE will have been considerably strengthened thereby .

The political commitment of the present Secretary of State for Scotland has added major impetus to the project backed by selective allocations of funds (including a small element for curriculum and staff development) from his own sources (£2.7 million so far over 2 financial years). The development of new degree programmes – in such areas as rural development and heritage studies suited to the cultural needs of the Highland and Islands area – has been eased by the relaxation of capping on entrants to HE courses of the network, and approval for the degree programmes by SOEID. One major unresolved issue is about recurrent funding for teaching. A consultant study of funding possibilities has been announced, but the policy issues arising from a single exception to the consolidation/capping regime have yet to be debated fully. Another key issue will be whether the Project can accomplish its recruitment ambitions. For young people the starting point for the Highlands and Islands is acknowledged to be levels of participation in HE already higher than in the rest of Scotland[17].

Conclusions

HE a decade hence may look quite different. The general expectation is that the outcome of the Committees of Inquiry into Higher Education will be a major reconfiguration of strategy, and roles of colleges and institutions, and of support for students in higher education. The much expanded contribution of colleges to FE and the level of capital funding committed to the UHI Project have reshaped the starting assumptions of the debate. Even greater concentration of colleges' and institutions' efforts on full-time study for degrees seems unlikely to be affordable for Government or students. Development of more diverse provision (maintaining but integrating all levels and type of HE including SVQ as well as HNC/HND), and promotion of part-time study should bring the colleges and institutions closer together. But the tighter funding gets the harder it will become to put collaboration plans for tomorrow ahead of survival plans for today.

References

1   FE colleges are referred to as "colleges" and higher education institutions including universities which award their own degrees as "institutions".

2　　SOEID Statistical Bulletin, Educational Series 13/1996, *Further Education Statistics 1994-95* (slightly different analysis of Table 5).

3　　Further and Higher Education (Scotland) Act 1992 c37 (HMSO).

4　　SOEID, Statistical Bulletin, Educational Series 12/1996, *Scottish Higher Education Statistics 1994-95.* (Numbers corresponding to percentage in table 2.)

5　　Source SOEID Annual Report 1995 and SOEID Education Statistics Division.

6　　SOEID, Statistical Bulletin, Educational Series 12/1996, *Scottish Higher Education Statistics 1994-95.* (Table 10.)

7　　SOEID, Statistical Bulletin, Educational Series 12/1996, *Scottish Higher Education Statistics 1994-95.* (para 4, 7.)

8　　SOEID Statistical Bulletin, Education Series, 6/1996, *First Destination of Graduates and Diplomates – 1994.*

9　　Gallacher J, Leahy J, Alexander H, Yule B (1996), *Further and Higher Education Links in Scotland,* First Report from the Patterns of Credit Transfer Research Project, Centre for Continuing Education and Department of Economics, Glasgow Caledonian University.

10　Ibid

11　Scottish Office Education Department (1995), *The Provision of Higher Education by Further Education Colleges,* Circular (FE) 9/95. Edinburgh, Scottish Office Education Department.

12　See inter alia

Gallacher J, Leahy J, Alexander H, Yule B, op cit

Gallacher J, Leahy J, Alexander H, Yule B (1996), *The Transition of Students from FEC to HEI,* First Interim Report for SOEID, Centre for Continuing Education and Department of Economics, Glasgow Caledonian University.

Gallacher J, Sharp N (1996), *Working Together: Aspects of FE/HE Links in Scotland.* In: Abramson M, Bird J, Stennet A (Eds), *Further and Higher Education Partnerships: the Future for Collaboration.* London: Society for Research into Higher Education and Open University Press.

Hanson A (1996), *Moving from FE to HE : the needs of part-time students,* FACE Occasional Paper, Number 3.

HEQC (1995), *Aspects of FE/HE Collaborative Links in Scotland.*

13　Further and Higher Education (Scotland) Act 1992, op cit.

14   Rawlinson S, Frost D, Walsh K (1996), *The FE/HE Interface: A UK Perspective*, A report to the CVCP, The Institute for Employment Studies.

15   Highlands and Islands Enterprise: Annual Report for 1995-96.

16   UHI Project note (July 1996).

17   Highlands and Islands Enterprise, op cit.

Mr Tom Kelly
Chief Officer, Association of Scottish Colleges

Tom Kelly took up the post as Chief Officer of ASC in April 1996 to take forward the wider lobbying and representational role which ASC had agreed in February 1996.

His background is in policy administration having spent 26 years in a wide variety of jobs in the Civil Service. His induction was in the Department of the Environment (1970-76). After joining the Scottish Office he worked in jobs dealing with public expenditure, European policy and funding, historic buildings, prisons and fisheries. In education policy, he was the Head of the Policy Division dealing with the introduction of SCOTVEC National Certificate and Standard Grade (to 1984) and policy, funding and reorganisation of Higher Education Institutions (1992-96).

Part II
Sharpening the focus

9

John Sizer

Strategic change: a SHEFC interpretation

Introduction

At the outset of any discussion of the Scottish Higher Education Funding Council's role in facilitating strategic change it is important to recognise that the institutions in receipt of Council funds are autonomous, and many generate significant funds from other sources. In meetings with Chairs of Governing Bodies, and in evidence to the Nolan Committee, the Council has emphasised the key role of the Governing Body in determining the strategic direction and approving the strategic plans of the institution. The Governing Body has the responsibility of ensuring that the institution maintains its academic vitality and financial viability in the longer term. On the other hand, the Council has to secure the most effective higher education system possible with the funds made available by the Secretary of State for Scotland, as well as implementing its Corporate Plan approved by the Secretary of State. Both have a common interest in maintaining the competitiveness of the Scottish higher education system in the global market for higher education as well as supporting the competitiveness of the Scottish economy.

When discussing the management of institutional transformation and change the Council is conscious of the tension between its role and responsibilities and those of the governing bodies. It wishes to optimise the congruence between the respective roles and work with institutions to facilitate institutional adaptation and change. It also recognises that if institutions are to implement strategic change, principals and their senior management teams must be agents for change, capable of carrying plans for change through senates and academic councils, securing ownership and commitment within institutions, and delivering their implementation. It is individual governing bodies and senior management teams who will drive the strategic management process not the Council.

In Circular Letter 16/96 (Main Grants in Support of Teaching and Research for 1996-97) the Council informed institutions of the reductions in funding in 1996-97, and of the further reductions in 1997-98 and beyond which underpin the Government's expenditure plans. They were advised that these reductions would require institutions to develop and implement innovative strategies for dealing with financial constraints over the longer term. These strategies will need to deliver cost reductions as well as sustained efforts to secure further improvements in the use of resources. Against this background, a major decision of the Council was to reduce significantly for 1996-97 the amount of resources top-sliced for time-limited initiatives, and to re-focus the remaining sum to support strategic change in the longer term. The Council therefore allocated a total of up to around £7M for grants to support strategic change in the sector in 1996-97 (of this sum around £1.2M was committed for initiatives to develop the Metropolitan Area Networks (MANs) and for Teaching and Learning innovation) and it has also decided to set aside about £10M each year (about 2% of the resources available) for this purpose after 1996-97.

The primary purpose of the Strategic Change Grant in 1996-97 is to encourage and enable institutions to conduct the analyses which will help determine their consideration of future strategies, and their preparation of the fully revised strategic plans which the Council will require to be presented in the summer of 1997. The Council's objectives, in the provision of Strategic Change Grant beyond 1996-97, will be to stimulate the strategic change which will be needed for institutions to respond to the needs of the next century within the constraints of limited public funds.

In May 1996 (Consultation Paper 02/96) the Council consulted institutions on the broad principles which the Council should adopt in allocating Strategic Change Grant in future years. The Strategic Change Grant is a relatively small fund when compared to the total resources allocated by the Council and it is important that it should be used effectively to facilitate strategic adaptation and change within and between institutions.

The consultation letter contained in Annex B a paper entitled 'The Management of Institutional Adaptation and Change' to promote discussion in higher education institutions about the rapidly changing environment in which they operate, and to consider the various measures institutions might take in this environment to maintain the quality of their teaching and research and to remain financially viable. The paper does not represent Council policy, but is intended to provide some indication of the issues which might be addressed through Strategic Change Grant, and to highlight aspects of scenario analyses, strategic analysis and strategy formulation which institutions might undertake as part of strategic planning. There was a broad welcome for the consultation paper, including the analytical models contained in Annex B, which a number of responses felt provided a stimulus for strategic thinking.

'Scenario analysis'

'Scenario analysis' is perhaps best defined as the process by which institutions examine the political, economic, technological, educational, demographic and other trends which will affect them in the foreseeable future. Effective scenario analysis and scenario planning may enable institutions to develop their strategic planning process through identification and evaluation of the various strategic options which are open to them. The process will, of course, identify areas of uncertainty, as well as providing information on possible future trends.

Clearly, institutions' most pressing concerns at present are financial. The Government's most recent expenditure plans indicated that units of resource were likely to continue to decline with, over a three year period, a reduction in funding of 10% in real terms or 11% per FTE. The continued pressures on other areas of public expenditure give little prospect to higher education institutions of a more favourable position in the next few years. The consequences of the public expenditure settlement for 1996-97 have included:

● a 0.25% reduction in the Council's funding of teaching, including a real reduction of 2.5% in teaching units of resource;

● no additional funded student places open for award by the Council, except for an allocation to reward excellent quality;

● level funding in cash terms for research and for equipment (a 2.75% reduction in real terms); and

● a considerable reduction in funding for time-limited 'initiatives' and no new programmes of capital funding.

There are a number of other external factors which may affect funding and student demand. These factors include:

● the outcome of the 1996 Research Assessment Exercise and its financial implications;

● the impact of the Technology Foresight Programme on funding for research;

- increased competition for students;

- the changes in financial support for students, including the withdrawal of the mature students' allowance and the increasing difficulties for students in funding attendance at taught postgraduate courses;

- pressures to increase proportion of sub-degree work and of three year undergraduate courses;

It is clear that a major challenge in future will be to maintain the current participation rate and the number of full time students at undergraduate degree level in Scotland. Achievement of these aims will require institutions to keep up the number of students who come to Scotland from other parts of the UK and beyond. There may also be an expansion of demand for 'lifelong learning', as people seek (with or without support from employers) to improve their qualifications and to bring their skills up to date. Institutions will have to be aware of changes in student demand, and be able to respond effectively to these changes. More sophisticated market research and analysis to inform micro-marketing strategies is likely to be needed.

Information technology

Two of the forces transforming the international business environment are widespread and rapid technological change and innovation (leading to increased globalisation and the proliferation of knowledge) and an increased focus on the needs of the consumer. These forces are also affecting higher education world wide. Although Scotland leads the UK in the development of wide-based communication highways and networks on a global scale such developments represent a new competitive threat as well as an opportunity. As illustrated in Figure 1, these networks have significant long-term implications for the ways in which teaching and learning material is developed (the **production** function) and how it is delivered (the **transmission** function). These two functions are separable and it may be an important part of institutions' scenario analysis to consider how they can specialise in, or withdraw from, the production function in various subject teaching programme areas, and how they can most effectively and efficiently undertake the transmission function.

Subject area analysis

Against the background of increased competition and continuing funding pressures, a major challenge for each institution's governors and senior managers is how to maintain the institution's capacity to adapt and innovate, while maintaining academic quality, national and international standing and financial

Figure 1

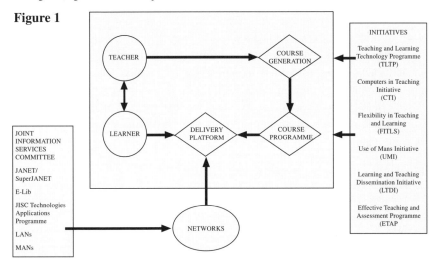

viability. In these circumstances the consensus within the institution may be to maintain the status quo; doing nothing is easier than making and implementing difficult strategic choices. Doing nothing is an untenable option.

Senior managers will need to consider strategic options for their core academic areas as part of their scenario analysis and planning, which may require them to undertake analysis of key markets linked to competitor profiling and benchmarking. This in turn may lead into strengths, weaknesses, opportunities and threats analysis (SWOT) and/or portfolio analyses. For the purposes of discussion, Annex B focuses on portfolio analysis. It is not intended to be prescriptive; the very process of rejecting the conceptual analysis and models in Annex B should inform discussion on strategy formulation within institutions.

Subject area or 'portfolio' analysis may involve institutions:

(i)   evaluating the strengths, weaknesses and potentials of their existing range of subject areas; and

(ii)   developing strategies for core subject areas which may lead to discussion with other institutions and the Funding Council on opportunities for regional and national collaboration and rationalisation.

Portfolio analysis may relate future subject area 'attractiveness' to an institution's relative strengths in that subject area. This process is shown, at a simplified level, in Figure 2. In practice, it is likely that at least the larger institutions would wish to undertake separate analyses for teaching and research. Individual institutions will also define 'strengths in the subject area' and 'subject area attractiveness' in a great variety of different ways. Subject areas may equate to organisational units, may be multi-disciplinary, or may be teaching programme based. In addition, it would not be reasonable to expect an analysis of this sort to be undertaken by monotechnic institutions or institutions with a very limited subject range.

Figure 2: Institutional directional policy matrix

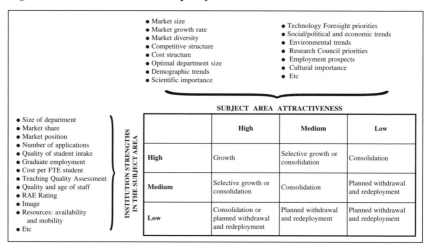

The range of options for institutions in each of their subject areas/organisational units may be summarised as follows:

●　Growth

●　Consolidation

●　Withdrawal

●　Redeployment

●　Development of emerging new priority areas

In practice, these options may not all be available. In a climate of financial stringency institutions may not be able to support new developments in emerging areas with high future attractiveness without the transfer of resources from other areas. Some areas of low strength and low attractiveness may be complementary to areas of strength. Withdrawal options will, in any case, tend to be expensive and, potentially, traumatic. An institution with a strong portfolio may be able to support a number of weaker areas without any disadvantage, particularly if they are not highly resource intensive and they complement strong areas, or if they are seen as central to the life of an institution. In addition, institutions may take into account the opportunities for rationalisation and collaboration with neighbouring institutions. There are also the problems which may arise if a number of institutions wish to withdraw from a particular subject area, leaving insufficient capacity to meet student demand. This gave rise to the question, in the consultation letter: "How can the Council maintain the balance between autonomous institutions concentrating on their strengths, and withdrawing from areas of relative weakness, whilst it ensures the appropriate subject diversity in national provision is maintained?" In other words, how do you optimise the congruence between the Funding Council's sector wide responsibilities and the sum of the actions of the institutions it funds? These are sensitive questions and the outcome of the consultation formed the basis of a discussion between Council members, chairs of governing bodies, and principals at the Council's 'Enabling Strategic Change' seminar held on 25 September 1996.

Figure 3

		Subject Area Attractiveness		
		High	Medium	Low
Institution strengths in subject area	High	(A)	B	(C)
	Medium	D	(E)	(F)
	Low		(G)	(I) (H)

( ) Proportional to resources deployed in subject areas

Figures 3 and 4 provide illustrative examples of the results of portfolio analysis. Figure 3 contains a simplified portfolio (in practice a university or college would have more subject areas). Assuming that the size of the circles is proportional to the resources deployed in the particular subject area, then the institution with the portfolio in Figure 3 might wish to withdraw from subject areas (I) and (H) to provide more support for (A), but might continue to support (F) and (G) because it has a number of strong positions in consolidation areas. The institution with the portfolio illustrated in Figure 4 is in a weaker position with many 'low attractiveness' areas and few growth and consolidation areas. However, it has three relatively small emerging priority areas, (A), (G) and (M). The institution might consider whether it can provide further support for these areas, particularly if other institutions have not established strong positions in these areas. If (A), (G) and (M) are resource-intensive areas, the institution may require to provide this additional support by withdrawing from a number of weaker areas. If the institution faces increasing financial stringency, the greater may be the need to have a sound strategy to withdraw resources from weaker areas in support of emerging priority areas.

Figure 4

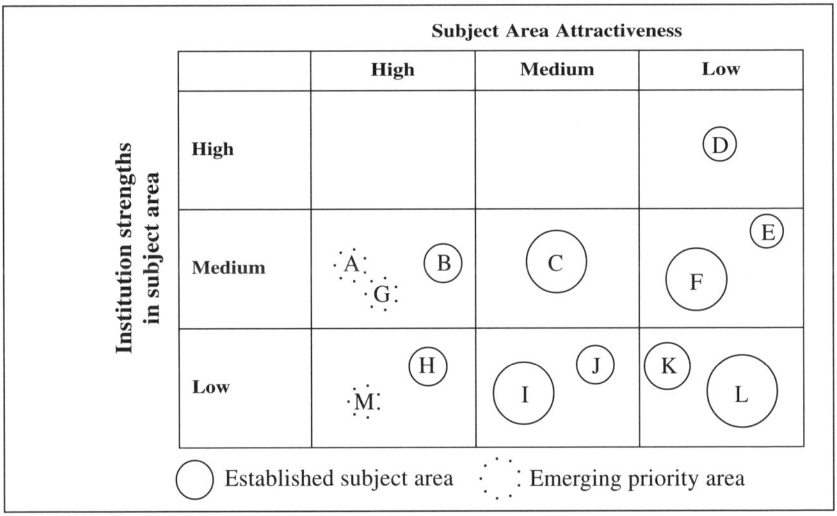

Figure 5 (which is not comprehensive) suggests that there is likely to be a range of options, falling short of complete withdrawal, which may be available for institutions to deal with areas of relative weakness. For example, there may be potential for beneficial co-operation with another institution. Such co-operation may be assisted by the opportunities made available through the development of the MANs, allowing some institutions to concentrate on **transmission**, rather than **production**.

Figure 5: Subject Area, Research and Teaching Programme Discontinuance and Alternate Options

Continuation	Alternatives		Termination
	Modification	Merger/Collaboration	

Contingent Continuation:
  Research Programme
  Teaching Programme
  Unit/Department
 	
Conditional Continuation:
  Research Programme
  Teaching Programme
  Unit/Department
	Changes in:
	  Nature of Research Programme
	  Structure of Teaching Programme
	  Curricular Design
	  Modes of Production
	  Modes of Delivery
	Budget Reductions
	Budget Increase
	Elimination of Specialist Options
	General Phase-Down
		Merger:
		  Internal
		  External
		  Generic
		  Thematic
		
		Strategic Alliance
		
		Consortia
		
		Collaboration:
		  Internal
		  External
			Phase → Down → Out
			
			Elimination:
			  Research Programme
			  Teaching Programme/Course
			
			Closure:
			  Unit/Department/Faculty
			  Institution

It will be recognised that the options and terms are not mutually exclusive but illustrate the options available to implement strategic decisions

Institutions undertaking portfolio analysis may 'map' on to it the effect of external events, such as the outcome of the 1996 Research Assessment Exercise (RAE), autumn 1996 student intakes and the 1997-98 funding round, before incorporating the analysis into their 1997 strategic plans. Figure 6 illustrates how the outcome of the 1996 RAE might be mapped onto department/ organisation unit strategies. Such an analysis might also form the basis of a proposal for support from the Strategic Change Grant, particularly if it can be presented as a detailed action plan. In assessing such proposals, it would seem reasonable for the Council to take account of 'sector-wide' issues, such as the preservation of minority subject areas and the surplus capacity which there may be in some other subject areas. This is why the Council consulted institutions on the extent to which it might be involved in addressing such issues – for example, where there is surplus capacity across the sector in an expensive subject area.

Figure 6: Departments/Organisational Units: Future Strategies for Teaching and Research

Research Assessment Units Strategies

Future Attractiveness Post RAE 1996 and Technology Foresight Priorities

		High	Medium	Low
Past Attractiveness	High	Expand/Protect	Consolidate	Redeploy
Pre RAE 1996 and TFP Priorities	Medium	Build	Consolidate	Withdraw and Redeploy
	Low	Build	Consolidate/Build	Withdraw and Redeploy

Informing: Departments/Organisational Units Strategies

Future Research Attractiveness

		High	Medium	Low
	High	T + R	T + R	T only
Future Teaching Attractiveness	**Medium**	T + R	T + R	T only or Withdraw and Redeploy
	Low	R only	R only or Withdraw and Redeploy	Withdraw and Redeploy

T = Teaching   R = Research

Governance, organisational structures, academic related and central services

The various parts of an effective planning process will place considerable demands on institutions' senior management teams, and on institutions' organisational and decision-taking structures. Members of senior management teams need to be high quality managers of strategic change who can secure ownership of the strategic planning process, its outcomes and its implementations. They will require to be supported by informed and active governing bodies. There may be a case for institutions reviewing how they ensure that they make the best use of the management skills which they have available. It is for institutions themselves to determine how effectiveness in management may be compatible with traditional forms of academic leadership and existing governing structures of committees and boards. A review of governance and organisational procedures might include examination of the potential for a simplification of hierarchical structures and ensuring that boundaries between disciplinary areas and areas of non-academic activity are not hindering effective management. There may be some value in looking at options for sub-contracting some academic and central services, as well as exploring thoroughly the options for collaboration with other higher education institutions. Institutions may also wish to look at whether they are making the best use of information technology in improving the dissemination of management information, in support of devolved decision-making and in monitoring performance against agreed action plans and budgets.

Priorities for the use of strategic change grant

The portfolio analysis may raise questions of how institutions can fund plans to re-focus resources into growth areas and emerging new priority areas. Figure

7 provides, at a theoretical level, an illustration of the range of 'strategic transformation and change actions' at which institutions might look. The Strategic Change Grant will have available a relatively low level of funds and therefore the Council is likely to be able to make only a marginal contribution to the costs of these plans. It is well known that plans involving staff severance can be particularly expensive. Rationalisation and relocation of staff and activities both within and across institutions may be more economical and may help strengthen the competitive position of Scottish higher education and individual institutions. The Council sought views on following order or priority for the use of funds:

(i)   implementation of regional and sectoral reviews;

(ii)   strategic actions which involve more than one institution (for example, involving the institutions in a particular region, a particular type of institution, or all institutions);

(iii)   internal action by institutions facing either significant reductions in student numbers and teaching grant, or a large reduction in research grant, or both;

(iv)   internal action by institutions where the reductions in funding are not particularly severe, and where the institutions may reasonably be expected to maintain sound financial health.

There was widespread support for the order of priority with the only significant reservations being on the position of (iii).

What actions might Strategic Change Grant support? In the case of **strategic actions involving more than one institution** the Council sought views on whether it might contribute to the costs of:

(i)   investigation of provision in particular subject areas, or particular types of course, or academic and central services;

(ii)   the appointment of 'facilitators' to assist in the development and implementation of action plans;

(iii)   relocation of staff and facilities, retraining, early retirements, redundancies;

(iv)   assisting mergers where there is mutual agreement by the parties.

Figure 7: Strategic Transformation and Change Actions

Organisation Level	Internal Actions	Joint Actions with other Institutions
Research and Teaching Programmes	Continuation, modification, merger, termination options per Figure 4	Buy in Course Material and Specialist Options Collaboration on development of course material Sharing of specialist research facilities Consortia for both teaching and research programmes Regional or sector rationalisation

Department/Unit (planned withdrawal/ redeployment/ consolidation areas)	Budget reductions and staff reductions
	    Phase down
	    Phase out
	    Internal merger
	    Internal restructuring
		External merger
		Consortia
		Regional or sector collaboration
		Regional or sector rationalisation

Department/Unit (emerging/existing priority areas)	Acquire new resources Redeploy existing teaching and research resources and facilities	Buy in course material Access external specialist research facilities Consortia in Scotland/UK Strategic alliances in Scotland/UK/international Regional or sector collaboration

Faculty	Internal restructuring:
	    within faculty
	    between faculties
	Rationalisation
	Closure
		External merger

Administration and central services/ governance and organisation structure	Re-engineer cost base Sub-contract services Review committee and governance structures Delayer and empower staff	External benchmarking with region or sector External benchmarking with third parties Regional and national collaboration Regional and national consortia
Institution	Restructure Close	Merger Strategic alliance Affiliation Regional or national collaboration

Support for **internal actions** could include contributions to the cost of:

(i)   development and implementation of teaching and learning strategies;

(ii)   consultancy studies on governance, committee structures, human resource management policies, reviews of the cost base etc;

(iii)   the development of emerging priority areas, through such measures as new blood schemes linked to early retirements in other areas;

(iv)   retraining, early retirements, redundancies.

There was broad support for the proposed actions.

The Council's main funding methods involve the application of relatively simple formulae. The advantages of this approach include visibility and a reasonable degree of predictability. However, such mechanistic formula funding can in particular circumstances have the undesirable effect of inhibiting major changes. The Council sought views on ways in which the existing main funding methods for teaching and research may be modified to improve their flexibility without losing visibility and predictability.

Commercial and entrepreneurial activities

Institutions may, of course, plan also to use resources generated by commercial and entrepreneurial activities to fund the development of emerging academic areas, or to subsidise existing areas which they wish to retain in their portfolios. There are likely to be other competing demands on these resources, including resources for implementation of estates strategies or for the maintenance of estates. Significant proportions of income streams may be necessary to service existing and new loan finance, including PFI schemes. It is important that institutions should make realistic assumptions of the amount of external income they can generate, and recognise the risks attached to this sort of income. Furthermore, given the continuing squeeze on government funding, it may be necessary for some institutions to build upon, rather than dilute, their financial reserves.

Strategic planning

The processes of scenario and portfolio analysis and strategy formulation which have been described in this paper may lead institutions to a set of strategic actions which they set out in strategic plans. These plans will be kept under review as the external environment changes further. In addition, the Council places considerable importance on institutions having well-developed contingency planning which provide both strategies for financial emergencies and for medium and longer term financial mobility. The need for sound balance sheet management and financing policies is equally important as institutions reduce their dependence on government funding. Their existence should ensure not only an appropriate **speed of response** to a rapidly charging environment but also increased **flexibility of response**.

Conclusion

This chapter has attempted to identify some of the most important factors influencing the higher education environment in Scotland over the next few years, and to put forward ways in which institutions may respond and adapt to changes in the environment. It has been emphasised that responsibility for ensuring effective responses and adaptation lies with institutions' governing bodies and senior managers. Aspects of strategic analysis and strategy formulation which institutions might undertake as part of strategic planning have been examined leading into a consideration of the means by which the Funding Council, principally through the allocation of Strategic Change Grant, can help institutions in the management of institutional change and adaptation, whilst at the same time recognising the tension between the responsibilities of the Council and those of governing bodies of autonomous institutions.

Professor John Sizer CBE
Chief Executive, Scottish Higher Education Funding Council

Professor John Sizer, D Litt has been Chief Executive of the Scottish Higher Education Funding Council since its establishment in 1992. He was Professor of Financial Management at Loughborough University from 1970 to 1996, having previously held posts at Edinburgh University and at the London Business School. He was a member of the University Grants Committee from 1984 to 1989, and is a former Chairman of the Directing Group of the OECD Institutional Management in Higher Education Programme and of the Society for Research into Higher Education.

10

Peter W Bush

The changing map of qualifications

Introduction: from simplicity to complexity

The expansion of higher education in the UK since the 1970s, and particularly since 1989, has been characterised by a greater diversity in the higher educational experiences and programmes of students and a greater range and complexity of pre-higher education qualifications. This is especially true in Scotland, despite the greater breadth and diversity of subject choice which has traditionally been open to school leavers through the Highers and Certificate of Sixth Year Studies (CSYS) offered by the Scottish Examination Board (SEB). During this period, the map of educational qualifications changed dramatically. Traditionally, students had entered the first year of a University or College degree programme having satisfied selectors on the basis of performance in the well recognised and understood Highers and CSYS school leaving qualifications. Indeed, the Scottish Universities Council on Entrance (SUCE) published annually detailed entry requirements, on a subject basis, for most courses offered by the eight pre-1992 Universities in Scotland. School leavers, their parents and advisers and higher education admissions tutors understood a system which was geared to deliver HE to a relatively small number of students whose education background was generally homogeneous. By 1996, new frameworks, emerging from different sources responsible to different departments of government, had been designed for differentiated segments of the population. Further changes are expected in 1998 with the launch of the Higher Still programme. The relatively simple and exclusive map has been transformed into a complex pattern of provision, offering alternative, though not mutually exclusive, routes into further and higher education and/or employment.

The raft of post-compulsory education qualifications

The period from 1984 witnessed a revolution in the range and nature of qualifications available at post-compulsory education levels and whilst it initially appeared to widen the distinction between 'vocational' and 'academic' awards, it increasingly questioned the validity of this dichotomy. During the same period, the school-based Ordinary Grade programmes were replaced by the Standard Grade in the early 1990s with its Foundation, General and Credit levels affording flexibility to reflect the different needs of a range of learners, whilst at the same time discussion on the reform of Highers intensified.

National Certificate

The launch of the National Certificate (NC) programme – initially by the Scottish Office in 1984 prior to responsibility being assumed by SCOTVEC – introduced a modular structure of courses at different levels expressed clearly in outcome based terms. These were initially of appeal to schools that exploited the NC's vocational orientation to provide an alternative curriculum for students unlikely to benefit from Higher Grade courses, although in recent years many school leaving students have presented a mixed portfolio of Highers and NCs. In 1995/96, 232,000 candidates, over half of whom were in secondary schools, enrolled for over 1.15 million modules. Whilst the number of candidates has remained fairly steady since 1990, the number of school-based candidates has increased by 60% during the same period[1].

Access Courses

As part of its drive to widen access, the Scottish Office launched in April 1988 the Scottish Wider Access Programmes (SWAP) and established partnerships between the then Regional Councils (as the main providers of school and Further Education), SCOTVEC, the universities and other institutions of higher education grouped on a regional consortium basis. The philosophy underpinning the SWAP-related access movement was to widen access to further and higher education; institutions of higher education themselves became more flexible and client-centred in their admissions policies and were key players in the development of the courses, usually based on an appropriate mix of SCOTVEC NC modules. SWAP was highly successful in easing the transition between vocational school based education/further education into higher education through the provision of FE/HE partnership Access courses in a variety of subjects. It did this by providing additional routes for non-traditional entrants into higher education and by securing more tangible links, through the access courses themselves, between NC provision and higher education. The Access courses were designed particularly for adults who had no recent experience of post-compulsory education or whose Higher Grade experience was of some years' standing. The SWAP consortia in the East, North and West of Scotland provided the impetus for the development of Access courses (either specific to a higher education institution or developed for the use of the consortium as a whole) and offered a mechanism for all participating students to obtain a place within the appropriate consortium. SWAP additionally adopted a quality assurance role through the use of the procedures in place in the higher education institutions or through SCOTVEC to the extent that formal CNAA – then HEQC – arrangements for the official recognition of Access courses were not deemed necessary in Scotland. Following the withdrawal of Scottish Office funding in 1994, the SWAP consortia have emerged as more informal networks with the development, approval, provision and recognition of access courses being more institutionally centred, a trend that was likely to develop following the incorporation of the Further Education Colleges in April 1993 and the eventual demise of the Regional Councils in 1996. Some higher education institutions additionally offer shorter more specific access courses in the form of 'summer schools' or 'taster courses'.

General Scottish Vocational Qualification (GSVQ)
The Government White Paper "Access and Opportunity" (1991)[2] presaged the introduction of a further range of SCOTVEC qualifications, the General Scottish Vocational Qualification (GSVQ), designed largely for the 16-19 age group to prepare candidates for a wide range of occupations (eg care, hospitality, leisure etc) and to offer the possibility of progression to higher education. About half a million candidates enrolled for GSVQ units in 1995/96[3]. Unlike its counterpart elsewhere in the UK, GSVQ grew out of the established modular provision at NC level. Attainment of GSVQ requires a demonstration of competence in numeracy, communication, IT and inter-personal skills and is offered at three levels. Level III offers entry, in principle, into higher education [4].

Scottish Vocational Qualifications (SVQs)
The more narrowly focused Scottish Vocational Qualifications (SVQs) were introduced in 1989 in response to the Government's drive to improve the skills of the UK workforce[5]. Although SVQs are awarded in the main by SCOTVEC, their standards are determined by some two hundred 'Lead Bodies', established by Government, and comprising employers, trades union representatives and practitioners to reflect the requirements of various industries. Standards are set by industry, via the Lead Bodies, with each SVQ relating to specific competencies required to carry out particular tasks. The SVQs consist usually of between six and ten units and may be awarded at five levels. The number of SVQ enrolments doubled between 1992/93 and 1995/96 to almost 30,000[6].

Level III has been considered to have broad parallels with the entry levels to undergraduate degree programmes[7], although this relationship is much more opaque than that linking GSQV with entry to the first undergraduate level.

A recent review[8] of 100 S/NVQs highlighted the need for greater clarity and simplicity in the language of the units. This review also saw merit in the separate certification of the 'knowledge and understanding' elements as against the separate 'competence' element, although greater integration of SVQs with the professional and academic programmes would obviate the need to create a still further SVQ award.

Howie and Higher Still

Whilst SVQ is not an education institution-based qualification and is open to all who seek a qualification certifying their competence to perform a range of work-based activities at different levels, its introduction further highlighted the growing range and complexity of qualifications covering the spectrum from academic institution-based on the one hand to specifically work-related and work-based on the other. The proposals of the Howie Committee (1992)[9] involved the introduction of two new school leaving awards, provisionally entitled the Scottish Certificate (SCOTCERT) and the Scottish Baccalaureate (SCOTBAC), modular in concept and facilitating credit transfer between them. However, whilst welcoming the penetrative analysis of secondary school education in Scotland, consultees to the proposals saw the arrangements as potentially widening rather than integrating 'academic' and 'professional' streams. The Government abandoned the structural proposals in the Report and set out to introduce 'Higher Still', launched under the title 'Opportunity for All', in 1994[10].

The introduction of Higher Still, scheduled for 1998, will replace the existing Highers, Certificate of Sixth Year Studies, National Certificate modules and the General Scottish Vocational Qualification within a common framework designed to encourage higher and broader achievement by all students. Qualifications will be available at five levels – Access, Intermediate I, Intermediate II, Higher and Advanced Higher. Certification will reflect achievement within courses (specific programmes of 160 hours of study), group awards (consisting of a coherent programme of courses) and core skills (ie personal effectiveness and problem solving, communication, numeracy and information technology). The Access and Intermediate Levels provide opportunities for progression for candidates whose performance at Standard Grade provides an inadequate underpinning for immediate access to Higher Level. The Higher is expected to remain the benchmark for entry into level 1 of Higher Education, although the relationship of Advanced Higher with higher education remains to be fully determined. Higher Still programmes will be accessed in schools and further education colleges, and, following the merger between SEB and SCOTVEC in 1997, will be overseen by a single awarding body, the Scottish Qualifications Authority (SQA). The implementation of Higher Still will thus establish in Scotland a single unit-based system of comprehensive education qualifications at levels between the compulsory and higher education frameworks. All qualifications will be based on a common approach to assessment and certification. Courses and qualifications will be designed so that one level links easily to the next: from Standard Grade through the new qualifications and on to higher education or Scottish Vocational Qualifications. The transition from school to further or higher education should thus be smoother.

Higher Education
Whilst the pattern of pre-higher education has changed significantly during the last ten years or so and is on the brink of structural change more fundamental and possibly more far reaching than recent developments, higher education itself was far from dormant. The range of provision increased significantly from the late 1970s with the development of vocational degree and honours degree programmes in those institutions (the majority of which were to become the 'post-1992' universities) whose degrees were, until 1992, awarded by the Council for National Academic Awards (CNAA) and, until the late 1980s, were required to be "approved" by the Scottish Education Department on grounds of resources and vocationalism. This provision, often reflected in relatively inflexible course structures, stressed the programme rather than the subject or discipline thereby complementing some of the provision available in the pre-1992 universities.

Since the beginning of the current decade, developments in higher education have been designed to afford greater flexibility for students to plan their own programmes in the light of their own experiences and anticipated needs. These developments clearly recognised and anticipated both the increased numbers and the diverse backgrounds of those entering higher education. The introduction of modularity (itself in part an extension of 'faculty' degrees in the ancient Universities); the freeing of students from the more extreme curriculum constraints imposed by subject Departments or Programme Boards; the increased opportunities to study part-time either on a specifically tailored programme or by 'sitting-in' on modules prepared initially for full-time students; the encouragement given to the preparation of non-certificated learning portfolios for the award of credit; and the growing recognition of work-based learning have been among the most potent changes to the higher education curriculum. As with the pre-higher education sectors, however, the greater availability of routes to qualifications has itself led to greater complexity and introduced barriers to the understanding of what had formerly been a relatively straightforward pattern of higher education.

Similar trends have characterised the development of the Higher National, rather than the Degree level, vocational qualifications which provided an alternative and usually discrete qualification offered in further and higher education institutions. These had been offered by the then Scottish Business Education Council (SCOTBEC) and the Scottish Technical Education Council (SCOTEC) which merged in 1985 to become the Scottish Vocational Education Council (SCOTVEC). The HN provision was rarely linked with degrees although HNC and HND programmes were offered alongside, but not integrated with, degree programmes in the then Scottish Central institutions.

In 1989/90, however, these programmes were redesigned into a modular format[11] which delivered both a range of individual units and appropriate combinations of these into Group Awards. This approach was influenced by the success and popularity of the modular NC provision and the awareness of increasing modularity in other parts of the higher education system. In recognising the practical implications of these changes, many institutions have developed or redesigned their programmes to ensure that there is a direct progression for students, without delay, from HNC/D into second or third years of degree programmes. Whilst the numbers of students following HNC/D provision in the post-1992 Universities has declined, the numbers following full-time Higher Education courses within Further Education institutions had more than doubled to over 22,000 between 1989 and 1995 with a smaller increase in the number of part-time students[12]. The greater articulation that flowed initially from the redesign of the HN units, the development of "2+1" and "2+2" degree courses offered jointly by an FEI and an HEI and the wider range of qualifications considered by HE Admissions Tutors have increasingly blurred the boundary between further and higher education. In the most recent (1995) review conducted by SCOTVEC on its Higher National provision[13], consultees stressed the importance of facilitating the transfer of credit between Higher

National programmes and higher education, significantly in both directions, and the possibility of the 'block' transfer of credit for pre-specified and agreed elements of programmes. There was continued support for the concept of modularity that offered flexibility with coherence through the integration of core skills increasingly within units or modules rather than as stand-alone assessed elements.

Underlying these changes in higher education – either explicitly or implicitly (and sometimes through a combination of both) – has been the principle of the accumulation of credit from a variety of sources towards an award. Credit accumulation can underpin degree programmes ranging from traditional subject based or multi-discipline awards to narrow, more vocational programmes with precise and often complex titles as well as forming the organising principle for modular-based programmes.

The SCOTCAT scheme[14] was originally developed to promote credit accumulation and transfer but it has increasingly become a fundamental principle underpinning an emerging framework for higher education. The framework basically consists of four undergraduate levels and a postgraduate level, each of which is associated with generic higher education awards and consists of 120 Scottish credit points. One credit point in the SCOTCAT framework is defined as equating to the learning achieved and assessed in ten hours of notional student effort. An agreement in 1989 between SCOTVEC and the then Council for National Academic Awards incorporated the SCOTVEC HN units into the scheme by recognising Higher National Certificate/Diploma awards as the equivalent of 120 general Scottish credit points at Scottish levels 1 and 2 respectively. The SCOTCAT system also caters for postgraduate awards of Postgraduate Certificate, Postgraduate Diploma and taught Masters within a single SM (ie Scottish Masters) level. It may be that the postgraduate element of SCOTCAT, which recognises progression within a taught postgraduate framework, will form a sound basis for a Scottish response to some of the recommendations in the recent Harris Report on postgraduate education[15].

SCOTCAT was developed by practitioners in Scotland as a route to:

i   crediting all assessed learning wherever and whenever it occurs, on-campus or off-campus;

ii   a greater sharing and acknowledgement of credit rating undertaken by institutions subscribing to SCOTCAT;

iii   developing clearer links between 'academic' and 'professional' vocational qualifications;

iv   sharing and developing good practice in credit rating and the operation of more flexible programmes of study.

These aspirations clearly invest in SCOTCAT far more than a tariff for credit transfer. All higher education institutions in Scotland (with the exception of the Royal Scottish Academy of Music and Drama) acknowledged the SCOTCAT system and its implications in 1991 by formally agreeing to honour its principles. This commitment was endorsed in 1994 at the invitation of the Scottish Advisory Committee on Credit and Access (SACCA). A number of institutions have subsequently expressed their own provision internally in terms of the SCOTCAT model; others have preferred to retain their course/programme structures but have accepted the implications of the accumulation concept within SCOTCAT. They have acknowledged the value of SCOTCAT as providing a single and easily understood currency for credit transfer both among and between FE and HE institutions and in the recognition of credit derived through assessed learning elsewhere. Nevertheless, institutions retain complete autonomy in the design and implementation of their own course structures and for the admission of students to their programmes. In Choosing to Change (1994), Robertson[16] called for the establishment of a national credit system. He failed to recognise that in SCOTCAT such a system has been in place in Scotland for some time with HE providers fully and positively recognising the principles, mutual responsibilities and architecture of SCOTCAT. The application of the SCOTCAT framework has clearly demonstrated its potential well beyond its initial focus on credit rating as providing a vehicle primarily for credit transfer.

The Babel of provision
The changes in post-compulsory education have been generally welcomed in making the curriculum more accessible and relevant to the needs of individuals. There is a variety of non-exclusive, straightforward or complex routes into higher education which increasingly offers greater choice and flexibility in terms of content, pace, place and timing of delivery and recognises that an individual's circumstances may require changes to any or all of these elements. In applauding these developments, the then Minister for Higher Education in Scotland, Lord James Douglas-Hamilton remarked (1995) that "a unified framework of qualifications is important in meeting the fast changing needs of employers" adding that "we cannot expect the public to understand the vast array

of different courses and awards if this is not set out clearly and helpfully to all those concerned"[17]. Confusion extends not only to students, parents and advisers but often to the educational institutions themselves who find the inter-relationships of pre-higher education awards difficult to understand and their links to appropriate higher education programmes at times almost impossible to articulate. There is a challenge to the education community to make more comprehensible the raft of post-compulsory education awards which individually have been welcomed but which collectively seem to present a tangled web of seemingly randomly interlocking threads.

Yet whilst the various developments outlined above have, on the whole, been free-standing, the general trend is clearly towards a model which embraces both initial and lifelong learning, and which is based on opportunity, choice, flexibility, the integration of the vocational and the academic, the need for credit transfer and the overall importance of moving towards a general culture of learning and training for all. Moreover, in terms of organisation and structures, the various awards frameworks in Scotland share a number of common approaches and features:

- identification of units or modules with stated learning outcomes;

- identification of levels or stages of awards, each governed by statements relating to the combination, amount, and levels of achievement required;

- opportunities for learners to devise individual programmes;

- greater emphasis on the learning of core and transferable skills;

- recognition of both vocational and academic achievement as relevant elements in an award;

- increasingly, the recording of achievement and performance at the unit and award levels;

- the use of "credit" as a means of describing achievement levels and group awards.

Nevertheless, learners are presented with a number of separate and discrete qualification frameworks. Each of these is expressed in its own language, and each presents an individual set of organising principles, structures, levels and awards. There are clear boundaries between the frameworks, but these boundaries are often perceived by potential users as barriers. Learning acquired and recognised through certification within one framework may sometimes permit "negotiated" entry to another framework, but more often it ceases to have any currency within the latter. Furthermore, differences in language and in the ways in which achievement is described and recorded hinder attempts by employers and learners to plan, relate and summarise educational achievements and opportunities.

A vision for the future

Each of the post-compulsory frameworks discussed recognises the need in Scotland for a more open and flexible system of education and training to encourage and support the progress of all learners. Each recognises and values individual achievement and provides greater opportunities for continuing and lifelong learning and training. Fundamentally, each scheme recognises that, within the terms of individual qualification frameworks, all appropriate achievement, provided it can be assessed, can be recognised in terms of national credit points. There is thus much commonality of principle and approach to provide a basis for the establishment of a national credit-based scheme for the recognition of all learning in Scotland. This scheme would embrace all post-compulsory education qualifications, locating each of these within an overall coherent structure for the recognition of lifelong learning opportunities and achievement.

Such a credit-based scheme would clearly have to be developed collaboratively by the main awarding bodies in Scotland. The scheme would draw on the common features of the autonomous qualification frameworks – which must continue to remain autonomous and distinctive – without in any way impinging on the separate structures and their diversity and flexibility. What is not proposed is a new system of awards. Rather, such a national credit scheme will provide a common language of credit points and levels to which learning within all awards frameworks can be related and will facilitate arrangements whereby awards can combine credit from a range of different sources and frameworks. All learners from age 15/16 onwards will thus be exposed to this scheme and begin to comprehend a common language within which lifelong learning opportunities can be readily presented and understood. Such a scheme should have significant potential in relation to educational guidance, information services and advice to employers.

It is not intended in this chapter to detail the architecture of such a system but rather to outline the aims, objectives and organising principles which might underpin any such scheme.

A national credit-based scheme should ideally seek:

- to support, promote and facilitate a more open and flexible system of diverse provision and the recognition of lifelong achievements;

- to promote opportunities for all to participate, as appropriate, within the system of Scottish awards frameworks;

- to enable the recognition of all academic, vocational and professional achievements, however achieved;

- to overcome barriers to progression, and to facilitate individual choice and routes to achievement;

- to embrace all qualification frameworks, and within the terms of their particular requirements, to facilitate arrangements for the award of credit in recognition of learning acquired elsewhere;

- to support parity of esteem in vocational and other qualifications;

- to support the individual, employers and others in defining and planning learning requirements and objectives.

More particularly, it should:

- build on the flexibility and opportunities inherent within each existing framework;

- make clearer the continuum of opportunities and extend to learners and others a common map/network of routes to achievement;

- offer a national agreement on credit points and levels;

- offer a common national format for the National Record of Achievement, the Record of Education and Training and for higher education transcripts;

- facilitate arrangements within the individual qualification frameworks for the recognition of non-certificated achievement;

- make clear and support emerging links between academic, vocational and professional qualification frameworks.

It is important that such a scheme should be developed and managed on the principles of agreement and co-operation between the awarding bodies, drawing on the common principles and structures that exist across the main qualification frameworks. It must, of course, be readily understandable, sensible, coherent and comprehensive from the user's perspective, enabling the development of a common approach to the description and recording of achievements. To be fully usable, it must include all qualifications and achievements including work-based learning, employers' programmes and the awards of professional and statutory bodies of the new Scottish Qualifications Authority (SQA) and of individual higher education institutions. Most importantly, it must neither undermine nor distort the autonomy of existing qualifications frameworks and awarding bodies.

Elements of the National Credit-Based Scheme
Given the development of the SCOTCAT scheme and network, its clear articulation with and involvement in the provision of the Further Education sector and the emergence of common principles underpinning the various qualification frameworks and SCOTCAT, it seems entirely logical that the proposed Scottish National credit-based scheme should be based on the principles and features of SCOTCAT. Whilst the proposed scheme is intended to provide a general and universal framework and a guide to levels of achievement, it should not be seen as drawing artificial equivalencies in either the types, purposes or standards of awards. However, the value in basing the framework on SCOTCAT will be the emergence of a shared understanding and a common format for the recording of achievement, together with the establishment of an agreed language and style for presenting applicants, learners and others with information on available provision and awards. Such arrangements would support, and would be supported by, national information and guidance services by describing all awards in terms of nationally agreed credit levels and credit points and by facilitating the development of a common transcript relating to the amount of credit gained and the levels of learning achieved.

It is interesting to speculate on the architecture of such a scheme and on the application of alpha/numerical scales to such a system. At this stage it is probably sufficient to expect the scheme to define the stages or levels of achievement through credit 'levels' and the amount of learning through credit 'points', the former reflecting a continuum of levels from the "Access" level of Higher Still through undergraduate to taught Masters. Learners will be offered throughout life a continuum of opportunities and progression within and across a coherent qualifications framework and will be able to define the levels (and amount) of achievement required of awards.

Whilst levels within the proposed scheme will describe the stage of achievement within the post-15/16 continuum, the sequence of levels should not necessarily equate to the sequence of post-compulsory learning. Levels are not necessarily linked to years of study, neither do they correlate to learner age. Learners will wish to access different levels within the scheme appropriate to their personal circumstances and will determine their pace, place and level of learning in the light of these.

With regard to credit points, the practice of recognising and describing units of achievement in terms of a common system of points provides learners, employers and education providers with a common means of quantifying, recognising and recording provision and achievement on the basis of learning achieved and demonstrated through assessment. In the SCOTCAT scheme, the outcomes expected to be achieved for each ten hours of notional student effort (including formal lectures/classes, self-directed/ private study, work-based learning, reflection, revision, preparation and assessment) deliver one credit point.

Conclusion

It is, of course, for the representatives of the awarding bodies to reflect on these proposals and to determine within the autonomous frameworks of their awards whether the vision of a Scottish National Credit Scheme, encapsulating the whole of the post-compulsory education provision is, in principle, of value to the consumers and their advisers, whilst remaining consistent with the aims and objectives of the individual frameworks. However, the advent of Higher Still, which will integrate the immediate post-compulsory provision, provides a rare opportunity to establish the scheme at an early date. The vision offers a possible solution to the apparent conflict between the self determination and internal coherence of the individual languages and the incontrovertible evidence that all users of the frameworks have a right to understand the relationships between these frameworks and to benefit by access to those elements appropriate to their own aspirations to lifelong learning.

Acknowledgements

I am most grateful to Norman Sharp (Assistant Director, HEQC Scottish Office), John Hart (Assistant Director, SCOTVEC), and Bob Bissell (Head of the Caledonian Education and Training Unit, Glasgow Caledonian University) for their very helpful comments on drafts of this paper. My thanks go also to those representatives of COSHEP, SACCA, SCOTVEC and SOEID who enthusiastically joined forces on a working group established by SACCA to consider post-compulsory education frameworks, and particularly to Dr David Bottomley, Senior Administrator at the HEQC Scottish Office, whose notes reflected a far greater coherence of views than seemed possible during our discussions! However, responsibility for the accuracy of the statements and the opinions expressed in the chapter is exclusively that of the author.

References

1   Communication from SCOTVEC, September 1996.

2   The Scottish Office (1991), Access and Opportunity.

3   See note 1.

4   SCOTVEC (1996), Aim for the Top: A Different Way to Succeed with GSVQs.

5   Gunning, D (1994), Scottish Education – Evolution Not Revolution, (Chemistry in Britain, pp296-298).

6   See note 1.

7   The Scottish Office Education Department (1992), An introduction to Vocational Qualifications in Scotland.

8   NCVQ (1996), Review of 100 NVQs and SVQs, Report of a Committee chaired by Gordon Beaumont.

9   The Scottish Office (1992), Upper Secondary Education in Scotland, Report of a Committee chaired by Professor John Howie.

10   The Scottish Office (1994), Higher Still: Opportunity for All.

11   SCOTVEC (1990), Advanced Courses Development Programme.

12   SOED Statistical Bulletins and SHEFC Statistical Bulletin No 5/95.

13   SCOTVEC (1996), Responses to Consultation Paper on SCOTVEC's Higher National Awards.

14   See, for example:

a   CNAA (1991), Scottish CATS regulations.

b   CNAA (1992), Scottish CATS: A flexible framework for higher education courses in Scotland.

c   HEQC (1995), The SCOTCAT Quality Assurance Handbook.

15   HEFCE, CVCP, SCOP (1995), Review of Postgraduate Education, Report of a Committee chaired by Professor Martin Harris.

16   HEQC (1994), Choosing to Change, Report on the HEQC CAT Development Project directed by Professor David Robertson.

17   HEQC/COSHEP (1995), Quality in Credit-based Learning: Ministerial address to national conference held to launch the SCOTCAT Quality Assurance Framework.

Professor Peter W Bush
Vice-Principal, Glasgow Caledonian University

Peter Bush was a founding member of the Geography Department at what is now Staffordshire University before being appointed Head of Humanities at Glasgow Polytechnic (then Glasgow College of Technology) in 1982. He became Assistant Principal in 1985 and is now Vice-Principal of Glasgow Caledonian University. In recent years his main interests have been in Adult and Continuing Education and Quality Assurance. He is the inaugural Chair of the Scottish Advisory Committee on Credit and Access (SACCA), a member of the Northern Ireland Higher Education Council (NIHEC), chairs the Universities Association for Continuing Education Scotland (UACES) and is an HEQC Academic Auditor. He was a member of both the Joint Planning Group (JPG) and the SHEFC/COSHEP Joint Review Group (the Miller Group) which have made recommendations on future arrangements for quality assurance.

11

John McClelland

A view from industry

In this chapter I describe the industrial background against which changes in our education system are contemplated, offer views as an industrialist of what we should expect from the system and touch on the implications these might have for existing mechanisms and processes.

The success or failure of any socio-economic grouping is highly dependent upon the knowledge and personal capability of its members. This statement is so much of a truism it hardly needs to be recorded. Yet in many aspects of our lives we have an expectation of success that is unrelated to the level of prior investment in knowledge and capabilities. It is always difficult to avoid the well worn analogy between socio-economic activity and sport. Being close to France in size of population we could have expected Britain to at least match France in the recent Atlanta Olympics. In the gloom of their more recent economic difficulties the French enjoyed great success in the Olympics thanks to an unprecedented prior focus and investment in every aspect of the nation's activities in athletics and other sports. Their Olympics success was the logical consequence of this programme. Britain's medal tally was the logical consequences of our prior investment in sports infrastructure.

Lest anyone concludes that I am comparing our nation's infrastructure for sport with our education system let me state categorically that this is not the case. Our education standards are amongst the best in the world. However, like our national reasoning when it comes to success in international sport we can also suffer from an overstated expectation level for output in education that is well beyond the intensity of our focus on investment at the input point.

The word "focus" is important. Whilst undoubtedly new investment in education and its associated infrastructure might be highly desirable I strongly believe that the focus of our existing investment must also be greatly improved. Given current and potentially long-term funding constraints this may be the only way forward.

If we examine the structure of our education system and the part it can play in creating economic and social wealth, what is the nature of the industrial environment in which graduates of the 21st century will be required to add their value?

Approaching the millennium it is fascinating to compare the industry and commerce graduates will join with the smokestack factories and technology-free offices of the past. However, despite the dramatic scientific and economic advances of the last hundred years or so, some of the economic or performance factors which created thriving industries and nations in the last century are as important today as they were then. British innovations created the Industrial Revolution in the 18th century and sustained it into the beginning of the 20th century. Our European neighbours rapidly learned from Britain's success and throughout the 19th century Europe led the world in science, technology and manufacturing – and hence in wealth creation.

Towards the end of the 19th century the balance changed and the United States, with its vast natural resources and an able, ambitious population, became the greatest industrial power in the world, surpassing Britain in the 1890s in steel and coal output, as well as raw cotton production, the contemporary measures of technological prowess. The US led in constructing new communication, transportation and power distribution infrastructures. It also learnt how to mass produce high quality, low cost articles for a rapidly expanding consumer marketplace.

Japan, with foresight far exceeding that of neighbouring Asian countries, laid the foundation for an advanced industrial economy at the beginning of the 20th century, and following the second world war, built on this by first copying, and then improving, American manufacturing methods. Japan recognised the significance of the coming revolution in manufacturing technology, materials, processes and devices. Major and sustained investments have resulted in her sharing global leadership with the US in many key technologies, including the all-important semiconductor technology.

As a consequence, the US and Japan are the major wealth creators in the world today. The US has displaced Europe as the leader in science, technology and manufacturing, while Japan is ahead of Europe in technology and manufacturing.

Britain, the cradle of the Industrial Revolution, no longer leads in these sectors, even in Europe.

A new threat is the emergence of low-wage economies which have become the "manufacturing capacity" for the technologies of more developed and technically skilled countries. The aggressive thrust and spectacular growth of the Pacific Rim has created a spectre that haunts governments and industries of the industrially developed world. Products from Pacific Rim countries can no longer be dismissed as inferior and of poor quality. Indeed, many western nations are relearning some of the key elements of efficient manufacturing from our low cost competitors. And now these so called tiger economies, having created their economic prosperity on the back of low wages and productivity, are becoming the high technology owners and investors of the late 20th century. One need only note the recent Taiwanese and Korean investments in Scotland to recognise this point. During these economic cycles and different point in time domination by nations or economic groupings we have seen technology, natural resources, low labour rates – and now again technology – holding the key to competitive advantage. The point I am making is that this is the UK's window of opportunity to regain the ground lost during the last century. If we could harness our technology and innovation strengths and convert these to gross domestic product and growth in our share of international trade then perhaps we could create again the type of success our nation enjoyed in the past.

Global trade and international cut-throat competitiveness are the key characteristics of the industrial environment in which we operate. However, in addition to the very obvious cross-border expansion of well known multi-national corporations which manufacture and market their products globally we also see creeping internationalism by specialist companies. Hungry for revenue and profit growth not easily available in home markets, they have acquired similar overseas companies. For example, the second largest supermarket operation in Massachusetts has just been acquired by one of Britain's household names in food retailing. And, of course, our Scottish banks have made overseas acquisitions and in some cases have themselves seen inward investment from abroad. This trend is different from global trading where often only a few key people in an organisation travel and trade and the others do as they did before. It can involve interlocking and meshing of businesses at every level. This need to be "internationalist" in our approach to business – and, therefore, in our education system – is a key feature of the world we operate in today and will become increasingly so.

What does this highly competitive global trading arena with more and more international ownership, even of small previously locally owned businesses, mean for Scotland? In my opinion we are well placed. We have traditional industries where we are natural world leaders, Scotch whisky being the most obvious of these. In addition, however, we have new industries like electronics and oil where our skills and ability to attract investment give us an edge that is the envy of other nations. This is against the backcloth of a strength in engineering and science-based industries that has been maintained and developed over the years. We also have the cultural heritage of being travellers and traders across the world.

In the context of the potential future competitive advantage of people skills and innovative culture we certainly have key strengths and therefore major opportunities to exploit – although like the rest of the UK we fail to turn enough of this innovation into local economic activity. Finally, like the rest of the UK, we have world competitive salary costs and flexible working practices which are essential for success. It is vital that our education system underpins exploitation of these advantages and opportunities and the changes contemplated must offer the flexibility to do so. Even more important, they must position us to take advantage of the "Technology Window" referred to earlier.

One might argue that the most important criteria by which we can measure the success of output from an education system is how well it satisfies industry's needs for employees who can contribute to successful business and, through that, to our economic well-being.

Given the environment in which the education system needs to be shaped what are the skills and capabilities that graduates entering industry and commerce should possess? It would overstretch my competence to attempt to develop a catalogue of skills most appropriate to Britain or, in particular, Scotland. At the same time, there are some critical characteristics that are consistent across much of our industrial and commercial activity. In making this assessment I have deliberately avoided existing terminology e.g. "Ordinary" or "Honours".

It may be useful to regard these needs as a hierarchy or pyramid of knowledge and capability. The foundation for the pyramid is a basic subject knowledge that is the outcome of a comprehensive education in the appropriate cognate area. If I take my own industry this might be in electronics or computer science. However, there are still many areas of industrial need not specifically covered by the education system. For example, some universities offer programmes in "manufacturing" yet there is not universal acceptance of this as a critical profession and industry is often left to add (for, say, mechanical engineering graduates) the wider business and other disciplinary aspects of manufacturing. This is only one example and there are many more. As already indicated, we have in Scotland industries that are especially strong in world terms but also highly specialised. We should ensure that our education system responds to these specialised needs, creating centres of competence which guarantee the ongoing provision of key skills.

Recent initiatives by some institutions offering degrees tailored to specific industrial needs (even for individual firms) are very encouraging. I believe this practice of offering education that exactly matches industry's cognate areas rather than holding to traditional institutional structures is an important one and its progress would be perceived as a major improvement for industry as well as offering the opportunity for the prioritisation of constrained resources . This is a topic I will return to later.

Ascending the pyramid, the next two blocks of needs rank equally and although quite different in nature are both essential in the rounding or staged finishing of the tertiary education process. The first is the basic skill to **apply** the education or knowledge. Industry prefers people who can contribute from day one and although I am not suggesting that job training should be anything other than an industry responsibility, the starting point for training has to be not only a knowledge of the subject but a capability to apply that knowledge in the day to day working environment. There are some commercial or industrial professions where this is difficult, but I believe these to be the exception and the education system should be able to simulate the workplace in equipping graduates with basic application skills. It is in this activity that the area of research should provide critical capability. I myself subscribe to the philosophy that some level of research is essential to good teaching and learning. However, I am also convinced that in the area of 'basic education and skills application' research must be keenly focused and supportive primarily of the teaching and learning mission in question.

The other equally important requirement is that of personal and interpersonal skill. I am not sure that its significance in a commercial or industrial environment is fully recognised, particularly by graduates themselves. The need to work effectively in a team environment is one of the most obvious needs. But it goes further than this. The personal commitment factor may be something we are born with, but I also believe that its relevance can be heavily emphasised at this stage in the development of individual careers. And, of course, in today's world personal communication skills are vital. The ability to communicate well in the multiple modes available today is essential. Within days of joining industry new employees will find themselves presenting business information to colleagues, superiors and even to customers. It is no secret that in this highly competitive and fast moving world, good personal communication skills are an enormous advantage, both for individual careers and for the business's success.

Any definition of personal skills must include computer literacy. It is amazing how many well educated and successful people in industry today are "computer illiterate". Sometimes the older and more senior we are the more difficult it seems to be to master that keyboard or understand the complexities of the software. This problem may solve itself as our primary and secondary schools educate our children in the use of computers. At the same time we need to be aware that we are fast approaching the point where computer illiteracy will be the latter day equivalent of signing one's name with a cross. Funding should be allocated as necessary to avoid that danger.

Where do second languages fit in this portfolio of personal skills? I believe this is a nettle that many of our institutions have grasped and recognise that it is possible to combine language learning with primary subject education. Given the much discussed global trade phenomenon, language capability is fast becoming an important personal skill. One aspect that needs some discussion, however, is the tendency to specialise in only one other language. Whilst this may be practical it can be restrictive. In recent years my reasonable personal competence in French was useless as I spoke to an assembly of Mexican employees in Guadalajara, negotiated with business driven Russians in Moscow and dealt with complex issues associated with my Japanese employees in Tokyo. My current operational responsibilities cover most of the world's nations so I could never be expected to be anywhere near proficient in so many languages. But a smattering of a number would have been a most useful personal capability.

How do students select the right language options from the outset? A job change, a corporate acquisition could render the original choice less useful overnight. I am advocating that our institutions should, in addition to current language provisions, offer basic programmes in languages of the world so that graduates can leave university with a working knowledge of multiple languages and cultures that can be the basis for specialisation as careers and business needs develop. Perhaps an offering in "internationalism" within the most appropriate cognate areas would be the answer to this need. Once again our primary and secondary education systems should complement this effort.

At the risk of stretching the personal skills category a little too far, a few brief words on "understanding business" may be relevant. Without some basic understanding of how national economies and businesses operate it is difficult to start to operate. Some degree courses will offer this as an inherent element of basic education. Where this does not happen a way must be found to guarantee that our graduates have a basic knowledge of how the finances and operations of national economies and business is structured and managed. I have deliberately avoided identifying this as 'economics'. It is a more practical and superficial knowledge to which I refer.

Finally, my underlying recommendation is that – together with enhanced content – within my portfolio personal skills should rank, and be measured equally with, other key elements of a degree programme.

At this stage my "hierarchy of business needs" from the point of view of the education system looks like this:

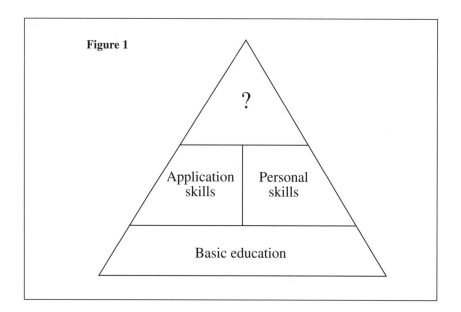

Figure 1

?

Application skills

Personal skills

Basic education

Whilst the entry point to the pyramid is obviously at the bottom the exit into employment would not generally be at the top. By depicting needs visually in this way I run the risk that I may be interpreted as advocating "incompleteness". This is certainly not the case. However, I am advocating the avoidance of "overcompleteness". I believe that the majority of industry's needs could be satisfied by graduates with a sound basic education linked to a genuinely practical capability to apply these skills and complemented by strong personal skills.

I will say now – and again later – that the timescale and resources allocated to offering this first level of degree should be more variable than at present and even be dependent upon the cognate area being provided.

Turning to the next stage of our hierarchy – and again risking the possibility of over-simplification – I see two alternative streams of activity. The first I would describe as "additional education" where the student adds significant new subject knowledge. It could be to add a business element to an engineering education or, alternatively, to allow further specialisation in one aspect of a wide profession. It could also afford the opportunity to add a complementary cognate area where there is overlap in the fundamental content between that second area and the student's primary subject choice. It could be to add a vitally important marketing skill to an engineering degree. Again, I do not record every aspect where this might apply but I do see it as the educational phase in which potential business and professional leaders equip themselves with hybrid capability to add a major competitive advantage both to their own career planning and to the business in which they will work.

The alternative stream is one that offers the opportunity for a more intense education in the existing cognate area. This is where extensive research would be conducted and where, through research programmes and investment in equipment and facilities, expertise and capability in advanced application skills could be created. Graduates from this stage would have a depth of subject expertise significantly incremental to the basic educational phase.

From an industrial point of view we would be creating researchers, leading-edge practitioners and industry experts who can provide industry and commerce with skills in technology and innovation key to long-term success. I have labelled this "advanced technical education".

So our hierarchy can be completed.

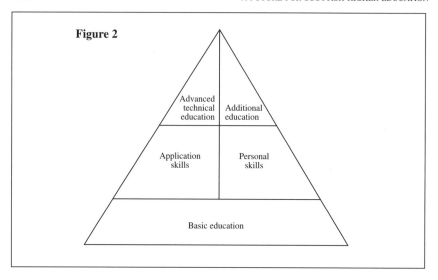

Figure 2

I am very sensitive to the possibility that the pyramid I have just created could easily crumble under better informed arguments. At the same time, in whatever way we portray the needs to be satisfied by our education system and its content, I do assert that we must recognise the variable or modular nature of the requirements of different individuals and different businesses and the fact that supplemental or specialised knowledge or skills may not be essential across the whole of the graduate population.

Let me now turn to some recommendations on how the Scottish system might continue to respond to these needs given two important considerations. The first is the well-recognised distinctiveness of the Scottish education system. The second is the reality of the funding environment we find ourselves in – exposing the fact that change is inevitable and should be managed.

One of the key changes that I believe worthy of further review would be to introduce the principle of driving the funding model primarily by cognate area. This would mean the funding body authorising institutions to provide offerings in a series of specific cognate areas. Changing this emphasis would support the need for greater focus on which cognate areas are funded, at what level and how the most efficient and effective delivery structure for the provision of that cognate area can be financed. It would also encourage the rationalisation of multiple provision points so that centres of excellence in specific subject areas could be encouraged.

Priority could be given to both British and Scottish business and social needs in establishing funding levels for each cognate area. In addition, highly specialised areas important to our own local economy could, where appropriate, be singled out for special attention. Even Scotland's need to support the growing internationalism of its industrial base could be addressed at the input point rather than be left as an ancillary topic.

This would not remove the Funding Councils' responsibility to understand and attend to the financial structure of institutions but it **would** recognise the already high and ever increasing proportion of non-governmental funding and the difficulty in finding the right long term formula at institutional level. The Funding Council would thus plan, manage and monitor primarily by cognate area for all that it funds.

I would also expect this mechanism to take account of the hierarchy of business needs by adopting a more flexible and variable approach to funding. For example, in addressing basic educational and personal skill needs the length of the course should vary by cognate area. However, where approved, the funding should be 100%. The mechanism should also cover research required to support this teaching and learning environment.

In moving up the hierarchy to the provision of advanced technical education there is more flexibility for **partial** or **selective** funding – partial where either industry or other funding source would supplement the financial provision or selective where in specific circumstances driven by the cognate area, the student population (or even institutional status) might not justify a taxpayer investment in the costs associated with this advanced, research-oriented stage of learning. Similar flexible funding principles would apply to additional education.

In developing this decision process one of the key considerations would be the national priority for skill and technology and in this respect I would expect that recent work like the Technology Foresight Programme would be a key driver.

Of course, I well appreciate that the funding of research (and the Research Assessment Exercise) is a problematical area. I am suggesting that, irrespective of the way in which the model is reshaped, it should have these elements of variability and an increased focus built in. However, I do believe that the funding infrastructure for research should be administered as part of a funding council mechanism rather than only through project related alternatives. In this way the relationship between teaching and the infrastructure for research can be progressively reconciled.

As we move forward there are some additional practices that I believe must be encouraged and in some cases at least partially funded. For example, from the identification of future skill needs, course content design, joint research programmes through to industrial placement it is essential that we have sound and constant liaison between institutions and industry. This must be woven into the fabric and there are many best in class examples which should be captured and used as the basis of formally co-ordinated work. Within this, the provision of industrial experience for undergraduates is vital. I recognise and applaud the significant progress made in this area by many institutions. Indeed, in some cases, it is industry that needs to ensure that it keeps pace with this progress.

I have touched upon many different issues in this short contribution. Most of these would have justified a more expansive review. I hope, however, that these personal views will contribute in a small way to the extensive analysis and debate taking place on the future of education in Scotland. As we approach this work there is one certainty: the education system that has served us so well in the past will only do so in the future if education providers and administrators, industry and government work together cohesively with common goals and a common sense of purpose.

Professor John McClelland CBE
Vice-President, Worldwide Manufacturing and Logistics
Digital Equipment

John McClelland is Vice-President responsible for the worldwide manufacturing and logistics functions of Digital's PC business. Prior to joining Digital in February 1995, he was Vice-President (Worldwide Manufacturing) for the IBM PC company. Professor McClelland is Chairman of the Confederation of British Industry's Technology and Innovation Committee, Chairman of the Scottish Higher Education Funding Council's Quality Assessment Committee, Chairman of the Quality Scotland Foundation Judging Panel, a Fellow of the Royal Society of Arts, Manufactures and Commerce and a Fellow of the Royal Society of Edinburgh. He is also a Fellow of and visiting Professor at the University of Paisley.

12

John Laver

The humanities: afterthought or cynosure?

This chapter offers a view of the contribution of the humanities to society through their place in higher education. The subjects that make up the humanities were historically the foundation of the university system in Britain, not just in Oxford and Cambridge, but notably in the four ancient Scottish universities as well. But public funding of the humanities is now the Cinderella of our national system of higher education. With the recent strong growth in emphasis by the Government on contributions to national prosperity and the material quality of life from research and training in science, engineering and technology, as exemplified in the 1993 White Paper on *Realising our Potential: A Strategy for Science, Engineering and Technology,* the marginalisation of the humanities in higher education has intensified. This has been to the detriment of the less tangible but no less important contribution of the humanities to the non-material quality of life of the nation. Research in the humanities in Britain is of international standing, has a wider relevance to material concerns than is often realised, and produces highly employable graduates and postgraduates. But above all, the humanities serve the wider function of higher education, that of enhancing the quality of mind of its graduates, to the social and civil benefit of society.

A basic tenet of this chapter is that the humanities participate fully in every significant function of the modern university system. The three major functions of a university are scholarship, teaching and research. If scholarship is the assimilation of knowledge, teaching is the delivery of knowledge, and research is the development of new knowledge. In every university all three functions should complement and nurture each other. A healthy system of higher education is one in which all three components co-exist in mutual support. The balance between the three will define the nature of the institution. The missions of some institutions will lead them to give greater emphasis to research than others, but no university should regard research as alien to its purpose as an institution of higher education.

Humanities research encompasses a very broad range of subjects. Research in the humanities includes the analytic, theoretical and historical study of (at least): American Studies; African Studies; Archaeology; Celtic Studies; Classics and Ancient History; Communication and Media Studies; Cultural Studies; Drama, Dance and Performing Arts; East and South Asian Studies; English Language and Literature, and the other Languages and Literatures of the world; European Studies; Film Studies; French Studies; German and Related Studies; Hispanic Studies; History; History of Ideas; History and Philosophy of Science; History of Art, Architecture and Design; Law; Italian Studies; Linguistics; Middle Eastern Studies; Music and the History of Music; Philosophy; Russian and Slavonic Studies; Scandinavian Studies; and Theology and Religious Studies. In brief, the humanities study every aspect of culture, ancient, medieval and modern.

Humanities scholars make up about 18% of all academic staff in institutions of higher education in Britain, with some 8,000 research-active staff, 4,000 of whom work in Departments rated 4 or 5 in the 1992 Research Assessment Exercise. 10% of the UK total of academic staff in the humanities work in Scottish institutions.

Table1 Full-time and part-time postgraduate students in the United Kingdom, 1994/95 *(data from HESA)*

	Total	PGR	PGT	Other	UK		Overseas	
					female	male	female	male
Full-time (Humanities)	20526	6447	7417	6532	6539	6658	3692	3637
Full-time (all subjects)	129711	44739	45987	38985	40851	48092	14997	25771
Humanities FT proportion	16%	14%	16%	17%	16%	14%	25%	14%
Part-time (Humanities)	20328	7228	9104	3996	8725	8450	1499	1654
Part-time (all subjects)	205614	42222	96178	67214	85214	91324	9294	19782
Humanities PT proportion	10%	17%	9%	6%	10%	9%	16%	8%

According to the Higher Education Statistics Agency figures for 1994/95, the numbers of on-course full-time and part-time postgraduate students in the humanities in the United Kingdom registered for research degrees (PGR), taught Masters courses (PGT) and other postgraduate qualifications are as shown in Table 1. The figures show that 40,854 full-time (FT) and part-time (PT) postgraduate students in the humanities make up some 12.2% of the overall total of 335,325 postgraduate students in all subjects. The 20,526 full-time students in the humanities divide into 13,197 from the UK and 7,329 from overseas. In both UK and overseas categories, numbers of female and male students in humanities subjects are broadly equal in proportion, very unlike the overall totals for all subjects, in which male students strongly predominate.

The greater part of the higher education system in the United Kingdom enjoys a dual support system, through Funding Councils with regional responsibilities and Research Councils with national scope. The block grant from the Funding Councils is said to support the needs of scholarship, by funding academic staff salaries, infrastructure facilities such as accommodation, libraries and basic information technology equipment, and limited institutional support for conference travel. Research Councils provide support for postgraduate studentships and project-based funding, with some support for equipment, distributed partly within themes reflecting priorities such as those of the Technology Foresight Programme (TFP) and partly in responsive mode. All disciplinary sectors except the humanities benefit from this double stream of funding.

The dual support system in the case of the humanities is asymmetric —the block grant from the Funding Council represents the main source of support. There is no Humanities Research Council sitting alongside the Research Councils for science, medicine and engineering. Instead, the Humanities Research Board of the British Academy, which was set up by the Academy in April 1994 after the Government's refusal to establish a Humanities Research Council, now distributes some £17.5M of funding annually to institutions. £16.5M of this is supplied by DfEE through the annual grant-in-aid of £24M to the Academy, and the Funding Councils provide a further £1M for a specific project-based programme. Compared with any Research Council budget, this is minimal funding.

The Humanities Research Board (HRB) spends just over £14M each year from its total of £17.5M to support a continuing stock of about 2,000 postgraduate studentships in the humanities, and to launch 1,000 new studentships in the humanities for students domiciled in England, Wales and Northern Ireland. There is an independent scheme for students domiciled in Scotland, funded from the Scottish Office Education and Industry Department. Cross-border traffic is not infrequent, with the net flow normally slightly in favour of Scotland. In addition, the Department for Education in Northern Ireland makes quota awards to Queen's University Belfast and the University of Ulster.

The HRB's resources for supporting postgraduate studentships might be thought to be of reasonable scale, though it should be pointed out that competition for these is extremely severe. The studentships are awarded to individual applicants on a competitive basis. In each of the last two years, more than 4,500 applicants competed for the 1,000 studentships available. In each year, less than half of the applicants with first class honours degrees were able to be funded – in 1990 an applicant with a first class degree was virtually assured of an award.

The very serious imbalance of funding for the humanities is specifically seen in the vestigial support available for advanced research. The HRB's programmes for project-based research, which are available for applicants from all parts of the United Kingdom, are limited to £3.3M per year. This amounts to a *per capita* amount annually for the 8,000 research-active staff in British universities of £412. Alpha-rated research applications to the HRB, which makes awards in responsive mode on a competitive, peer-reviewed basis, typically already exceed available funding by a ratio of more than 4 to 1.

The British Academy also distributes a further £5.6M for the support of a number of special schemes of research in the humanities and the social sciences. About £3.7M of this sum goes to the humanities, since the social sciences are able to call on funding from the Economic and Social Research Council (ESRC). The funds available from the Academy include support for competitive post-doctoral and senior fellowships analogous to those of the Royal Society; overseas exchange schemes; academic symposia; research in the overseas Academy-sponsored Institutes and Societies, such as the British School at Rome; and the development of the New Dictionary of National Biography.

The combined total for the national support of advanced research in the humanities through the British Academy, including the funds distributed by the Humanities Research Board, is thus about £7M per year. This yields an overall average of about £875 per research-active member of academic staff in UK universities. The analogue of this £7M in the ESRC budget for the social sciences, for the support of the advanced research of about 7,500 research-active staff, out of its total budget of some £63M per year, is about £36.5M. The *per capita* support for advanced research for academic staff in the social sciences in the United Kingdom is thus of the order of £4,850, compared with the figure of about £875 for the humanities.

Some of this discrepancy can be explained by the fact that there is currently much less (expensive) collaborative research in the humanities than in the social sciences. Research by singleton scholars is still by far the major mode of research in the humanities. But it is arguable that this is at least in part a consequence of funding constraints, and that the humanities are inhibited from exploring the benefits of other modes of research. The residual explanation is the apparent Government opinion that the chief need for funding in the humanities, apart from support for postgraduate studentships, is not for original research, but for scholarship. The implicit view that all that academic staff in the humanities need is time and library facilities seems to be deep-seated in the mind of Government. This view is quite out of date, and substantially ignores the nature and requirements of modern research of international quality in the humanities.

The current straitjacket of funding means that many important areas of research in the humanities are unable to benefit from research assistance or from project support lasting longer than a single year, with all the inefficiencies of the use of public funds that entails. In addition, the information technology needs of a number of humanities disciplines now rival in processing power and bandwidth required those in the social sciences and some of the natural sciences. This is especially true of image-processing, where humanities research needs computer-enhanced images of faint or damaged manuscripts, illegible inscriptions and old paintings. The development that will undoubtedly most influence the nature of research across all humanities subjects is the growth of networked computing for communication, access to resources and dissemination of information. The information technology of JANET and SuperJANET and the Internet, electronic mail, databases, image banks, text archives, bibliographic resources and on-line catalogues has over the last decade begun to transform the practice of humanities research.

In the wake of the Follett Report on the future of academic libraries, the launch in 1996 of the Arts and Humanities Data Service by the Joint Information

Systems Committee (JISC) of the Funding Councils, partly on the model of the ESRC Data Archive and the existing History Data Unit, will eventually make several thousand electronic databases available to the humanities research community. But to take effective advantage of this, institutions and funding agencies will need to recognise the requirement for humanities researchers to have access to high resolution multimedia workstations, with suitable network connections, to view good quality images of manuscripts and artefacts in libraries, museum and gallery collections around the world. It is a truism that the library is the laboratory of the humanities. The unification of the world's libraries into a single virtual collection, at least at the level of their catalogues, with a swiftly growing proportion of digitised textual and other material made widely available over the network, promises to recast the laboratory of the humanities into one of global scale.

It has to be acknowledged that, like other disciplinary sectors, the humanities also have access to competitive research funding from the charities, trusts and foundations. These notably include Leverhulme, Nuffield, Wellcome (for the history of science), Carnegie and others, including international sources. In addition, organisations such as the British Museum and the British Library provide some access to research funds. But the comparative figures presented above for the HRB and ESRC as the nearest neighbour in the Research Councils retain their main point – research in the humanities is prevented from realising its full potential by severe inadequacies of funding in an inequitable dual support system. This is a waste of national talent.

The broad picture is that research in the humanities is both marginalised, and impeded by severe limitations of funding, from making its full potential contribution to the quality of life of the nation, in the best sense of that phrase. What then are the arguments that reveal the nature of the contribution to socio-economic and civil benefits to society that humanities research could make, given more realistic levels of public funding?

An economic argument notes that humanities graduates are now employed in a very wide range of occupations – in 1989-93, only 24% of doctoral graduates who had received British Academy studentships went into academic posts, including school teaching. The contribution of the remaining 76% to the economic welfare of administration, industry and commerce is substantial.

The recruitment of overseas students in the humanities also makes a tangible if smaller contribution to invisible exports. On the conservative assumption that each overseas student spends on average £10,000 per year in the British economy, including fees, then the total annual contribution of the 15,000+ overseas full-time and part-time students in the humanities is in excess of £150M. Part of the cultural argument developed below also relates to this economic theme.

A diplomatic argument focuses on the influence abroad that our overseas graduates can exercise to promote an understanding of the attitudes and priorities of this country in interactions on the world stage. Similarly, work in a wide range of humanities subjects contributing to area studies enhances the ability of British commerce to sell its goods abroad, through access to the knowledge and understanding of the language of the country concerned, and of its customs, culture, politics and religion.

The subject-specific skills acquired by doctoral humanities graduates, such as competence in languages, are obviously highly marketable. But an educational argument suggests that, while science graduates are usually initially employed for the content of their dissertations, a PhD in the humanities is more often taken by employers as a measure of the quality of mind that the graduate has acquired in the process of the research. Skills of arguing from evidence, of persuasion and presentation, and of evaluation and decision-making are of commercial value. Institutions are properly now paying more and more attention to equipping their doctoral graduates with these subject-general skills relevant to their future employability outside academic life. One valuable outcome of acquiring these skills, not least, is in making the humanities graduate a very trainable employee.

An argument which focuses on the non-material quality of life proposes that experience of the humanities encourages the development of two distinctive attributes in its postgraduates: reflectiveness, leading to a thoughtful tolerance that is one of the hallmarks of a civilised culture, and a sense of being rooted in a cultural and historical context. While scientists and technologists give the community increasing control over the external, material world, humanities graduates can perhaps render the internal world more intelligible. They can, to some extent, explain the world of crisis to the community, and can hope to make some sense of the role and nature of personal, national and international turmoil. Noteworthy here is also the contribution that the humanities can make to general social and political debates, not least in trying to ensure that such debates are conducted on a rational basis. Examples of this come from philosophy, concerning the acceptability of abortion or euthanasia, or the question of balancing personal liberty against democratic needs.

This leads on to one of the most important types of argument for the value of the humanities, which one might call the public policy formation argument. The humanities contribute towards the many kinds of understanding necessary if public policy is to be accurately informed and realistically directed to its purposes. Government would no doubt acknowledge the contribution of the social sciences to policy-formation. But the extent to which the social sciences are themselves informed by the humanities in relevant areas (most obviously but not only by historical studies) deserves to be stressed. Some transparent examples come from areas of policy where historical knowledge is directly relevant. Studies of nationalism, nation states, supra-national organisations, religious and ethnic groups have an obvious and necessary utility if events in the United Kingdom, eastern Europe, the old Soviet empire, the Middle East, Africa and Asia are to be properly understood, and if an appropriate policy response is to be constructed. Such examples could no doubt be multiplied for most aspects of public policy, in a context where we need to understand ourselves in time and space, and in relation to the different cultures of the world with which we interact.

A cultural argument suggests that humanities graduates are the disseminators to society of the British understanding of life, education, values, culture, law, natural justice. They talk, argue and persuade as part of their employment in a huge variety of careers, and carry the ideas forged in the crucible of their humanities degrees wherever they involve themselves in civic life. Such an argument goes on to identify the importance of the humanities, of the most direct economic relevance to the tourism and leisure industries, in preserving our multicultural heritage, which is both unique and immensely rich. It is in large part conserved and accessed in libraries, museums and monuments, and analysed reflectively in the humanities departments of our universities. One of the attributes of a civilised society is that it seeks to understand, interpret, and with discrimination conserve its heritage from the past, in all its forms, from buildings and the landscape to books, manuscripts, paintings and other forms of media. This plainly involves all, or almost all of the humanities. Understanding, interpreting and conserving are also widely valued as goods in themselves – not just by scholars, or by pressure-groups in the conservation lobby, but also by the population at large which is interested in the whole heritage from battlefields to museums and galleries.

In this more material sense of the quality of life, graduates in the humanities are likely to have a particular role to play in the future, as our post-industrial society evolves, in providing the research and administrative base for a range of increasing opportunities for leisure, especially for an ageing population which now typically retains a lively intelligence well beyond the point of retirement.

Combining this cultural argument with the diplomatic argument mentioned earlier, one can say that much of the history and culture of this country has made a world-wide impact, through the spread of the English language for example, and through emigration of so many people from Britain (and especially from Scotland) over many centuries. Many overseas countries turn to this country in order to learn something about our cultural heritage. The standing of this nation in the eyes of the world is in no small part dependent upon the image that we project of British society both present and past. Projecting this image requires a supply of well qualified researchers in the humanities who can promote and communicate scholarship of the highest quality, and who can in addition transmit their skills to future generations of scholars in the humanities. The benefits to Britain are realised at both the national and the international levels.

A market forces argument based on public demand has two elements – student demand and popular demand. In terms of student demand, humanities subjects are amongst the hardest-pressed by applicants both at undergraduate and postgraduate levels. One should perhaps see this student demand for humanities courses as part of the wider public demand for the attributes of a civilised society. Public demand here is evidence of the value widely attached to non-utilitarian goods. One could cite popular interest in a whole range of humanities, even if in diluted, leisure-related, 'popular' form – exhibited in societies for local and family history, the performing arts, and the like. That popular interest needs to be informed and constantly reinvigorated by scholarly work if it is not to become prejudiced, ignorant and ossified.

Within a science and engineering-based perspective, the humanities have an important contribution to make by providing an understanding of the historical and cultural context which will partly determine whether new scientific and technical advances will be accepted. Philosophy has a much-needed ethical contribution to make to acceptable developments in fields such as pharmaceuticals and genetic engineering, and indeed to the ethos of business in general. More directly, archaeology has an excellent record of achievements in collaboration with the construction industry and the oil industry, for the conservation of our cultural heritage. Linguistics is central to the development of intelligent automated information services using speech technology and natural language processing, which are likely to proliferate in the telecommunications, education and entertainment sectors supporting an information-based society. In a European context, languages, linguistics and translation all have a vital and economically fruitful role to play in ensuring that this rapidly developing information society is fully multi-lingual, and does not exclude those citizens of Europe who are unable to read and write English.

All these arguments reinforce the view that humanities graduates have much to offer society. Some of the economic benefits have been described. But ultimately it is the benefits to a civilised society that need emphasis. Selecting points from all of the arguments mentioned above, one can offer a broader view of transferable skills in this context. Transferable skills are normally thought of as basic competence in navigating electronic and printed information, together with skills of literate, rational and persuasive presentation. However, the transferable skills most valuable to society are likely to be those which are most intrinsic to a graduate education in the humanities. They result in graduates who are:

● trained and experienced in clarity of argument, and able to subject their own lives and their own experiences, and those of others, to critical analysis and understanding

● able to recognise and discount bias and prejudice when they encounter them, and recognise and suppress them in their own work

● able to reflect critically on communal goals and values, in a way that is informed by a clear sense of the historical origins and background of these, and able to participate in debates about these goals and values in an informed, reflective and dispassionate way.

Surely these skills are those which make valuable citizens, willing and able to settle disagreement by rational debate rather than by violence.

Conclusion

Even though humanities research has a wider relevance to material concerns than is often realised, the riches produced by the humanities are usually more intangible than those produced by the activities of research in science and technology. This chapter has tried to show that these less tangible results of humanities research are just as important for the long-term health of a civilised society, and for our quality of life, as the more material benefits of science and technology. The present funding structures of higher education marginalise the humanities, in giving inadequate support to their advanced research. Humanities research deserves to be recognised for the national social and cultural asset it represents, and should be funded accordingly.

Acknowledgement

The wide variety of types of argument supporting the value of the humanities reported in the chapter arose in widespread consultations with more than eighty professional associations and individual universities that the HRB has undertaken since its inception in 1994. Individual members of the Humanities Research Board itself have also contributed extensively to the arguments presented.

Professor John Laver
Vice-Principal, University of Edinburgh

Professor John Laver FBA, FRSE is the first Chairman of the Humanities Research Board of the British Academy, and Vice-Principal of the University of Edinburgh with strategic responsibility for research and postgraduate studies. He is an adviser to the Research Working Group of the National Committee of Inquiry into Higher Education (Dearing Committee). He is also a SHEFC-nominated member of the Joint Information Systems Committee.

13

Gordon Kirk

Teacher education

Introduction

The schools of Scotland, like those in other countries, are experiencing change on an unprecedented scale. The central thrust of these changes, manifested in a series of national government initiatives, is to enhance the quality of pupils' learning; to make the educational system more responsive to the changing requirements of a complex society; to meet the ever more demanding expectations of parents, politicians, and others; to raise the level of pupils' achievements; and to enable all young people, not simply a selected few, to achieve their best potential both in their own interests and to promote the well-being of the community.

It is now widely acknowledged that the revitalisation of the schools depends pre-eminently on the quality of teachers. There are those who argue, and there is evidence to support their claim, that socio-economic factors exert a powerful influence on pupils' achievements. However, the burgeoning literature on school effectiveness confirms what we know intuitively, that good teaching makes a difference. As the pressures for change intensify, with the corresponding increase in the range and complexity of the teacher's task, it becomes even more urgently necessary to ensure that the education of teachers is of the highest quality. What mechanisms are in place to ensure the quality of teacher education in Scotland? How effective are these? Does teacher education provision fully reflect the demanding challenges teachers are expected to meet? How might quality be enhanced? These are the questions to be addressed in the present chapter. The thesis to be argued is that, while reasonably robust mechanisms to protect quality are in place, paradoxically there are several tensions that need to be resolved if Scottish schools are to be able to recruit and retain the quality of teacher they need and to which their pupils are entitled.

Political control: the role of the Secretary of State

The Secretary of State for Scotland is responsible for the educational service in Scotland. That responsibility, it is claimed, cannot be fully exercised without having control of the education of teachers. The Secretary of State's powers in that regard are extensive. They include the entitlement to determine qualifications for entry to teacher education programmes; to fix the number of students to be admitted each year; and to approve all courses leading to the award of a teaching qualification. Since the early 1980s the Secretary of State has exercised this last responsibility by developing guidelines for teacher education courses and stipulating that one of the criteria to be applied in the approval of courses is that they are compatible with the national guidelines.

Critics of the Secretary of State's role in teacher education contend that it constitutes an unnecessary degree of political interference and weakens the claim of teachers to enjoy professional status. On the other hand, it is argued that, if the public has an entitlement to determine the curriculum framework of schools, it is reasonable for the public, through the office of the Secretary of State, to be satisfied that teachers are educated in a way that enables them to operate effectively within that national curriculum framework. Besides, the guidelines are the product of consultation and seek to reflect a professional consensus about the education of teachers. Nor are they highly prescriptive: a study of the different programmes of teacher education in Scotland demonstrates that, far from resulting in a procrustean uniformity, the guidelines allow course planners ample scope for their resourcefulness.

The most serious attack on the national guidelines has been mounted in response to the revisions made in 1993 when, for the first time, the Secretary of State included a set of competences which all courses were obliged to develop.[1] Based on a rudimentary functional analysis of teaching, the competences were divided into four categories:

- competences relating to subject and content of teaching
- competences relating to the classroom (sub-divided into communication, methodology, classroom management, and assessment)
- competences relating to the school
- competences relating to professionalism.

Each of the main categories was sub-divided to create, in total, forty separate competences which all intending teachers were expected to acquire as a condition of the award of the teaching qualification.

While the Secretary of State's initiative is interpretable as an attempt to systematise teacher education and to ensure that programmes are directed towards the achievement of essential occupational competences, critics responded to the revised guidelines with suspicion and hostility.[2] Some saw the emphasis on competence as evidence of a reductionist over-simplification of the complexities of the teacher's role that was motivated by a political commitment to de-skill teachers and to reduce them to the status of low-level functionaries, trained in a narrow range of practical manoeuvres. There are two responses to that analysis. First, it fails to recognise that the competences may be seen as minimalist, as essential components within a more wide-reaching programme. Secondly, as the preamble to the guidelines makes clear, the term "competence" was taken to refer to "knowledge, understanding, critical thinking and positive attitudes, as well as to practical skills". It went on: "In order to teach satisfactorily, certain craft skills have undoubtedly to be mastered. But, in addition, teachers must have a knowledge and understanding, both of the content of their teaching and of the relationship between their methods and children's learning, and must be able to evaluate and justify their procedures to others." In line with that claim, the list of competences makes repeated reference to the need "to be informed about" and to be able "to evaluate and to justify". Moreover, the list of competences includes a wide-ranging set of "commitments", which encompass the student's relationship with pupils, with colleagues, and with the wider educational community.

It is noteworthy that that approach to competences differs in significant ways from the approach adopted south of the border. There the Secretary of State appears to have assumed a much more confrontational stance; to have proceeded with minimum consultation; to be committed to the introduction not simply of a general framework for programmes but to the rigid specification of the content of the teacher education curriculum; and even to prefer the decoupling of teacher education from the university.

Professional control: the role of the General Teaching Council
Established in 1966, the General Teaching Council (GTC), which consists of a majority of practising teachers, may be said to be the voice of the teaching profession in Scotland. It discharges a range of responsibilities with regard to teacher education; it is the Secretary of State's principal advisory body on teacher education; it regularly visits teacher education institutions to report on their work; it nominates members to the governing bodies of teacher education establishments; it ensures that those appointed to teacher education institutions

are themselves registered teachers; and, finally, it maintains a register of those who are entitled to teach in Scottish schools. However, the GTC's most direct impact on teacher education is through its accreditation of all teacher education courses.

The GTC has been criticised on the grounds that only about a third of teachers participate in the election to members of the Council and on the grounds that, allegedly, the discussion is dominated by the principals of teacher education establishments. Such observations scarcely weaken the standing of the Council as an accrediting agency. Nevertheless, it is important not to over-emphasise the power of the GTC. It is widely believed that the GTC controls entry to the profession in Scotland. However, the legislation establishing the Council gave the Secretary of State the authority to prescribe to the GTC the criteria governing registration. Notwithstanding the existence of the GTC, ultimate responsibility for teacher education therefore rests with the Secretary of State and, if the Secretary of State were determined to introduce changes – for example, of the kind that have been introduced in England and Wales – the GTC could not prevent him. However, to date, relationships between the GTC and the Scottish Office have been collegial rather than confrontational, which no doubt lends some credence to the charge that the relationships are too cosy.

Academic control: the role of the university
Teacher education in Scotland developed independently of the universities, in separate self-governing colleges of education; and, throughout the twentieth century, the Scottish Office has sought to prevent the universities from any involvement in teacher education, with the single exception of the establishment of a small teacher education function at the University of Stirling. Since the Second World War there have been four major studies of the institutional context of teacher education. The last of these – the STEAC report of 1985[3] – provided a vigorous defence of the principle that teacher education should be provided in "thriving specialist establishments". Since then, partly in response to the demise of the CNAA, and partly out of a concern to gain the advantages of membership of larger academic communities, all of teacher education in Scotland now falls under the aegis of the universities. While the precise nature of the constitutional relationship varies, in each case teacher education courses lead to awards of the senate of a university and are therefore subject to all the disciplines that that entails. In consequence, like all other university studies, teacher education is open to the independent scrutiny of the Scottish Higher Education Funding Council, through its quality assessment arrangements, and of the Higher

Education Quality Council, through the quality audit process. Moreover, the quality of the research activities of teacher education establishments is evaluated through the triennial Research Assessment Exercise.

It is entirely appropriate that the education of teachers – like that of the other professions of medicine, the church, law, engineering, and commerce – should be located within a university context. Universities are centres of rational enquiry and reflection. They perform a key function in subjecting social institutions and public policy to critical examination. As the apex of the educational system, universities are bound to have a concern with the quality of the work of the schools, and surely have a responsibility to ensure that their expertise and research skills are able to address the problems which confront teachers. There is something hugely beneficial in the incorporation of teaching within the university environment and within that culture of critical discussion which a university exists to sustain.

Relationship between three forms of control
These three systems of control ensure that the public interest is protected, that courses carry the support of the teaching profession itself, and that they meet the standards set by university senates. In addition, if there were any fear that the role of the Secretary of State in teacher education was too intrusive, both the GTC and the universities could exert a countervailing influence. Thus, it is unlikely that the Secretary of State would introduce criteria for teacher education courses that were unacceptable to the GTC or, indeed, to the universities. For example, courses that were exclusively concerned with the performative aspects of the competency-based model and were thought to threaten the professionalism of teaching simply would not be approved by the GTC or by a university. By the same token, if it was felt that the incorporation of teacher education within the university would threaten the strong links that teacher education institutions have with schools, or that courses had acquired such a heavy academic bias that insufficient attention was given to the practice of teaching, the GTC and the Secretary of State would find it difficult to grant approval. There exist, therefore, sufficient checks and balances to ensure that all relevant interests are protected.

Current provision
That three-fold structure of quality control might be thought to provide a secure protection of academic and professional standards and to lead to a level of provision that was of high quality. The quality assessment of initial teacher education undertaken in the course of session 1994/95, concluded that, in

general, provision was "highly satisfactory".[4] That verdict implies that further enhancement of quality is necessary. Without relying on the quality assessment report itself, it is arguable that there are three areas where further progress is required.

Firstly, the Primary BEd degree is required by the national guidelines to provide a professional preparation for teaching pupils from the age of three to twelve, and across the whole primary school curriculum. Indeed, the commitment to a generalist primary teacher is strongly supported in Scotland. In 1994, the present writer raised with the GTC the question of whether it was appropriate in an honours degree to have quite the curricular span that the present degree seeks to encompass. Since then, there have been major national initiatives in foreign languages, in Scottish literature and history, in health education, and in science and technology. It seems reasonably clear that, if all of these areas are to be given even greater prominence in the degree, the structure may become unworkable. The present course may be appropriate for teaching in the early years of the primary school but stronger curricular specialisation may be necessary if the degree is not to become superficial and to provide an inadequate basis for the heavy demands imposed by the 5-14 Development Programme in schools.

Secondly, the one-year postgraduate programmes are proving to be extremely condensed. Entrants to these courses have a very strong academic base and the task is to ensure that they are fully equipped to exploit their subject expertise to enhance the learning of pupils with varying characteristics, including significant differences in the rate at which they learn. In other countries, for example in North America and Australia, the practice is growing of requiring two years of professional education beyond the first degree, one of these being spent almost entirely in schools. In Scotland, preference seems to be given to an alternative route into secondary teaching which follows the tradition established at Stirling University, where the study of academic subject(s) proceeds in parallel with educational study and periods of school placement, thus allowing a progressive maturing of professional understanding in a way that is impossible in the forcing-house of the PGCE.

Thirdly, there are serious difficulties about the post-initial education of teachers in Scotland. The evidence is clear that arrangements for probation are extremely uneven, partly because teachers are unable to find permanent employment and must move during the first two years through a succession of schools, thus making it extremely difficult for a coherent induction into teaching to be obtained.[5] Despite strenuous efforts by the GTC to systematise probation and to provide attractive materials for probationary teachers and their supervisors,[6] research findings indicate that too many schools have inadequate arrangements in place. There is a clear case for requiring schools to develop, in association with teacher education institutions, a programme of induction which builds on initial training and, without loss of educational momentum, leads to a valid assessment at the end of the probationary period.

Arrangements for the continuing professional development of teachers beyond probation are also in need of systematisation, particularly now that the designated funding for in-service programmes for teachers appears to be under threat. There is, however, evidence of a significant increase in the number of teachers, frequently at their own expense, attending programmes of professional development provided by the teacher education centres. These are all organised on a modular basis and lead to a national system of awards at certificate, diploma or master's degree level. A significant feature of these programmes is that, while they require course members to demonstrate that level of cognitive and conceptual understanding that is necessary for postgraduate work, they have a strong professional focus, encouraging teachers and others to adopt a more critical approach to their work. Regrettably, however, that provision does not yet require to be accredited by the GTC.

The partnership principle
The involvement of schools is an established feature of teacher education in Scotland. That involvement is based on the assumption that cognitive achievements, however impressive in themselves, must issue in intelligent practice. Learning to teach is therefore assumed to require sustained periods of school placement under the supervision of experienced teachers. Partly in response to the New Right's unfair but influential critique of colleges of education as centres of irrelevant, subversive or, in the words of a former Minister for Education, "barmy" theory,[7] and partly in recognition of the importance of the work-place in the acquisition of professional understanding and skill, there has been a widespread movement to give the school a more substantial role in the training process. Scotland's experience of this development has not been entirely happy. Following a pilot study at Moray House,[8] the Minister announced in December 1994 a new national initiative in which a larger part of the total programme for secondary teachers would take

place in schools under the responsibility of trained mentors. In response to strong professional opposition, that initiative was withdrawn in October 1995. Instead, the GTC was asked to undertake a study and to report on the development of partnership. That is expected in March 1997.

The principles underpinning the proposed initiative were not in themselves objectionable, based as they were on the extremely successful and innovative Oxford Internship Scheme.[9] Besides, the idea of a pilot project was welcomed, not so much to demonstrate the superiority of the proposed approach as to provide evidence of its practicability in a Scottish context. Even the injection of additional funding of £2m to cover the start-up costs was acclaimed. Why then, was it necessary for the initiative to be withdrawn? Some saw the initiative as undermining the theoretical basis of teacher education. Some college of education staff – mistakenly, in my view – felt that they were not only expected to participate in the transfer of their work to the schools but also to undertake the training of those who would take over their responsibilities, thus hastening their own professional demise, like turkeys engaging busily and enthusiastically in the Christmas preparations. For their part, many teachers interpreted the scheme as yet another imposition and one for which insufficient resources were allocated, even at the rate of £1,000 per student. All of these reactions certainly helped to generate a climate of opposition. However, it is arguable that the scheme was rejected mainly because it was the creation of a Conservative administration. From that point of view, the episode is perhaps yet another illustration of the crisis of legitimacy which the Conservative government faces in Scotland, and the decision to invite the GTC to take the initiative forward acknowledges that that body is more likely to come forward with proposals that reflect a professional consensus. What vision is the GTC likely to offer?

There is now common ground that schools and universities have distinctive and complementary contributions to make to the education of teachers. One leading commentator has maintained that "classrooms are necessarily the dominant context for student teachers' learning".[10] It is through engaging in work with pupils that students' growing professional understanding is developed. It is in the classroom that students access the "craft" knowledge of the accomplished teacher, the knowledge that is grounded in the cumulative experience of the classroom. However, teaching is not simply a craft: it is underpinned by an extensive range of theoretical understandings. It is the function of the university to engage students in the analysis of the theoretical underpinnings of teaching, to familiarise them with the insights derived from research, and from the academic literature on the theory and practice of education. The challenge is to find a way in which these two distinctive but complementary knowledge bases are to be co-ordinated to form a coherent programme of professional preparation. What is the most appropriate context for that co-ordination?

The literature on partnership includes reports from a number of countries on highly innovative patterns of collaboration between schools and universities.[11] This "collaborative partnership" has a number of features. First, it sees collaboration on teacher education as part of a wider network of collaborative activities such as research, consultancy and continuing professional development. Secondly, it is based on the principle of reciprocity: universities acquire placement opportunities for their students and a ready context for research and other initiatives; for their part, schools benefit from being in touch with developments in pedagogy and can secure the involvement of university colleagues with expertise that can be used to support the schools in the monitoring of their educational effectiveness, and in their strategies for enhancing the quality of their work. Thirdly, a formal mechanism is established, involving the university, education authorities and schools, which reflects a commitment to the sharing of power rather than the maintenance of traditional status differences: universities acknowledge that successful teacher education programmes require the endorsement of the schools operating under the aegis of an accrediting body; and schools acknowledge the importance of obtaining university-level awards for teachers. Collaborative partnership envisages the universities working in close association with a network of federated schools, sustaining, through joint staff initiatives, co-operative teaching, and academic interchange of various kinds, a culture of professional co-operation and development. Through these various points of contact and joint activity the universities become partners in the revitalisation of the work of the schools and teachers come to enjoy the benefits of engaging in the life and work of the university.

That vision ought not to be dismissed as an impossible dream. It has been realised in other places, and Scotland is a compact enough educational entity for it to be realised here. Besides, teachers have a strong commitment to teacher education: they recognise that their standing as a professional community requires that they participate in the induction of new members; and they are pragmatic enough to be concerned to help to shape the development of their future colleagues. For their part, teacher education specialists have demonstrated, through nearly two decades of what even a former Secretary of the Scottish Education Department called a "period of turmoil", that they are resourceful and committed professionals.

However, collaborative partnership will require the investment of additional resources. The evidence is now clear that, unless these additional resources are made available, teachers will not participate in any new major initiative. If, on the other hand, the additional resources are obtained by transferring funds from the teacher education centres, then these centres will simply not survive.

Of course, it is acknowledged that funds for higher education are finite and that the pressure to obtain value for money is inescapable. That said, it is regrettable that we must serve under a political leadership that asserts that a major initiative in teacher education has to have a "financially neutral" effect, as if the *summum bonum* was the achievement of "efficiency gains" and as if the world of commerce did not frequently make additional investments to underpin important new ventures. If the Scottish Office will not be persuaded to fund the enhancement of the partnership arrangements, it is to be hoped that the Scottish Higher Education Funding Council will adopt a more positive stance. The collaborative partnership described could be seen as a way of finally realising the intention behind the Further and Higher Education (Scotland) Act of 1992. That legislation "repatriated" the universities: collaborative partnership would integrate them fully into the educational life of Scotland. Of course, universities are members of an international community of scholarship and derive sustenance from that membership; but they are also embedded in local communities. Their roots, which constitute another source of sustenance, need to be extended into the schools. For schools, and for the universities themselves, that extension of contact, communication and influence would be invigorating. If it really is essential to express the liberating and humanising mission of the educational system in financial terms, the added financial investment would be modest, perhaps a fraction of 1% of SHEFC's funds. But the return on that investment would be incalculable.

References

1   Scottish Office Education Department, *Guidelines for Teacher Training Courses,* December 1993.

2   For example, Carr D, *Is Understanding the Professional Knowledge of Teachers a Theory/Practice Problem?,* Journal of Philosophy of Education, Vol 29, No 3, 1995 and Humes W M, *Towards a New Agenda for Teacher Education,* Paper presented at ATEE Conference, University of Strathclyde, September 1996.

3   Scottish Tertiary Education Advisory Council Report, *Future Strategy for Higher Education in Scotland,* HMSO, Edinburgh, 1985.

4   Scottish Higher Education Funding Council, *Reports of Quality Assessment in Initial Teacher Training,* 1995.

5   Draper J, Fraser H, and Taylor W, *Teachers at work: early experiences of professional development,* Paper presented to European Conference on Educational Research, September 1996.

6   The General Teaching Council for Scotland, *Training Units for First Year Probationer Teachers: Primary/Nursery* and *Welcome to Teaching for First Year Probationer Teachers: Secondary,* Edinburgh, 1992.

7   The most recent of the "genre" is *All must have prizes* by Melanie Phillips (1996).

8   Cameron-Jones M and O'Hara P, *The Scottish Pilot PGCE (Secondary) Course 1992/93,* Edinburgh, Moray House Institute of Education, Heriot-Watt University, 1993.

9   McIntyre D, "The Oxford Internship Scheme and the Cambridge Analytical Framework: models of partnership in initial teacher education" in *Partnership in Initial Teacher Training,* edited by Booth M, Furlong J and Wilkin M, 1990.

10   McIntyre D, "Classrooms as learning environments for beginning teachers": in *Collaboration and Transition in Initial Teacher Education,* edited by Wilkin M and Sankey D, Cogan Page, London, 1994.

11   Some examples are:

         (a)   Fullan M G, "Reshaping the Teaching Profession: Address to Scottish Association for Educational Management and Administration Conference", 29 March 1996.

         (b)   Furlong J, Whitty G, Whiting C, Miles S, Barton L and Barrett E, "Redefining Partnership: Revolution or Reform in Initial Teacher Education" in *Journal of Education for Teaching,* Volume 22, No 1, pp 39-55, 1996.

         (c)   The Holmes Group, *Tomorrow's Schools of Education,* East Lansing, USA, 1995.

Professor Gordon Kirk
Principal, Moray House Institute of Education

Professor Kirk has been Principal of Moray House Institute of Education since 1981. He is a former chairman of the Scottish Council for Research in Education, the Educational Broadcasting Council for Scotland, and the In-Service Teacher Education Board of the Council for National Academic Awards. He has also served as a member of the Scottish Examination Board and of the Consultative Committee on the Curriculum. He is the Vice-Convener of the General Teaching Council for Scotland. Professor Kirk has written extensively on teacher education and is co-editor of the series *Professional Issues In Education,* a 16-volume commentary on current developments in Scottish education.

14

Chris Carter

Art and Design

Introduction

In writing about the future of Art and Design in higher education in Scotland, I am conscious that there is a big difference between what the future could be if the Art and Design sector was properly funded, and what the future looks likely to be if the funding cuts and underinvestment of the last few years are allowed to continue. It is not my intention to set out a blueprint for any particular future date, as that would make presumptions about decisions which autonomous institutions will make. Nor am I going to attempt to second-guess proposals which may emerge from the Strategic Change Initiative for which SHEFC has announced funding over the next three years.

I shall instead attempt a variation of a SWOT analysis, to show the main strengths of the Art and Design sector, the main issues it faces, the major threats to the future, and certain opportunities for change and development which could be achieved if perceptions of the role and potential of Art and Design in HE can be changed, and if funding can be made available to initiate that change.

For the purposes of clarification, my definition of the Art and Design sector relates largely to that provision which is made under the headings of Fine Art, Design and immediately related subject areas within the four Scottish Colleges of Art. It excludes other subject areas taught within the Colleges of Art (for example Architecture and Town Planning) and excludes the performing arts which, in Scotland, are taught in institutions other than Colleges of Art.

The four Colleges are: Duncan of Jordanstone College of Art and Design, which is part of the University of Dundee, Edinburgh College of Art, Glasgow School of Art and Gray's School of Art which is part of The Robert Gordon University, Aberdeen.

In the Art and Design sector as defined above, there are slightly in excess of 3000 home and EU students representing 2.6% of the students in HE in Scotland as a whole. SHEFC currently (1996/97) allocates 2.76% of its Teaching funding and 1.6% of its Research funding to the Art and Design sector.

The distinctiveness of art and design education in the Scottish Colleges of Art

The following is a summary of the main characteristics of Art and Design education in the Scottish Colleges of Art:

● The four year integral honours degree in which the first year, a diagnostic year, is part of the degree programme and not a separate foundation year as is the case elsewhere in the UK. This enables students to select their specialisms and supporting subjects from a more informed perspective thereby contributing to the low dropout rates and the small number of transfers between specialisms.

● The maintenance of traditional skills with considerable importance attached to drawing, to life classes, to the teaching of anatomy and to inputs from practising artists and designers. Elsewhere this solid foundation has been undermined by a tendency to follow short-term objectives.

● An approach to teaching and learning which mostly involves one-to-one contact between students and staff in the studio. In Art and Design education, learning is largely by "doing"; it involves experimentation and develops through the acquisition of practical skills, understanding and creativity in problem-solving, rather than the accumulation of existing knowledge.

● A reluctance to modularise provision, which does not reflect an unwillingness to change, but rather a concern to maintain the coherence, the integrity and the progression of skills development throughout degree programmes.

● The development of a strong practice-based research ethos especially among those Colleges which did well in the 1992 RAE. Recurrent funding for research in Art and Design in Scotland has been more generous than in England and Wales, but it has been at the expense of a reduction in funding for teaching.

● The offering of a wide range of non-vocational day and evening courses. This provision is a vital way in which the Art Colleges work with their local communities, giving access to specialist studios, equipment and expertise not available elsewhere within the localities.

- A location in Scotland which offers distinctive resources to influence and inspire the students. Scotland also offers a range of high quality national galleries and museums, while distance from London often creates a greater willingness to look to Europe and North America to broaden the experience.

Strengths and weaknesses: issues facing higher education in art and design
The distinctive characteristics of Scottish Art and Design education point towards certain of its strengths. Some of these very strengths, however, are beset by weaknesses which are not of the Colleges' making, but relate to the context within which they operate. These include a widespread misperception externally of what Art and Design education is all about, and of the contribution Art and Design can make to the economic, social, and cultural well-being of Scotland.

Teaching and Learning
Teaching and learning have traditionally been regarded as strengths of the Scottish Art and Design sector. The cuts in funding over the last few years, following a period of rapid growth in student numbers, have had a particularly severe impact on Art and Design. This is partly because a disproportionately high percentage of the Art Colleges' income has been subject to the cuts, and partly because of the nature of Art and Design provision, with its emphasis on studio-based teaching and learning with high contact hours, high space requirements, high materials costs, stringent health and safety requirements, a dependency on specialist equipment and workshop facilities with technical support, and a heavy demand for applications of technology. As a result, the cuts in funding have weakened the provision to the point where the quality of the students' experience of teaching and learning is seriously at risk. This has already been commented upon by some external examiners, while certain gradings in some of the quality assessment reports clearly reflect a concern over resources.

Teaching and learning in Fine Art and part of Design (Graphics and Textile Design) were subjected to Quality Assessment by SHEFC in 1994/95. Whatever the benefits of the process, there is a serious questionmark over whether the overall outcome served the Scottish Colleges of Art well. Out of nine assessments (five in Design and four in Fine Art) only one was graded "Excellent". This may or may not have fairly represented the comparative merits of provision within Scotland, but it raises the issue of whether the gradings are appropriate in a UK context.

Quality assessments in Fine Art and Design in the rest of the UK have yet to be undertaken, but it will be interesting to see whether the English and Welsh

Funding Councils, unfettered by having to award additional funding for "Excellent" gradings, are so parsimonious. If they are not, as appears likely in view of comparisons in other subject areas, the Scottish Colleges of Art will have one of their traditional strengths interpreted as a relative weakness by prospective students from the rest of the UK and overseas.

Research

Reference was made above to the emerging strength of research in Art and Design in Scotland. Achievement of the full potential, however, has hardly begun. Having been funded, prior to 1993, only for teaching, the Art Colleges have little or no infrastructure in place to support the working methods of visual research. Without this infrastructure, the capability of developing applied research which will attract external funding and the interest of industry is severely limited. In addition, the traditionally high teaching contact hours and the greatly increased student numbers mean that staff availability for research is constrained. Only significant changes to a much valued approach to teaching can yield staff time for research.

This position of disadvantage is compounded by the absence of a research council to fund research in Art and Design. As a result there is little new or additional money available to support research. In these circumstances not only is the ability to generate research funding greatly constrained, but the ability to enable students to achieve their potential through contact with a research environment is reduced.

Hitherto, with some notable exceptions, industry and other research funding agencies have been largely unaware of the high levels and range of expertise available within the Art Colleges, while other research oriented disciplines in universities have not thought to seek collaboration. A new realisation is slowly beginning to emerge as a result of growing research activity through the post-1993 SHEFC research funding, through the IDEAS (Industry & Design Education Action Scotland) initiative and through the related project funded via the Regional Strategic Initiative involving the six Scottish Schools of Design together with numerous industrial concerns.

This is a start, but the weaknesses of inadequate financial support and inadequate infrastructure for research remain, and create a danger that the Art Colleges will be seen as "second class" in the strongly research competitive higher education environment. This indicates that the previous focus on funding only for teaching was flawed, as it led to a perception of Art and Design being solely vocationally oriented disciplines, undervaluing the importance of intellectual development and research. As Ammundsen has said in discussing Design education in Denmark:

> "The promotion of research is necessary to maintain the development of the Design profession and to keep the best teaching staff . . . ".[1]

Links with industry

Mention has already been made of the strength which teaching programmes derive from their links with industry and practice. Such links are considered essential but, by and large, their ability to generate significant additional income is limited. The real potential for links with industry has yet to be exploited, but will only occur if the Art and Design sector is given the technological capability to deliver the right kind of research, and if British industry can be persuaded both to understand the significance of Art and Design and to integrate it into the product formulation process. As Jones has indicated:

> "The success story of British art and design has been sadly but consistently overlooked by sectors of British industry and by our parliamentary masters who have yet to fully realise the brilliance and international acclaim of British design companies and the effect they could have, if engaged, on the economic regeneration of our nation."[2]

Industry must be persuaded away from the notion that design is an afterthought to make products look better, or that its role is confined to the packaging and advertising of products. This lack of understanding, not only by much of industry, but also by government, of the role design can play in the manufacturing process, has contributed to the serious under-capitalisation of design education. Investment in computer aided design (CAD) has taken place in varying degrees in different Art Colleges but is insufficient; more importantly, investment in computer aided manufacture (CAM) is largely absent and is urgently needed. This would be an investment both in the sector's graduates to enable them to play a more central role in industry, and in the Art Colleges' staff to enable them to engage in income generating research in collaboration with industry.

CAM, in particular, offers one of the key applications of technology and one of the key ways in which higher education in design can relate to manufacturing industry. Certain of Britain's competitor countries in Europe and the Pacific Rim have not been slow to recognise this. They are able to see the ways in which Art and Design can contribute to their economic development through the ability of artists and designers to apply their intelligence to the generation of innovative solutions to longstanding problems. This will facilitate change within their economies; change which will be essential to ensure that they meet the demands of rapidly changing markets. They see Art and Design as major drivers of this change and, as a result, are in some cases investing vast sums of money in CAD and CAM facilities in their Art and Design institutions. It is ironic, however, that these very countries are keen to send students to the UK to develop their intellectual capabilities, while they provide them with the technology and the opportunities to collaborate with industry so that their graduates' full potential can be realised. If we are unable to recognise this, we will be the progenitors of growing economies elsewhere, but not of our own.

Technology
The discussion above has indicated that although the Art and Design sector has embraced technology as far as current funding levels permit, considerable capital investment is needed if the full potential in terms of both teaching and research is to be realised. It was extremely disappointing that the Technology Foresight Programme failed to recognise this, bracketing Art and Design with Humanities and seeing the sector as contributors only to "the quality of life" rather than as major drivers of economic change and development.

There is also a significant role for artists and designers in developing the technology itself. As the President of one Japanese technological company put it:

"Art students get to the edges of technology in the first five minutes."

This is echoed by the Finnish designer Sotamaa who has stated:

"The developers of digital technology are increasingly employing artists to research the borders of technology and visual and acoustic possibilities."[3]

A separate issue is whether technology can contribute to the delivery of Art and Design education and whether in doing so it can reduce the costs. The evidence to date suggests that it can significantly enhance the student's learning experience, but that it will provide no substitute for the development of creativity and will not change the need for the acquisition of skills through experience. In addition, it will not reduce costs. As Greenhaigh observes, the proponents of technology

> ". . . deceive themselves into believing that the technology is the important element, whereas it is the materials the technology dispenses and the teachers involved . . . who remain the key."[4]

The contribution to Scotland's economic and social well-being

Even though there is a far greater potential that could be achieved, it is an important strength of the Art and Design sector that it can point to the contribution the arts already make both to the Scottish economy and to its culture. A weakness is that this message does not seem to be widely understood. The Charter for the Arts in Scotland expresses the view that:

> ". . . the quality of our cultural life depends fundamentally on the creative energy and insight of artists."[5]

A number of recent studies have demonstrated that cultural activities have the potential to generate significant direct economic returns for relatively low levels of investment and can give rise to a high multiplier effect, contributing to indirect and induced income and employment (Dundee City Council, 1996).[6] This was amply demonstrated for Glasgow by the Myerscough Report in 1988.[7] Indeed, the major milestones in the transformation of the image of Glasgow since the early 1980s have frequently been related to the arts: the advent of Mayfest (1982), the housing of the Burrell Collection (1983), the building of the Concert Hall (1990), the European City of Culture (1990) and the opening of the new Gallery of Modern Art (1996). Such is the confidence of Glasgow in this arena, that it currently has posters on buses **in Edinburgh** saying "Art belongs to Glasgow"!

Dundee, having achieved much through its Public Art Programme, is now attempting to emulate Glasgow by developing a Strategy for the Arts, a key element of which is the establishment of a new £8 million City Arts Centre.

These observations underline the importance for Scotland in having a high quality Art and Design sector in higher education which will ensure a continued and growing contribution to the nation's economic and cultural life.

Pressures for change: threats and opportunities

Pressures for change arise from a number of factors. Some are seen as threats to the well tried and tested and highly successful approach to Art and Design education in Scotland; others represent opportunities to develop new strengths which are appropriate to the changing nature of higher education in the UK in general, and to the need to ensure that a strongly technologically based Art and Design sector is able to play a full part in the research competitive environment.

Funding cuts

By far the biggest threat comes from the expectation that the cuts in funding, to which reference has already been made, will continue for the foreseeable future. The pressure, which falls on staffing costs in particular, will erode further either the extent of the one-to-one teaching and learning in the studio, or the availability of staff to undertake research, or, as seems likely, both. In addition, an increasing inability to afford part-time staffing will severely reduce a key way in which interaction with industry and the professions takes place.

Pressures on space and on materials and equipment may inhibit the choice of specialisms for students, thereby further diminishing the quality of their learning experience and changing the balance of provision, which currently accords with student demand.

Rationalisation

Continuing severe financial constraint, and consideration of strategic change throughout higher education in Scotland, is likely to raise the issue of subject coverage among institutions (ie whether there is scope for rationalisation). This question arose in relation to provision in the four Art Colleges in 1985 during the consultation period for the Scottish Tertiary Education Advisory Committee (STEAC) Report. It was firmly rejected then; the argument being that breadth of subject coverage was essential and that, without it, the institutions concerned, could not genuinely be considered "Colleges (or Schools) of Art".

The argument still holds force today. Scotland has only four Colleges of Art and they are widely geographically separated. The possibilities, therefore, for students to broaden their experience by studying in more than one College at the same time – even through the SCOTCAT scheme – is not feasible. In addition, in recent years, the many subject boundaries in Art and Design have come more blurred, and scope for students to support their specialism with experimentation in related areas has greatly increased. Without such opportunities, in geographical proximity, the scope for innovation and creativity is diminished.

In addition, because the costs of provision in Art and Design rise on a per capita basis, there would not be significant savings from rationalisation unless student numbers and concomitant staffing were reduced accordingly. But as Scotland already has a disproportionately low number of students in the Art and Design sector, (proportionately about half of the number in England), and as demand for places remains extraordinarily high, it would seem inappropriate to deny even more young Scots (and older ones!) the opportunity to study Art and Design. Furthermore, rationalisation on the basis of related subject areas and existing strengths might not only stifle change, but could result in some Colleges finding themselves supporting a group of high cost subjects in which excellence could not be sustained.

Student financial hardship
Students in Art and Design are experiencing similar problems of financial hardship to those in other subject areas, but the problem is made significantly worse by the high and rising costs of materials. Art and Design students' performance is largely assessed on the basis of artefacts produced. The final year assessments for all students involves the display of work in exhibitions open to the public. No other disciplines subject themselves to such scrutiny, and for many this is a showcase for gaining commissions or subsequent employment. The costs of mounting such exhibitions, however, are very high.

The impact of student hardship on Art and Design is well summarised by Kirkpatrick who states:

> "In Design, the successful outcome of many projects depends upon maintaining an analytical, voyeuristic respect for fellow human beings who are end product users. So much design activity is predicated on equanimity, introspection and regard for humanity, society and the many different ways people choose to live . . . It's very difficult to obtain a broad experience of living or be tolerant and understanding of different lifestyles if you exist in abject poverty, if your view of the world is warped by a lack of funds".[8]

Art and design provision at school and FE levels
The integral four year honours degree to which attention has been drawn as a distinctive characteristic and strength of provision in Scotland is under threat. At a time of increasing financial constraint for higher education, the emergence of the two year SCE Advanced Higher, on the one hand, and the growing willingness of FE Colleges to provide Art and Design education to the equivalent of first year level on the other, may lead some to the conclusion that first year provision could be offered more cheaply elsewhere. Such a step would be

retrograde, creating the division between foundation courses and degree programmes that exists elsewhere in the UK.

Changes in funding for non-vocational programmes
SHEFC's decision to invite all Scottish HE institutions to convert their Continuing Personal Education (CPE) provision to credit-bearing has put the non-vocational programmes in the Colleges of Art at risk. The Colleges of Art have decided that the great majority of their provision is not at degree equivalent level and have, as a result, not converted to credit-bearing status. Some institutions other than the Colleges of Art have, however, been allowed to convert similar provision in Art and Design to credit-bearing. This secures their CPE funding even though no Art College would recognise the credits awarded by these courses. Art College CPE funding meanwhile is rendered open to competition and to shifts in priority by SHEFC, thereby placing it under threat.

Change and development: the role for research
If the anticipated funding trends continue, the quality of the tried and tested approach to teaching and learning simply cannot be maintained. If Scotland's Art Colleges are going to survive, therefore, they have to change, and the key to that change is the development of research. This presents an opportunity for change which will not only improve the prospects for the Art and Design sector, but will also develop a much greater understanding by industry and government of the contribution the sector can make to economic and cultural development.

A higher level of research activity will add a new dimension to the teaching and learning environment, it will carry the potential for new income generation, it will enable more fruitful links with industry to develop, and it will encourage inter-disciplinary collaboration within institutions on a much wider scale. To enable this to happen, however, Art and Design cannot continue to be penalised by having no research council or equivalent body to fund deserving projects, and it cannot undertake the required level and amount of research, without significant investment in the appropriate infrastructure. This particularly means investment in technology, especially CAD/CAM, and it is vital that the importance of this is understood when funding under the Technology Foresight Programme is allocated. Something akin to the Switch Programme for Engineering is what is needed for Art and Design. To facilitate change on such a scale, serious consideration should, in addition, be given to providing funding through the Strategic Change Initiative to support structural adjustments to staffing, staff development and curriculum review.

The challenge
The key questions are: Does Scotland value its Colleges of Art, and does it wish to retain them? Is the potential for Art and Design to contribute to Scotland's economic and cultural development recognised? The present quality of the learning experience for students cannot be maintained in the face of anticipated continuing cuts in funding. Whilst this is to be regretted, there is an opportunity to enable the Colleges of Art to take a new direction to achieve their potential, but this will require substantial investment and the continuing support of a research council or equivalent body. Will those responsible for allocating the funding recognise that some of our competitor nations are already investing heavily in technology for Art and Design in precisely this way, such that if the same challenge is not accepted in Scotland, a significant potential competitive advantage will be lost?

References
1   Ammundsen, K. (1994) *The Danish College of Design* in Higher Education in Design and Crafts in the Scandinavian Countries. Gothenburg University Press. pp 13-17.

2   Jones, A. (1996) "Darwin's Dodo, Part II" *Royal Society of Arts Journal.* Vol CXLIV No 5471. pp 31-42.

3   Sotamaa, Y. (1994) *Art, Crafts, and Design in Finland: the University of Art and Design, Helsinki* in Higher Education in Design and Crafts in the Scandinavian Countries. Gothenburg University Press. pp 25-28.

4   Greenhaigh, M. (1996) *Pictures tell more than one story in Multimedia Features,* The Times Higher Educational Supplement, 8 March 1996. p V

5   Scottish Arts Council, et al (1993). *The Charter for the Arts in Scotland* HMSO. p 19.

6   Dundee City Council (1996) *Cultural Industries and local economic development* A report to the Dundee Partnership. Unpublished.

7   Myerscough, J. (1988) *The Economic Importance of the Arts in Britain* Policy Studies Institute.

8   Kirkpatrick, J. (1996) *Starting all over again* Design Week, 17 May. p 12.

Dr Chris Carter
Deputy Principal, University of Dundee

Chris Carter worked as a Town Planning Assistant for Cumbernauld Development Corporation and for the City of Glasgow before beginning his academic career in the Planning Department at Glasgow School of Art. After a brief spell at Coventry Polytechnic in the mid-1970s he came to the School of Town and Regional Planning at Duncan of Jordanstone College of Art in 1978, becoming Head of the School the following year. He was appointed Vice-Principal of the College in 1981 and became Principal in 1993. Following merger with the University of Dundee in 1994, he became Director of the College and Deputy Principal of the University. He was a member of the UFC's Scottish Committee from 1988 to 1992 and a member of SHEFC from 1992 to 1994.

15

John Daniel

The Open University and Scotland

Established by Royal Charter in 1969, the Open University [OU] has pioneered open and distance learning at university level in the UK. In twenty-five years, it has become Britain's largest university. Nearly twenty-thousand adults in Scotland will be studying Open University courses and study packs this year; ten times that number will be studying with the OU elsewhere in the UK and Europe.

The OU can be said to have been born in Scotland. It was in a speech at Glasgow in 1963 that Harold Wilson, then Leader of the Opposition, first launched the idea of a "University of the Air" – a consortium of existing universities using broadcasting and correspondence tuition to bring their teaching to adult students in their own homes. Under the Labour Government of 1964, it fell to Jennie Lee, a Scot by birth and education, to take the proposal forward. Under her, a new concept emerged of an autonomous, independent university using the techniques of distance learning to bring higher education within the reach of adults living throughout the UK.

The task of realising this vision fell to another Scot, Walter Perry (now Lord Perry), who left the acting Vice-Chancellorship of Edinburgh University to take on the task of planning and leading this new institution. He brought with him two Scottish passions – for breadth of learning and for education of the highest quality – which have endured as guiding principles of the OU to this day.

The OU today offers a broadly-based, modular curriculum that provides an open learning route to most of the major academic disciplines. It blends high quality, multi-media teaching materials with locally-based tutorial and counselling support to provide an integrated system of supported open learning. And it has established a reputation for the quality of its teaching and research which is internationally recognised.

Many of the techniques which the OU has developed over the past twenty-five years are now being taken up by other HE providers as they seek to meet the now escalating demand for higher education and lifelong learning in new, more flexible and more cost-effective ways. It is instructive, therefore, to look at the three legs of open learning upon which the OU's success is based – high quality course materials; local and personal student support; and highly professional logistics.

Course materials

When the OU was established, there was considerable scepticism about its ability to provide a learning experience for its students equal in quality to that enjoyed by full-time students in conventional institutions. Correspondence tuition, as it was then perceived, had a poor reputation.

The OU therefore took as one of its top priorities the development of instructional materials of the very highest quality. Academics from other universities were appointed to the University's establishment; they and colleagues from other institutions, brought in as contributing authors and tv lecturers, set about the planning of an HE curriculum and the development of courses of university-level standard. Courses were written by teams rather than by individuals, ensuring that what was written was considered, consistent and reliable in quality. Qualified educational technologists, BBC producers and OU editors and designers ensured that the courses were pedagogically sound and professionally produced to the highest standards. External assessors from other universities ensured that the academic standards were consistent with the rest of the sector. And small groups of students were asked to developmentally test the materials before they were formally issued.

The practice of building teams of academic, pedagogic and technical experts continues to this day. The teams are constituted slightly differently to include those versed in the new knowledge media and in the application of video, computer and communication technologies to teaching and learning. But the principles of co-operative working remain the same. Indeed, collaboration between colleagues of different institutions is now being extended to include co-operation between the OU and other institutions in the production of common materials. In Scotland, for example, the OU and the University of Dundee are currently engaged in the production of a distance learning course in Modern Scottish History which will be offered by Dundee and will also be eligible for credit within the OU.

This multi-skilled approach of the OU course team has led to the production of courses which use a wide range of teaching media, with elements combined in various different ways to achieve different learning objectives. At the heart of most courses is a series of specially-produced text books (known as 'units' within the OU). They are linked in most cases to course readers and text books and to recommended reading. They are closely integrated, too, with other specially-prepared materials: radio and television programmes, audio and video tapes, home experiment kits for science and technology courses, and computer-based media.

Student support

The development of high quality learning materials has been only one plank of the OU's success. The OU also attaches great importance to the local and personal support it provides to its students. It has successfully developed a national system of tutorial support, assessment and counselling that allows for interaction between students and tutors in a variety of ways. Tutors mark the assignments submitted by students and provide detailed written feedback on each essay. They meet students in tutorials and day schools and they keep in contact through telephone and computer, either individually or collectively through audio/computer conferencing. The latter is particularly important for students in the remote areas of Scotland who are unlikely to be able to meet regularly for tutorials. Residential schools held at various places around the UK over a weekend or a week are also an integral part of many OU courses.

OU students also have access to an academic counsellor who is available to help students plan their learning and to relate it to their personal and career goals, to help them develop their study skills and transferable competences, and to attend to any study difficulties they may encounter. They also arrange for additional services to be provided to students with disabilities.

Tutors and counsellors make a contribution to the students' learning experience as great as that of the learning materials. Consequently, much care is taken with the selection and appointment of suitable candidates, and with their training and development. All newly- appointed staff receive thorough briefing and training about the nature of teaching with the OU and about the particular course to which they are appointed. In addition, they are advised and supported by a mentor and their progress is regularly reviewed before, during, and at the end of their probationary two-year period. Staff are encouraged to undertake further training and development during their period of appointment with the OU.

As in course development and production, the OU draws heavily on the rest of the HE system in Scotland and elsewhere to help present its courses and support its students. Staff from other institutions serve as tutors and examiners, and universities and colleges provide premises for study centres, residential schools and examinations. In return, the OU provides for its tutors the UK's largest and most comprehensive staff development programme. OU learning materials are also used extensively by other universities, most of which have recording licences for its TV programmes. In some cases, the OU works in partnership with other providers to extend the reach of its programmes and its support systems, as in 1995 when, with funding from SHEFC, it worked with the Workers Educational Association and the Tayside Regional Council Community Education Department to provide return to learning and access routes based on OU materials.

Logistics

The University's administrative and operational processes provide the underpinning essential to ensure the quality and effectiveness of its materials and student support. Wherever students live – whether in Kelso or Edinburgh – the courses they take have the same high quality content and are taught to the same high standards. There is a sensitive balance between what is done in the University's central headquarters at Milton Keynes and what is done regionally and locally.

Roughly three-quarters of the University's 850 academic staff and most of its 900 administrative staff and 1500 clerical staff work at Milton Keynes. They plan, prepare, produce and distribute the course materials using mass production and delivery systems. Some services (such as editing and design) are provided in-house; others (notably printing and publishing) are contracted-out. The OU has a long-standing partnership with the BBC for the production and transmission of broadcast programmes.

The rest of the University's staff are located in 13 Regional Centres, three of which cover nation-regions (ie Scotland, Wales and Northern Ireland). The regional centre for the OU in Scotland is located in Edinburgh. It deals with all matters which concern the way in which courses are presented to students. Academic staff in the Centre select, brief, train and monitor tutorial and counselling staff, arrange tutorial timetables, deal with student enquiries and admissions, handle complaints and appeals, and attend to personal difficulties and special circumstances. Administrative staff allocate students to tutors, secure suitable study centre sites and examination centres, and organise residential schools and graduation ceremonies within the region. The whole operation is supported by data handling systems of enormous size and complexity.

Output

What, then, does all this amount to? What is the impact of the OU? The answer is that it has provided opportunities to individuals on a large scale. Over 130,000 people have received degrees from the OU in the past twenty years and another 30,000 have received other qualifications. Roughly one-tenth were from Scotland. Most of them express profound gratitude to the OU for the opportunities it gave them. Many graduates had few other options, particularly those with disabilities, those living in remote areas and those – they are about a third of each year's graduates – who left school as youngsters without the qualifications necessary to be admitted to a conventional university.

Furthermore, the OU has shown that open entry works and that conventional higher education exaggerates the importance of prerequisites at all levels. Notwithstanding its open entry policy, about 80% of finally registered undergraduates pass their first year exams and more than half successfully graduate within three to eight years. The OU has proved, with tens of thousands of examples, that motivated adults can succeed in university study despite shortcomings in their earlier schooling.

The OU has also demonstrated the extremely positive relationship between open learning and employment. Over 80% of graduates report that studying with the University had a 'great' or 'enormous' benefit for their lives and over 80% reported a beneficial effect on their careers. One third change their occupational category while they are students. Twelve per cent of students are full-time housewives when they begin their studies and six out of ten of them enter or return to paid employment during or following their studies. One in three graduates use their OU qualification as a springboard for further training. The success rate of OU graduates applying to postgraduate programmes at other universities is one of the highest in the country.

Finally, the OU has shown that open and distance learning can combine high quality and low cost. The OU is at the top of the quality league for teaching: of the 70 universities assessed by the HEFCE in more than ten subjects only 15, of which the OU was one, were rated excellent in most subjects. In three of those subjects (Geology, Music and Social Policy) the OU accounts for the majority of **all** students taking excellent-rated courses. At the same time, the cost to the Exchequer of teaching each full-time equivalent student at the OU is about half the average for the rest of the HE system.

Learning from success

What lessons can be learned from the OU experience that are relevant to the rest of the sector and to other institutions that are embarking on or further developing open learning programmes? Three major conclusions suggest themselves.

First, open learning is not cheap. Though the direct costs of teaching are relatively low, the development of high quality learning systems and resources incurs high initiation costs and continuing high levels of fixed costs. Open learning courses can only become cost-efficient, therefore, when they are studied by large numbers of students.

Second, the effectiveness of open learning courses (as measured by the numbers of students who successfully complete their learning objectives) critically depends on the quality of the course materials and of the learning support that students receive. This in turn depends in large measure on the quality of the staff. It is this factor more than any other that has enabled the OU to achieve higher completion and success rates than any other distance teaching or correspondence teaching institution.

Third, open learning, linked to modular programmes and schemes of credit accumulation and transfer, has proved itself popular with mature students. It enables them to study at times and in places which cause minimum disruption to their life and work, to construct learning programmes that best fit their individual needs, and to study at a rate that best suits their changing circumstances. Not all study need be taken in one institution.

Open learning, then, has significant potential in helping the transition to mass higher education and to lifetime learning in Scotland as elsewhere. It has the potential to contain costs, enhance quality and widen choice. But to be truly cost-effective, it needs to achieve critical mass and to generate economies of scale. Many institutions do not have student numbers large enough to achieve such economies. Even an organisation the size of the OU may not achieve critical mass in some subjects at some levels. There is considerable scope, therefore, for collaboration and partnership.

Initiatives such as SHEFC's 'Flexibility in Teaching and Learning Scheme' (FITLS) have helpfully encouraged such initiatives. However, funding councils are not best placed to determine educational strategy and evaluate its effectiveness. A more determined national approach is required that draws in a broader range of stakeholders. A Learning Board, along the lines suggested in the MacFarlane Report, could provide the vehicle for such an initiative and could help the sector to work more effectively together in creating, sharing and using open learning materials, in developing a delivery network of study centres, laboratories, computer networks etc, and in commissioning the development of appropriate support services, including staff development programmes.

The OU's experience of collaboration with other higher education institutions has expanded rapidly since it inherited a major accreditation and validation function from the former Council for National Academic Awards. Open University Validation Services (OUVS) has a number of accredited institutions in Scotland, of which the largest is Northern College, and registers doctoral students in a range of sponsoring institutions. Senior Scottish academics play key roles in the operation of OUVS, which is also an Awarding Body for Scottish Vocational Qualifications.

The scale and variety of its own activities make the OU a useful partner in joint ventures of many kinds. For example, the OU has been closely involved with the project for the University of the Highlands and Islands since its inception, making available course materials, validation expertise and staff development opportunities, as well as choosing the Highlands region for one of the OU's own developments in advanced technology-based teaching. The OU looks forward to joining with other Scottish universities in helping to create a new, exciting and innovative model for higher education in the next millennium.

A system of higher education built on flexibility and partnership needs to be underpinned by a method of institutional funding that encourages innovation and collaboration and by a system of student awards that treats all students equitably, irrespective of their mode of study. It is essential that the Dearing Inquiry uses its authority and influence to bring about these most important changes in higher education. Ever since the 1992 Higher Education Act created an integrated system, funding methodologies have promoted competition between institutions. Considerable efficiencies have resulted across the higher education sector. However, the future will also require mechanisms for collaboration if we are to unlock the potential of the new technologies that the OU calls the knowledge media. The challenge for all of us is to build together a system of higher education that combines quality and cost-effectiveness in the service of lifelong learning.

Sir John Daniel
Vice-Chancellor, The Open University

Sir John Daniel was educated at Christ's Hospital and St Edmund Hall, Oxford where he studied metallurgy. After a doctorate at the University of Paris he began an academic career at the Université de Montréal. Part-time study in educational technology and an internship at the infant Open University led him to reorient his career and help establish two of Canada's distance teaching institutions, Quebec's Télé-université and Alberta's Athabasca University. In the 1980s he was vice-rector of Concordia University, Montreal and president of Laurentian University in Ontario. He moved to the UK as vice-chancellor of the Open University in 1990. His book *Mega-universities and Knowledge Media: Technology Strategies for Higher Education* was published in 1996.

16

Maria Slowey

Continuing education – A bridge to the learning society

"Continuing education is at the cutting edge as universities become more fully 'learning organisations'." (Duke, 1992, p 4)

Introduction

In 1994 the Scottish Community Education Council published a paper entitled *Scotland as a Learning Society: Myths, Reality and Challenge*. This report set out a vision of Scotland as ". . . a society whose citizens value, support and engage in learning as a matter of course, in all areas of activity." (p 3). While highlighting many areas of good practice, the report emphasises that the achievement of this vision has to contend with the contrast between the high value which Scottish people often place on education, and the mixed feelings and reactions which many of them display towards it in practice. This point is illustrated by a large scale survey of the population aged 21 or over which indicated that the percentage of those who had recently participated in some form of adult education activity in Scotland was not only significantly below areas such as Yorkshire (50% as opposed to 38% in Scotland) and London (44%) but was even below the national average (40%). (Tuckett and Sargent, 1996)

Higher education clearly is one of the key players in any strategy which seeks to translate general interest in learning into the actual participation required for the achievement of a learning society. A quick glance at the statistics can easily lead to the complacent view that higher education is already well on the way to playing its role in relation to delivering the vision – the age participation rate of young people has increased significantly; the proportion of mature entrants has increased rapidly to a level where they now constitute about half of all students in higher education; the number of part-time students has also increased dramatically; there is even – at last – some evidence which points to increasing levels of participation in higher education courses from those from social groups IV and V. (COSHEP, 1996)

As usual, however, the statistics conceal as much as they reveal. While the age participation rate for cohorts of young people leaving school may now sit at over 40%, for the vast majority of the population, that is those aged 21 or over, estimates of the age participation rate lie somewhere in the region of 3-5%. (Osborne and Gallacher, 1995) Can a system which is, in spite of all the rhetoric, still so overwhelmingly front loaded, really play a major role in the delivery of a learning society?

It is the central argument of this chapter that unless the essential principles and approaches which underpin the activities currently encompassed with the broad field of *continuing education* – in all their rich diversity of forms – are taken seriously in shaping the future, then the role of the higher education system as a whole is in danger of becoming increasingly marginalised as it fails to meet the social and economic demands placed upon it. (Barnett, 1994) points to some of the key weaknesses of the present system in this regard.

"In a world of change, in the so-called post-Fordist world where 'flexibility' is the watchword, the wider world, despite itself, is coming to just such an appreciation of just those wider skills and capacities of human reason traditionally espoused in the university . . . the only problem is that the university fails to practice what it preaches. The gulf between theories – in-use and espoused theories which the critical academics love to observe in others is to be found in glaringly sharp form in the academy. Having trapped itself into narrow definitions of knowledge, it is unable to provide the wider definitions of knowing and intellectual development which it supremely should have been in a position to supply and which are now required by society."
(Barnett, 1994, p 24)

In making the case for the lessons to be learned from continuing education, the broader policy context of the need for lifelong learning is taken as a given. While there are differences in emphasis in documents such as the European Commission's White Paper on Teaching and Learning (1995) or the DfEE/ SOEID paper on Lifetime Education (1996), they share a common analysis that economic, technological and social forces all point to increasing need for learning over the lifetime.

But what do we mean by continuing education? Does the term resonate within the context of moves towards a mass higher education system? The first part of this chapter points to the broad range of activities which currently tend to be included within definitions of "continuing education". While not in any way representing a comprehensive survey of such activities within higher education institutions in Scotland, it does point to the diversity and richness of this area of work. The second section identifies certain key principles and features which characterise continuing education activity and, it is argued here, provide crucial lessons for the future direction of the system as a whole. The final section focuses on the policy implications. Inevitably, given the fact that the funding of the present system is geared towards the norm of the full-time student (both in terms of institutional and student funding), questions about resourcing part-time studies lie at the heart of this discussion.

Continuing Education – the basis of a coherent approach to lifelong learning?

The diversity of forms of provision and activities encompassed within continuing education make precise definition difficult. In general terms, continuing education tends to refer to activities which are targeted at learners other than those progressing directly to higher education from full-time initial studies. While the emphasis is on part-time and mixed-mode forms of provision, the category is usually extended to include mature students on full-time access courses and related higher education courses.

In a briefing document prepared for the Scottish Higher Education Funding Council by the Universities Association for Continuing Education (Scotland) the following definition was used:

> "University continuing education provides quality higher education for adults returning to study predominantly part-time. It emphasises education for personal and professional development, in the world of work and the community, and the widening of learning opportunities in higher education for all who wish and are able to benefit from it. It serves personal, social and economic ends. . . . University continuing education ranges from research-based professional development and technological training through community-based work with disadvantaged groups, liberal adult education and access courses, to part-time undergraduate and postgraduate degrees."
> (UACE(S), 1993, p 2)

Dissemination of higher education to the broader community has a long tradition in Scotland. In 1727 for example, the Professor of Natural Philosophy in the University of Glasgow was required to provide public lectures for the benefit of the "manufacturers and artificers in Glasgow". (Cited by Bryant, 1984, p 3)

Bell and Tight (1993) in their account of the "closing" of higher education over the centuries draw particularly on this Scottish tradition. They argue that much of today's debates about the role and functions of higher education, particularly as they relate to the widening of access and part-time studies, are all too frequently influenced by a faulty view of the practice and conventions of higher education in the past. Into the last century in Scotland any male was free to matriculate, regardless of his previous qualifications. Furthermore, it was possible for (male) individuals to attend lectures on a drop-in basis, even if they had not matriculated. They argue that common (mistaken) perceptions of Oxford and Cambridge have been very influential in shaping a view that the present system, with its emphasis on full-time, residential study and formal entry qualifications, has emerged from a longer tradition than is in fact the case. The erosion of the more open traditions over the century up to the 1970s (including the introduction of formal entry qualifications) enabled those who argue against moves to wider access to see themselves as defenders of a higher education tradition that is actually relatively recent. The activities relating to the field of access and continuing education tend therefore to be regarded as breaking new ground, with all the dangers of marginalisation which such a role carries with it.

That said, a review of continuing education activity in higher education institutions in Scotland in the mid-1990s reveals a diverse and vibrant picture. In the area of *access*, to take one significant example, in contrast to the situation in England, Scottish universities are themselves major providers of access courses. Access courses were introduced into Scottish universities in 1978, and by 1992 over 1,200 students were enrolled on university part-time access courses. These courses continued to complement those later developed under the auspices of the Scottish Wider Access Programme within further education colleges. (Gallacher and Osborne, 1991) *Mature students'* participation in higher education, represents another major dimension of continuing education. In Scotland, as in other parts of the UK, the absolute numbers and proportions of such students in higher education have been increasing steadily over the last decade. Between 1985 and 1991, for example, the proportion of new entrants to full-time higher education courses who were aged 21 or over increased from 20.4% to 31.4%. (Osborne and Gallacher, 1995)

Recent years have also seen an expansion of *part-time* higher education programmes which are overwhelmingly attended by those aged 21 or over. Currently, the most significant contribution to part-time mature entry to higher education comprises those taking advanced courses other than degree programmes, often located within further education colleges. These figures are likely to be augmented considerably in the near future as a result of the "conversion" into credit-bearing programmes, equivalent to SCOTCAT Level 1 or above, of much of the *liberal adult education* provision offered by the Universities of Aberdeen, Dundee, Edinburgh, Glasgow, St Andrews, Stirling and Strathclyde. Following on from the report of the Committee of Enquiry into Adult Education (the "Alexander" Report) (1975) a particularly strong dimension of the liberal adult education tradition in Scotland involves collaboration with the community education services of local authorities and other relevant bodies in providing educational opportunities targeted at *disadvantaged sections of the community*. These usually take the form of outreach activities which are located in areas of multiple deprivation, providing the potential for valuable links between universities and urban and rural regeneration initiatives.

The scale of provision is impressive. In recent years over 40,000 adults enrolled on courses defined by the Scottish Higher Education Funding Council as Continuing Personal Education (CPE) in the universities mentioned above. These courses have played a significant role in bringing university education opportunities to the wider public and have provided an important point of contact between universities and the broader community. However, just at a time when the demand for this type of continuing education opportunity has never been stronger there is considerable concern about the impact which recent funding changes will have on this work in the future. These changes derive from two main sources – SHEFC pressures to convert liberal adult education and community based provision into credit-bearing activities (Scottish Higher Education Funding Council, 1994) coupled with the impact of local government reorganisation. As much continuing education is post-experience, or offers a first step on the rung of higher level learning or involves work by universities in disadvantaged communities, it does not fit easily into credit frameworks derived from the four-year degree downwards. The threat posed to large areas of existing work which cater for important personal and social needs is therefore a matter which has attracted considerable attention and debate. [See, for example, Duke and Taylor (1994); Skinner and Osborne (1995); Barr (1996); Taylor (1996)]

There is perhaps less debate and more consensus about the area of increasingly important contact between universities and the community at large through the provision of *continuing professional development* programmes to industry, commerce and the professions. Definitional problems abound in this area also, and precise figures are difficult to obtain. However, recent estimates from the Scottish Higher Education Funding Council indicate that Scottish universities provided over 2.7 million student contact hours of continuing professional development activity in 1995/96, and generated a further 770 FTEs through related credit-bearing courses. (Scottish Higher Education Funding Council, 1996)

This is a growing area of activity for universities and is clearly of strategic importance in relation to economic development. As Davies states:

> "Thirty years ago, when the Robbins Report stated its objectives for Higher Education, the manpower needs of the economy were not explicitly highlighted. Since then, the world of work has changed substantially. People no longer stay within one job, or even one career, throughout their working life, and there is an increasing need for continual updating and retraining, and growing demand from certain professions for professional development." (Davies, 1996, p 7)

At one level, therefore, continuing education activities in Scottish universities are thriving. Statistically, the numbers of mature students on full-time courses and numbers of part-time students across the system (including, of course, the Open University) are growing in both absolute and relative terms. However, as Coffield, points out, these observations convey ". . . the impression that the character and role of higher education has been successfully transformed and the battles over access, participation and enlarged mission have all been won". (Coffield, 1996, p.6) The reality is very different.

Lessons from continuing education for the future shape of higher education
It is a truism to state that continuing education has operated on the margins of higher education. However, it is this "marginal" status which has facilitated many of the innovatory developments which, it is argued here, offer signposts

for the future of the higher education system as a whole. In its response to the consultation exercise conducted by the National Committee of Inquiry into Higher Education, UACE points to the increasingly important role which continuing education will have in higher education in the 21st Century in:

● developing the higher education lifelong learning opportunities for the whole community

● meeting diverse and social needs

● fostering the values of a civilised citizenship within a democratic society.

(UACE, 1996)

There are three particular features of continuing education which I believe offer valuable experience on which the system as a whole can usefully draw. These relate to (i) responsiveness and flexibility; (ii) equality of opportunity and the promotion of social justice; (iii) the dissemination of knowledge and skills to the broader community.

(i)   *Responsiveness and flexibility*
A high priority for higher education at present is the achievement of an appropriate balance between responding to the various interests which it serves, while at the same time rejecting an ideology which transforms "students" into "clients". As the most market orientated part of higher education, continuing education has long experience in managing this tension. It could be argued in fact that many (if not most) of the creative developments fostered by continuing education have been generated by finding ways of working with this potential area of conflict – responding to the demands of different sections of society, while maintaining the critical, independent approach which is fundamental to academic integrity.

Whether it is responding to the needs of employers and individuals for professional and updating activities, or to the interests of social movements for widening access, continuing education has had to find ways of identifying which activities are appropriate for a higher education environment and delivering these in ways which meet the very diverse demands which are placed upon it. In doing so a case could be made that continuing education is simply a part of higher education which goes back to some of its most ancient roots. To quote Bell and Tight again, until this century the higher education tradition in Scotland was:

"... very much a buyer's market into which the Scottish universities, unlike their ancient English counterparts, had shown a willingness to launch almost any new and relatively respectable subject that seemed likely to draw an audience." (Bell and Tight, 1993, p 23)

Illustrated below are just four examples of ways in which continuing education practice is responsive and innovative and, in my view, offers a model from which the whole system has much to learn.

- Firstly, in terms of *mode of delivery* – continuing education has always recognised that its student body includes people with significant work, domestic and social commitments. These commitments are not seen as "problems" which students have, but rather as the source of a valuable resource and a strength which students bring to their learning – as evidence that the students are engaged in making their contribution to the broader economic and social well-being of the community. Not only is full-time study impossible for the majority of the population, it is also not appropriate for many of their learning needs. Continuing education, therefore, effectively acts as a test-bed for new modes of delivery based on a wide variety of part-time, flexible approaches, increasingly including distance education and the use of IT.

- Secondly, because continuing education starts from an identification of the learner's interest, it adopts almost by definition a *multi-disciplinary* approach. Not being constrained by traditional academic boundaries, the opportunities for curriculum innovation and development become wide open. As a result, many new curricular areas which have become incorporated into the mainstream of higher education provision have their origins within continuing education.

- Thirdly, considerable emphasis is placed in continuing education on *educational guidance*. As the system becomes more diverse, as the range of opportunities expands and as fewer students enter as part of a cohort, but rather come as individuals with learning needs which change throughout their lifetime, the provision of high quality, impartial educational guidance becomes a matter of increasing significance for the system as a whole.

- Fourthly, the responsive nature of continuing education activities offers considerable experience in working in *partnership* with a wide variety of external bodies including employers, professional organisations, voluntary organisations, local authorities, other public and private sector bodies. These partnerships assist in building bridges between higher education and broader societal interests.

Clearly there are tensions to be managed between the independence of the academy and the demands of the market, and also tensions between the interests of the different communities served by higher education. The present uncertainty about the future of higher education arises not just from resourcing issues but also from questions about the contribution which higher education can and should make to the broader society. However, as Elliott et al. (1996) comment, what is certain amidst all the current uncertainty ". . . is that increasing numbers of influential voices are scrutinising the role of the universities to arrive at a general conclusion: they must become more responsive to the social and economic needs of the wider society . . . that responsiveness must ensure that universities are, to borrow from contemporary jargon, in the mainstream rather than at the margins of societal change . . .". (p. xiv)

(ii)   *Equality of opportunity and the promotion of social justice*
One particularly strong dimension of the continuing education tradition lies in a commitment to the social purpose of higher education. This tradition has manifested itself in different ways, in particular between the pre and post 1992 universities. In the latter case the emphasis has particularly been placed on seeking ways to provide greater equality of opportunity for individuals from different social backgrounds, for members of different minority ethnic groups and for women to gain access to higher education. Adult education departments in the pre-1992 universities, in addition to sharing an involvement in initiatives aimed at widening access, included in many cases also a traditional commitment to the social purposes of higher education which included links with the Trades Union movement, with women's educational groups and many community based initiatives. This is not to suggest the existence of a monolithic or consensual approach within continuing education. In fact, quite different ideologies underpin traditions which place an emphasis on social and economic mobility for individuals in contrast to those which seek to promote wider social benefits through the community. (See, for example, Wallis, 1996; Fieldhouse, 1993)

There is, however, much which continuing education has to offer in terms of the role which universities can play in relation to the extension of knowledge and skills which will not just lead to the enrichment of the lives of individuals, but, more broadly, contribute to the well-being of society at large. In the context of globalisation and increasing levels of inequality it is ever more vital that higher education adopts a pro-active stance in seeking to identify and highlight the major problems created by social, gender, ethnic and racial inequalities. While not ascribing to the higher education system a more powerful role than it actually holds in society, the fact remains that individual universities *are* powerful institutions within their own communities. As such, they have a responsibility to make whatever contribution they can to the enhancement of learning opportunities for all members of these communities – either directly or indirectly.

(iii) *Dissemination of knowledge and skills to the wider community*
Internationally, very different balances are achieved between the three major functions of universities – research, the education of students and service to the community. Within the higher education systems of individual countries, different parts of the sectors also place different emphases on these different functions. Through continuing education there is the opportunity for these three dimensions to be brought together in relation to the dissemination of knowledge generated by the research taking place within higher education. In spite of the fact that much of the original research function is now located in non-university research institutions, research and the generation of knowledge still lie at the centre of the higher education system.

Schuetze (1996) identifies three main barriers which inhibit universities from transferring knowledge to the wider community in general, and to the industrial community in particular. The first of these is the prevalence of a *linear model* within higher education. Essentially this views knowledge as a commodity which is developed within universities and handed over (or down) to the outside world for application. Continuing education, in contrast, offers a view of knowledge as dynamic, multi-faceted and requiring multiple interaction and constant feedback. This allows for interaction between researchers and practitioners rather than a producer/consumer relationship.

The second barrier identified by Schuetze relates to the fact that much provision *lacks multi-disciplinarity*. Scientific and technological developments tend to be isolated from the humanities and social sciences. By bringing together a wide range of disciplines within one organisation, higher education institutions should be the best placed societal institutions to offer genuinely multi-disciplinary perspectives. Outside continuing education, however, how frequently is this potential realised in practice?

Thirdly, in discussing technology transfer, Schuetze argues that there is too often a separation of *knowledge and learning*. Ideally the transfer of knowledge needs to be supported by organised, systematic learning. Continuing education, in other words, ties in with dissemination of knowledge and skills to industry, commerce, the professions and the community at large in a very significant way.

Policy Implications

This chapter has argued the case for a higher education system which has a unique role to play in enhancing the quality of life of individuals and civic society through the generation and dissemination of knowledge and higher level skills in dynamic interaction with the broader community. Many of the necessary elements are already in place. In particular, much can be learned from the student responsive tradition which lies at the core of continuing education.

Resourcing levels and methodologies are obviously crucial to the delivery of higher education. Leaving to one side the inadequacy of funding levels, present funding methodologies for both institutions and students are not neutral. They are overwhelmingly geared towards the model of the young, residential full-time student. The Universities Association for Continuing Education (Scotland) response to the National Committee of Inquiry into Higher Education takes as one of its axioms that:

> "The full-time/part-time distinction will disappear and higher education needs to be ready for this, in its financing systems, its curricular structures and its teaching approach." (UACE(S) 1996)

Funding is important, but the latter two areas of the curriculum and teaching methods are, in my view, of equal significance. A major cultural shift is required to deliver a higher education system orientated towards lifelong learning needs. This is by no means to suggest that higher education should simply comply in an uncritical way with the demands placed upon it but, as Barnett expresses it, higher education ". . . cannot seriously entertain the prospect of promoting a self-critical, mutually self-informing society unless it takes on something of that form itself." (Barnett, 1994, p 24)

Part of the development of this self-informing society involves bringing the university into the community in various ways, including on occasion literally. Historically many Scottish universities, in particular the University of Glasgow, have traditions of bringing intellectually challenging and critical curricula out to disadvantaged communities. Today, university lecturers are involved in bringing philosophy, history, ecological studies and English literature to, to take one of many examples, the Govan area of Glasgow. The positive outcomes of such activities are well documented. (Hamilton, 1994, SOEID, 1996) What is needed is a real commitment from those who shape policy at the national *and* at the institutional level to a major expansion of this type of initiative and complementary forms of provision.

It appears that this is a commitment which is now shared by Sir Ron Dearing. He is quoted in The Higher as saying:

> "I'm told in some working-class estates there isn't an HE culture. In fact, there might even be an anti-HE culture. We've got to go in and establish units there." (THES, 25 October, 1996)

While the tone of this statement may not strike quite the right chord with all continuing educators, the sentiments which underlie it are to be warmly welcomed. We can only hope that such views will find their way into the heart of the policies which will shape the higher education system of the future.

References

Barnett, R. (1994) *The Limits of Competence; Knowledge, Higher Education and Society,* Open University Press, Milton Keynes.

Barr, J. (1996) "The Scottish Higher Education Funding Council Review of Continuing Education", *International Journal of Lifelong Learning,* Vol. 15, No. 6.

Bell, R. & Tight, M. (1993) *Open Universities: A British Tradition?* Open University Press, Milton Keynes.

Bryant, I. (1984) *Radicals and Respectables: the adult education experience in Scotland,* Scottish Institute of Adult and Continuing Education, Edinburgh.

Committee of Enquiry into Adult Education (1975) *Adult Education, the Challenge of Change,* (The "Alexander" Report), HMSO, Edinburgh.

Coffield, F. (1996) *Higher Education in a Learning Society*, University of Durham.

COSHEP (1996) *Higher Education for Scotland: A Vision for the Future* Submission to the Dearing Inquiry, Committee of Scottish Higher Education Principals, Glasgow.

DfEE/SOEID (1996) *Lifetime Learning,* DfEE, London.

Davies, G. (1996) "The Role of the Higher Education Funding Councils and their support for CVE", *Proceedings of the 1995 UACE CVE Conference held at the University of Lancaster,* UACE Occasional Paper No 18, Universities Association for Continuing Education.

Duke, C. (1992) *The Learning University,* Open University Press, Milton Keynes.

Duke, C. and Taylor, R. (1994) "The Higher Education Funding Council (England) Review and the Funding of Continuing Education", *Studies in the Education of Adults,* Vol. 26, No. 1.

Elliott, J., Francis, H., Humphreys, R., Istance, D. (eds.) (1996) *Communities and their Universities – the challenge of lifelong learning,* Lawrence and Wishart, London.

European Commission (1996) *Teaching and Learning – Towards the Learning Society*, European Commission, 1995.

Fieldhouse, R. (1993) *Optimism and Joyful Irreverence*, NIACE, Leicester.

Gallacher, J., and Osborne, M. J. (1991) "Differing National Models of Access Provision: a comparison between Scotland and England", *Journal of Access Studies,* Vol 6, No. 2, pp 147-164.

Hamilton, R. (1994) "Outreach Pre-Access – A Case Study of Collaboration between Universities and Local Authorities", *Scottish Journal of Adult and Continuing Education,* Vol. 1, No. 2.

The Higher (1996) "Dearing Aims to Enthuse the Poor", *The Times Higher Education Supplement*, 25 October 1996.

NIACE (1993) *An Adult Higher Education: a vision. A policy discussion paper,* National Institute of Adult Continuing Education, Leicester.

Osborne, M. J., and Gallacher, J. (1995) "Scotland", in P. Davies (ed.) *Adults in Higher Education: International Perspectives in Access and Participation,* Jessica Kingsley, London.

SCEC (1994) *Scotland as a Learning Society: Myths, Reality and Challenge,* Scottish Community Education Council, Edinburgh.

Schuetze, H. G. (1996) "Knowledge, Innovation, and Technology Transfer: Universities and their industrial community" in J. Elliot et al, *Communities and their Universities – the challenge of lifelong learning.*

SHEFC, (1994) *Continuing Education – Circular Letter 53/94,* Scottish Higher Education Funding Council, Edinburgh.

SHEFC, (1996) *Allocation of CPD Funding for 1996/97 – Circular Letter 25/96,* Scottish Higher Education Funding Council, Edinburgh.

Skinner, A., and Osborne, M. J. (1995) "Response to Scottish Higher Education Funding Council Circular 53/94 on Continuing Education", *Scottish Journal of Adult and Continuing Education,* Vol. 2. No. 1.

SOEID, (1996) *Lifelong Learning in the Community,* Scottish Office Education and Industry Department, Edinburgh.

Taylor, R. (1996) "Preserving the Liberal Tradition in "New Times"" in J. Wallis (ed) *Liberal Adult Education – the End of an Era?* University of Nottingham, Nottingham.

Tuckett, A., and Sargent, N. (1996) *Creating Two Nations?* NIACE, Leicester.

UACE, (1996) *Executive response to the National Committee of Inquiry into Higher Education,* Universities Association for Continuing Education, unpublished paper.

UACE(S), (1993) *Continuing Education in Scottish Universities – a briefing document for the Scottish Higher Education Funding Council,* Universities Association for Continuing Education (Scotland), unpublished paper.

UACE(S), (1996) *Response to the National Committee of Inquiry into Higher Education,* Universities Association for Continuing Education (Scotland), unpublished paper.

Wallis, J. (1996) *Liberal Adult Education: The End of an Era?* Continuing Education Press, University of Nottingham.

Professor Maria Slowey
Director of Adult and Continuing Education, University of Glasgow

Professor Maria Slowey is Director of the Department of Adult and Continuing Education at the University of Glasgow. Her particular interests lie in research and policy development in relation to the participation of adults in higher education. Prior to taking up her post in the University of Glasgow in 1992, Professor Slowey was Head of the Centre for External Relations and Continuing Education at the University of Northumbria. She has acted as consultant on adult education and training to a range of bodies including the OECD, the EC and the Council of Europe.

She is honorary Specialist Advisor on Continuing Education to COSHEP.

17

William Duncan

How the RSE can help Scottish higher education

Origins and development[1]

The Royal Society of Edinburgh (RSE) is Scotland's foremost learned Society and was established in 1783, by Royal Charter granted by George III, for the "Advancement of Learning and Useful Knowledge." The RSE's roots lie in bodies such as the Rankenian Club (formed in 1716 for literary social meetings), the Society for the Improvement of Medical Knowledge (instituted in 1731) and the Philosophical Society of Edinburgh (founded in 1737). The range of interests of these precursor bodies is reflected in the breadth of interests in the RSE, which continues to represent all branches of learning.The RSE was originally divided into a Literary class (93 members) and a Physical class (72 members), giving 165 founding members. The Literary class included Adam Smith, Henry MacKenzie and Sir Robert Liston, while the Physical class included Joseph Black, James Hutton, James Watt, James Gregory and Sir James Hall. Following the Presidency of Sir Walter Scott in 1832, the separation of the fellowship into two classes ceased. This also coincided with a long term decline in the activity of the Literary class, from which it has only recently emerged. It was overshadowed by the Physical class which flourished as a direct consequence of the important scientific discoveries reported to the Society during the 19th century by Fellows such as Brewster, Clerk-Maxwell, Forbes, Kelvin and Tait. Although concern continued to be expressed from time to time about the domination of the Sciences, it was not until the 1970s that corrective measures were taken, (and continue to be taken) to achieve a more even balance between the interests of all branches of learning.

Currently, there are nearly 1100 Fellows drawn from all disciplines and 70 Honorary Fellows, many from overseas. All Fellows are expected to have a connection with, or strong interest in, Scotland, but there are no nationality requirements.

Although the RSE was founded and is based in Edinburgh, from the earliest days its Fellows have been drawn from all parts of Scotland and beyond. Edinburgh and its institutions have had an important role in shaping the RSE, but other cities, especially Glasgow, have contributed much. Several of the founding Fellows had strong links with Glasgow and Lord Kelvin was President for a total of 21 years on three separate occasions between 1873 and 1907. Fellowship of the RSE is still widely distributed throughout Scotland and the RSE can claim, with considerable justification, to be the "Royal Society of Scotland." Indeed, *The Glasgow Herald* felt able to comment about the RSE: "Intercity rivalry or jealousy is as foreign to its history as the forbidden topics of religion or politics"! It is this continuing ability to stand above the rivalries and tensions, and yet not be aloof, which is one of the RSE's most useful assets. "It is generally acknowledged that the most important function of the Society is to afford a unique opportunity in Scotland for scientists and scholars of all disciplines and persuasions to meet. It thus acts not only as a 'mutual stimulus of association and discussion', but also as an integrative influence".

The RSE is a wholly independent body, governed by an elected Council of 25 Fellows, including nine honorary office bearers, led by the President. There is a small group of paid staff headed by the Executive Secretary. The RSE's premises in George Street, Edinburgh were extensively refurbished during the 1980s to convert what had become a rather antiquated library into modern lecture and conference facilities. This transformation of the RSE's rooms coincided with, and partly stimulated, a resurgence of activity and the RSE now occupies an important role at the heart of learning and scholarship in Scotland. In recent years such has been the growth in the range and volume of activities that additional accommodation was required and the opportunity was taken recently to acquire adjoining premises in George Street. The development of the new premises will allow further expansion of the RSE's public benefit role and provide a show-case for the best of the research in Scottish HEIs.

The RSE is now funded from a wide variety of sources: the single most important of these remains grant-in-aid from the Scottish Office although the proportion of public funding has declined significantly in recent years. The recent expansion of the RSE has largely been through securing new sources of private and charitable income and these now provide the majority of recurring funds. In addition, Fellows contribute much: not only financially through annual subscriptions and appeals for capital funds, but particularly through the time and effort they provide in supporting the Society's diverse range of activities.

Indeed, the health of the RSE critically depends on a willing and committed Fellowship.

From the earliest days, the RSE has enjoyed cordial relations with the Scottish universities, but has not been dominated by them. Although a leading figure behind the creation of the RSE was the Reverend Dr William Robertson, Principal of the University of Edinburgh, he did not hold high office in the Society. University Principals who have been Presidents include: Sir David Brewster (1864-68), Sir William Turner (1908-13), Sir James Ewing (1924-29) and Sir Alwyn Williams (1985-88). The Fellowship has included, and still includes, many of the leading researchers and teachers from all disciplines in the Scottish universities, but the Fellowship draws more widely and also includes highly distinguished people from the professions, business and public sector. It is this unique breadth which hallmarks the RSE and is the source of much of its usefulness to higher education and scholarship in Scotland

Main activities in support of higher education in Scotland
The principal function of the RSE is the promotion of research and scholarship: in doing so it is mindful of its Royal Charter which emphasises the equal importance of advancing "Useful Knowledge" and "Learning". The RSE provides an important forum for inter-disciplinary activity as a counterbalance to the growing tendency of ever smaller specialisations and sub-disciplines. Indeed, the RSE's role in maintaining a strong inter-disciplinary emphasis has never been more important, and it has been its deliberate policy of seeking to address complex and often controversial issues which require a broadly-based approach. The breadth of the Fellowship also helps promote stronger links between the academic and business communities, to the mutual benefit of both. It is by being able to act as an independent, well-informed body that the RSE is able to fulfil these essential roles for the intellectual well-being of all of Scotland.

The specific activities which the RSE carries out for the benefit of the wider higher education community in Scotland are these:

● awarding research fellowships, scholarships and prizes to promote research

● organising inter-disciplinary meetings and specialist symposia

● providing an independent forum in Scotland for consideration of matters affecting the well-being of the nation

- giving advice to Parliament, Government and its agencies on relevant policy issues

- developing better links between industry and commerce and the academic community

- publishing scholarly journals.

Awarding Research Fellowships, scholarships and prizes to promote research

Currently well over 40% of the RSE's expenditure is directed towards supporting a broad range of post-doctoral research fellowships in Scottish HEIs, as well as supporting several postgraduate studentships in specific disciplines. The research fellowships are a relatively new and expanding activity.

As part of the recompense to the RSE for the transfer of its library to create the core of the Scottish Science Library (SSL), the grant-in-aid from the Scottish Office was increased to cover the cost of post-doctoral research fellowships, each for up to three years, in Scottish universities. The scheme was later enlarged to include support fellowships – one year sabbaticals for academic staff. These Scottish Office funded fellowships cover all disciplines, but currently there is a preference for topics identified as Technology Foresight priorities. Since the inception of the Scottish Office funded schemes in the 1980s, 26 post-doctoral research fellowships and 16 support fellows have been appointed.

The success of the Scottish Office funded schemes encouraged other non-public sources to create parallel research fellowships. In 1988, BP endowed a series of postdoctoral research fellowships in specified science and engineering subjects and, to date, 14 research fellows have been appointed. In 1988 the Wellcome Trust created a senior clinical research fellowship with the RSE. In 1990, the Caledonian Research Foundation (CRF) agreed to create post-doctoral and support fellowships in the bio-medical sciences and 11 research fellows have since been appointed. Subsequently, CRF also created a series of visiting research fellowships in Arts and Letters, to establish a two-way flow of scholars between Scotland and Continental Europe. The James Weir Foundation also created a 3 year research fellowship in Environmental Sciences.

As part of the implementation of the recent strategy for improving commercialisation of the Scottish science and engineering base, Scottish Enterprise has agreed to fund a pilot scheme of Enterprise Fellowships in Optoelectronics.

Many RSE research fellows have become well recognised for the quality of their work and have been appointed to senior academic posts: a few have been elected FRSE. There is intense competition for each of the research fellowships which are administered by the RSE at arm's length from the donors. Selection is strictly by merit and determined by specialist selection boards consisting mainly of RSE Fellows. These research fellowships are an invaluable additional source of research opportunity for those wishing to carry out academic research in Scotland. There are no nationality restrictions on applicants and the various schemes attract able overseas researchers wanting to work in Scotland or those wishing to return to Scotland, as well as others keen to continue their researches here.

About one-third of the funding for these fellowship schemes comes from public sources (through the Scottish Office Education and Industry Department) and this clearly demonstrates the way in which judicious and innovative use of public funds can be used to attract even greater support for the benefit of higher education in Scotland.

In addition to these post-doctoral research fellowships, the RSE also offers a few postgraduate studentships in astronomy, engineering and physiology. These are all funded from bequests or legacies to the RSE and not from public funds. The subjects covered by these awards reflect the donors' wishes.

The RSE also awards various prizes and medals to recognise outstanding scholarship and the list of previous prize-winners reflects some of the pinnacles of achievement in Scottish sciences. A more recent development has been the creation of prize lectureships funded by BP, CRF and others

Organising inter-disciplinary meetings and specialist symposia
Communication of the latest discoveries was, and remains, one of the core purposes of the Royal Society of Edinburgh. Despite great improvements in communication technology, effective communication between the disciplines has never been more challenging. When the RSE was created in 1783, scholars could meet regularly and usually converse freely on the basis of an assumed shared body of scientific and literary knowledge. Early Fellows could move from discipline to discipline with relative ease; for example, William Cullen (1710-90) moved smoothly from being Professor of Medicine at Glasgow University to being Professor of Chemistry and Physics at Edinburgh University.

Not only are there, nowadays, the problems of communication between the so called "Two Cultures" – the Humanities and the Sciences, there are difficulties in maintaining adequate communication between different branches of related subjects. A particular emphasis of the RSE's programmes of lectures, symposia, workshops and conferences is to try to bring together a wide range of people from different backgrounds to consider common issues. Given how frequently important discoveries have been made at the interface of different disciplines, rather than at the centre of any one of them, it is essential to create these cross-disciplinary opportunities.

The RSE premises in George Street are now well suited to holding symposia, research seminars and workshops, and there is a busy varied programme of such events. Because of the range of skills and professional expertise vested in the Society's Fellowship, it is uniquely competent to organise meetings which involve participation by specialists from many different fields.

One of many possible recent examples of meetings which illustrate this broadly-based approach was a two day international meeting on "To Treat or Not To Treat?: Dilemmas Posed by the Hopelessly Ill". The medical issues were introduced by a Professor of Neurosurgery from Glasgow, the ethical issues by a Professor of Philosophy from Glasgow and the legal issues by a Professor of Law from the Free University of Berlin. The programme included discussion of issues such as handling acute crises (discussed by annaesthetist), the effects of brain damage (discussed by a mental health specialist), and the particular problems of children and the elderly. On the second day, discussions widened and included contributions concerning medical decisions at the end of life, based upon experiences in the Netherlands and the USA. This breadth of treatment, as well as its depth, could not have been adequately achieved from within the confines of one medical or biological discipline. By bringing together this range of specialists it was possible, for example, to focus on inappropriate use of treatments when a reasonable recovery is not possible, or when prolonging life appears not to be in the patient's best interests. It was recognised that the ethical issues raised are often troubling to doctors as well as worrying to the public. In addition, there can be legal implications particularly if the patient is not competent to express preferences about his or her management. Such a conference, bringing together doctors, nurses, lawyers, philosophers, social scientists and members of the public was timely and enlightening.

Providing an independent forum in Scotland for consideration of matters affecting the well-being of the nation

Complex issues, especially those relating to different aspects of social, scientific or environmental policy demand a many-sided inter-disciplinary approach. As feelings may run high on such sensitive issues, the RSE fulfils an important role by providing a neutral setting, without any prior political commitment or bias and can, therefore, act as "Honest Broker". Intellectual adversaries can be brought together in an effort to find common ground for a better understanding of different points of view.

Recent examples of such meetings are:

- Engineering: Scotland's future

- The future organisation and funding of Scottish Higher Education

- The economic, social and legal consequences of 1992 in Scotland

- The science base: underpinning the future of Scotland

Self evidently, all of these topics have considerable relevance to the higher education sector in Scotland. The attendance and structure of discussions at the RSE enable those in higher education to meet and discuss freely with those in industry, commerce, the professions and the public sector similarly concerned with such complex issues.

Giving advice to Parliament, Government and its Agencies on relevant policy issues

The RSE is increasingly invited to comment on matters of public concern. This is a complementary role to organising meetings on public policy issues. Although consultation with Fellows and the establishment of Working Parties to prepare reports – often at short notice – places a heavy burden on Fellows, this is a particularly important role for the Society. The independent status and range of experience represented through its Fellowship give a breadth of approach which is unique within the learned societies in Great Britain and enables the RSE to adopt a holistic view on complex issues – not just a Scottish perspective. The RSE is particularly pleased to welcome Parliamentary Select Committees to its rooms when they take evidence in Scotland, as this can help improve understanding of the Scottish dimensions within the issues under consideration.

Many of the topics on which the Society has given evidence in recent years have been of particular interest to the higher education community, but care has been taken to ensure careful balance and independent chairmanship of the working parties involved in the preparation of evidence. Topics of particular interest include:

- White Paper on Higher Education – a new Framework. Working party chaired by Lord Emslie. Comments were also given on the Further and Higher Education (Scotland) Bill.

- Report on Upper Secondary Education in Scotland – The Howie Report.

- White Paper on Science and Technology. Working Party chaired by Lord Balfour of Burleigh.

- Priorities for the Science Base. Working Party chaired by Professor David Tedford

- Scrutiny Review of Public Sector Research Establishments and subsequent Prior Options Reviews. Working Party chaired by Professor John Forty.

Developing better links between industry and commerce and the academic community

The RSE Fellowship, although well represented by the academic community in Scotland, has always been drawn more widely and includes prominent Scots active in industry and commerce.

Improving the links between business and academe has been given a particular emphasis recently through the Technology Foresight programme and the joint enquiry with Scottish Enterprise into commercialisation of the Scottish science and engineering base. The commercialisation enquiry led to a national strategy report entitled "Technology Ventures". Both these programmes have particular importance to the higher education community as they share a common objective of improving wealth creation from the research base.

In the course of the commercialisation enquiry, several factors inhibiting the effective exploitation of the research base emerged. The RSE will continue to work closely with Scottish Enterprise and SHEFC to improve understanding and dissemination of technology processes. The RSE will be arranging a series of Foresight seminars to help improve the links between Scottish universities and multi-national corporate R&D directors. Although there are improving links between Scottish based firms and academics, there is comparatively little industrial R&D carried out in Scotland and Foresight seminars seek to address such issues.

Publishing scholarly journals

As part of its core role of communicating research, the RSE has published scholarly journals from the outset. The lectures and discussions of the Society were published in the *Transactions* and *Proceedings*. With ever increasing specialisation of scientific research, these journals have also become more specialist in their subject content.

Transactions is now an earth sciences journal and is a well recognised medium for papers in palaeontology.

Proceedings A is now devoted to mathematics, particularly algebra, and is widely recognised as an international journal of considerable standing. The future of both journals depends critically on the quality and support of Scottish research specialists in the fields covered by these journals and the Editorial Boards draw heavily on staff in Scottish universities.

Because of declining sales, the RSE recently ceased production of *Proceedings B* which had remained a broadly-based journal in the biological sciences. This has been replaced, in part, by a series of "Occasional Papers" many of which derive from symposia themes on issues of broad ranging topical concern. Recent titles have included Leukemia Clusters and Gene Therapy; the content of these publications reflects the broadly inter-disciplinary approach of the originating meetings.

Future roles

In addition to continuing to develop many of the themes noted above, the recent acquisition of adjoining premises in George Street will lead to new areas of further activity involving the higher education sector in Scotland. The most apparent of these will be the creation of Windows on Research. This will be a public show case of outstanding research taking place in Scottish Universities and research institutes and how this will affect peoples' lives. There will be a series of themed exhibitions and associated events dealing with particular aspects. Topics to be covered will include:

● biomedical research

● transport and communication

● technology and the disabled.

Each of these themed exhibitions will last about 9 months and will seek to attract a broad cross section of the public interest. The opportunity to present leading edge research from Scottish universities will be an important contribution not only to the greater public understanding of science, engineering and technology, but will also help stimulate the improved links between business and the academic communities.

Agreement has been obtained, in principle, from most Scottish universities to take part in relevant Windows on Research displays and the RSE will seek to highlight the best research taking place throughout Scottish HEIs.

To help promote the development of the Society's public outreach and to facilitate the development of the adjoining premises, the Society has created a separate charitable trust called RSE Scotland Foundation. This is expected to become an increasingly important vehicle for expression of the aspirations to advance "Useful Knowledge".

Reference
The Royal Society of Edinburgh: the First Two Hundred Years by Neil Campbell and R. Martin S. Smellie (RSE, 1983).

Dr William Duncan
Executive Secretary, Royal Society of Edinburgh

William Duncan, BSc, PhD, GradIPD, has been Executive Secretary of the RSE since 1985. He is also head of paid staff and principal policy adviser to the Council, responsible for all aspects of the efficient running of the Society's business. He is formerly a Principal Officer, Lothian Regional Council and Administrative Officer, Treasurer's Department, Greater London Council.

Index

2 Topics